THE HIDDEN FACE OF GLOBAL GEOPOLITICS

RAUL OJEDA

Raul Ojeda, first edition ©2016
Ojeda.raul.antonio@gmail.com
ISBN-13: 978-1520136066
Editor Code: A3CRW5DWBRD7GK

Mirelvis Nazareth Gutierrez
General Review
Cover illustration
Diagramming
Mirelvisgutierrez@gmail.com

THE HIDDEN FACE OF GLOBAL GEOPOLITICS

For my family
And all those who
Have been victims of
New world order

RAUL OJEDA

WHY THIS BOOK?

"Nothing in Geopolitics happens by chance, and if it happens it has been previously planned". Franklin Delano Roosevelt

The reason is simple: if you are in doubt about what is going on in the world, if you love good and truth, this book is a good start. The world needs to know the reality on the dark side of the **'World Geopolitics'**; you must know that behind every global event there are very powerful organizations that have previously planned, not by chance. It is necessary for the whole world to awaken their sleeping consciousness by the invasion of our minds through the media and other weapons of psychological destruction.

You should know as 'powerful' have created and implemented the **"New World Order"** through the Think Tank, among which will be addressed: **the Bilderbergers Club, the Project for a New American Century, the Trilateral**

Commission, the European Troika (conformed by the European Commission, the European Central Bank and International Monetary Fund), and **the Council on Foreign Relations**; you must also understand the truth about Israeli Zionism, the False Flags and the Financing of Terrorists to destabilize the African Continent and the Middle East. In turn with the same geostrategic importance you should know as US imperialism attempts to destabilize progressive governments in Latin America through the reissue of **'New Plan Condor'**.

And longing to make clear in this book: "Yes we are Palestinian, yes we are Iraqis, yes we Libyans, yes we Syrians, yes we are Afghans, yes we are Africans, yes we are American, yes we are brothers and yes we are humanists", and nobody can stop Our struggle against a system implanted since the Great World Powers, let alone avoid the awakening of the millions of dormant and slave consciences to the present system.

Dear reader: It is time to understand that we live in a world where material matters more than spiritual, where the physical aspect matters more than the feelings. We live in a world where there is a Nobel Peace Prize that is awarded to a genocide, we live in a world where International Organizations approve resolutions to create chaos in today's society, we live in a world where selfishness is the main feeling skin deep, we live in a world where an entire village snatches their land and almost 70 years later is still suffering the greatest abuses to which it may be subjected a human being, like the giant of

THE HIDDEN FACE OF GLOBAL GEOPOLITICS

Latin America **Eduardo Galeano** he said in his book "Muddled: School's World Upside Down" (1998):

"The world upside teaches us to suffer reality rather than change it, to forget the past rather than listen and accept the future rather than imagine: well practiced crime, and so recommends. At her school, school crime, are mandatory classes impotence, amnesia and resignation".

Palestine Exists and Resists!

The author

RAUL OJEDA

INDEX

RAUL OJEDA

PROLOGUE

The world we know on maps, books and newsreels is the result of dreams, struggles and betrayals to the aspirations of peoples. In meeting rooms, bank offices, embassies, and government far from television cameras, the press and social networks are obscurely knit the destinies of nations and their social processes, without considering in most cases the real interests and legitimate of the same peoples.

This game of public and private alliances and intrigues where economic, political and ideological interests are involved involving the different nations of the world is called geopolitics and exists within the necessary relations between the different nations of the real world, however there is a Hidden side that explains that nothing or almost nothing of what happens in the international scene is the result of chance, on the contrary is the logical consequence of the action of multiple actors and opposing interests: Cold War, the fall of the socialist bloc that wanted To give way to "the end of history" and to the so-called "new world order" I try to impose for the benefit of the USA a unique vision in the economic and political sphere governed by the large corporations and multilateral financial institutions that like the IMF and The WB with the support of the "factual powers" create a media matrix of good and bad governments, good and bad world leaders in the minds of people and peoples, are a demonstration of the manipulation of geopolitics in its most hidden face. Today it is intended to justify coups, legal and illegal wars, military interventions to impose peace, let us see as normal the unjustified shame of the 21st century as the new apartheid against the Palestinian people or the oblivion to which the Saharawis are subjected While waiting in refugee camps for UN support that will never come.

The hidden face of global geopolitics of our young and restless Raul Ojeda is then an honest effort to understand and know the result of the political intrigues of the great powers against the struggle of the peoples, for being free and sovereign of the tutelages of The external powers and that as critical individuals we must make known to a collective alien to the manipulations of a global world.

Pedro Luis Martínez
Mayor of the Municipality Bolivariano Guanipa
Venezuela

THE WORLD AFTER THE COLD WAR

"That's where the cold war ended, but here's the hot war" Jaime Garzón

Initiate commenting something interesting that can not know: **Adolf Hitler** "predicted" the Cold War. The document known as the original name **Bormann Vermerke** (Notes Bormann) has been published in different languages.Here is presented with the title of French, Hitler's political testament. Indeed, they are notes that **Martin Bormann** (private secretary of Adolf Hitler) take expressions that Adolf Hitler said between 1941 to 1944 and are an important part of thinking about the future Führer of Germany. The fact of being transcribed and annotated by Bormann confers more force to these dispositions, given the intimacy and the reliability that he felt to him by Hitler.

This document contains the latest reflections on the war that, at the time of being made, had already been lost; As well as the certainty of the realization of a Reich that would last forever. But, it is not an "official testament"; is the very entrainment of man turning in words collected by the last and most faithful man of confidence; By one who would not have dared to change anything to the dictates of his idol.

Martin Bormann signed these documents to close the possibility that something was added. Hitler's testament, thought and character had been exposed and nothing and no one could change them. This quote was taken from the work of **François Genoud in 1961,The Testament of Adolf Hitler: Hitler-documents Bormann.**

"There will continue to exist in the world only two great powers capable of facing each other: the United States and the Soviet Union. The laws of history and geography will force these two powers to a test of force, whether military or in the fields of economics and ideology. These same laws make it inevitable that both powers become enemies of Europe. And it is equally true that these two powers eventually seek the support of the only surviving great nation in Europe, the German people" [Extract].

Now, it is fair and necessary to make a count of that time, since for many people around the world especially the Americans and Soviets, the Cold War was a reality that accompanied their day to day for several decades, and their end in the nineties he represented the beginning of a "New

World Order" conceived and imposed by US (Now the sole superpower).

But what was the controversial Cold War? – It can be highlighted by the absence of direct battles, deployment of armies or large human losses. It consisted of a long period of apparent tense calm between the United States and the Soviet Union, an economic, geopolitical and ideological confrontation from the end of the Second World War to the early 1990s. The conflict materialized in an arms race. The concept of superpower was born, and both countries competed for being the most powerful in terms of nuclear weapons, as well as in space technology. Unable to deal directly (it would have meant the end of the human race given the characteristics of the missiles), they undertook petty squabbles, provocative gestures as US support The Mujahideen insurgents in Afghan conflict, or the missile crisis in Cuba.

TERM OF 'COLD WAR'

It is imperative to point out that the main differences in the historiographic proposals of the 'Cold War' lie mainly in the area of chronology and causality. In order to structure the main historiographical tendencies, these have been organized into two large groups. In the first of them, all the authors who consider the Cold War as the conflict promoted between the United States are incorporated. And the USSR after World War II, while in the second group are located the authors who consider the starting point of the Cold War in the year 1917. In the first place, each of these historiographic tendencies will be explained in a general way, for Then introduce the proposals of the selected authors, trying to highlight the particularities, points in common and differences between each one of them.

It is interesting that the term 'Cold War' was universalized in 1945 to denominate geopolitical tensions (political, economic, social, military, informative and even sports) between the so – called Western bloc (capitalist) led by US and Eastern (Communist) bloc led by the USSR. First appeared on October 19, 1945 in an article by **George Orwell** titled "You and the atomic bomb 'in the British newspaper' Tribune', which argued:" One can infer from several symptoms that the Russians do not have the Secret of the making of the atomic bomb. On the other hand, the general opinion is that they will own it in a few years. What we have before us, therefore, is the project of two or three monstrous super states, who possess a weapon with which millions of people can be wiped off the face of the earth in a few seconds, and divide the world including "In this situation Orwell called it" cold war. However, e n the specific sense of pointing geopolitical tensions between the Soviet Union and the United States, the term Cold War has been attributed to American financier and presidential adviser Bernard Baruch. On April 16, 1947, Baruch gave a speech in which he said "Make no mistake: we are in a cold war". The term was also reported by columnist Walter Lippmann with the 1947 edition of a book entitled 'Cold War'.

American historian **Ronald Powaski** summarizes the historiographical schools of the Cold War into three main trends: **orthodox, revisionist and posrevisionista.**

1. Orthodox: the Soviet Union is considered the main culprit in Western historiographical schools, and the United States had no choice but to restrain and, where possible, disrupt the expansion of an aggressive communist state that sought above all to overthrow the capitalism, democracy and other aspects of Western culture.

2. Revisionists: United States of America was responsible for the Cold War and the USSR country was forced to react to the aggression of a country that was determined to promote the expansion of capitalism ensuring unlimited access to markets and resources of the world determined to crush the revolutionary and leftist movements that threaten its interest.

3. Posrevisionista: US believes that both As the USSR are responsible for the tension at the end of World War II, since their actions inevitably provoked hostile reactions from both sides and this created a kind of action–reaction cycle in which the level of "animosity" rose periodically to levels Dangerous and even came to the brink of a total nuclear war that neither side wanted.

THE HIDDEN FACE OF GLOBAL GEOPOLITICS

BUT WHAT IS ESTABLISHED HISTORIOGRAPHY?

In the group of historians who consider the Cold War as a result of World War II, two aspects are clearly identified. The West was characterized by experiencing a progressive evolution towards interpretive and Soviet objectivity, which for a long time maintained its rigidity and orthodoxy.

According to the dissertation of **Juan Pereira** (Pereira Castaneda, Juan, The Origins of the Cold War, Editorial Arco, Madrid 1997), the firmness of the Soviet interpretations remained until the late seventies and the early of The eighties where there was finally a relaxation of tension and improved relations between Moscow and Washington, allowing to give nuances to historical interpretations in the context of the Cold War. However, it was with Mikhail Gorbachev's Perestroika proposal, which contributed to a more critical interpretation of Soviet performance during this period.

However, for the **Soviet interpretation** is a Cold War prism of class struggle internationally transplanted, pursuant to which world capitalism and represent countries that would have begun an attack on all fronts against the socialist world. Soviet analysts establish an official position on which we insist on the unilateral nature of the causes of the Cold War, blaming what they call 'American savage capitalism'. As already pointed out, internal criticism was only evidenced by Mikhail Gorbachev's arrival in power in the 1980s.

For the purposes of this book they have been considered definitions and proposals in the following works: **"Compendium of History of the USSR"** (1966), **'Great Soviet Encyclopedia'** (1970) **",History of Foreign Policy of the USSR '** (1971), **and 'in Confidence: Moscow's ambassador to the six US presidents of the cold war'** (1998). Of these works, only the latter could be considered as a critical analysis that tries to seek answers in a more objective way, since unlike the previous ones, it is not subject to the demands imposed by the Soviet State, that was in charge to establish The orientations of the historiography, having this one to conform strictly to the official interpretation.

In the case of **Western interpretation,** it experienced a remarkable evolution over the years in which the Cold War spreads. In the early years, studies devoted to the Cold War had a great connection to the orthodox tendency, establishing unambiguously unilateral explanations, where the main causes were essentially Soviet aggressiveness and its expansionist zeal over the rest of the world. From this perspective, the United States is considered legitimate defender of the **'Free World'**, which was supposed to protect, thus avoiding the significant progress of the communist forces that threatened to spread throughout the world.

According to this vile perspective, the Cold War is an instrument of world communism, which hopes to achieve the subversion of the masses in Western countries, in order to achieve its objectives, the communist world used preferably non-military means, for example propaganda. However, the use of military means was not ruled out. In this way the action of the United States is explained as part of the legitimate defense against an imminent danger that the aggressive and expansionist interests of the communist world mean to the Western world.

For a better critical understanding, the oldest work that was published in 1989, when the Soviet Union was still standing, although already suffering many of the symptoms that led to the collapse, will be analyzed. The evolution experienced by Western historiography be known from the aforementioned works of **Juan Pereira Castañeda** through **'History and Present of the Cold War'** (1989) and **'Origins of the Cold War'** (1997), in both works The evolution of the historiography related to the Cold War from 1947 to the moment in which each book is published is presented roughly. Authors such as **Eric Hobsbawm** and **Rafael Aracil,** provide a general analysis of the most important aspects of the Cold War. While through **Henry Kissinger** and **George Kennan** you may know the perceptions of two prominent protagonists of the Cold War, which, through their works try to approach analytically to study the period in which for various reasons were directly involved. Let's see.

SOVIET INTERPRETATION

According to this, world capitalism and the countries that represented it would have begun an attack on all fronts against the socialist world. Soviet analyses are official and insist on the one – sidedness of the causes of the Cold War, blaming what they call 'American imperialist capitalism'. As already noted, the internal criticism only seen with the advent of **Mikhail Gorbachev** to power in the eighties. In the **Great Soviet Encyclopedia** The explanatory one–sidedness on the causes that originated the conflict denominated Cold War becomes remarkable.

"The Cold War is an aggressive political course taken by the reactionary circles of the imperialist powers, under the leadership of the United States and England, following World War II 1939–1945 (...) The Cold War is oriented not to allow the Peaceful coexistence between states of different social systems, to exacerbate international tension and create the conditions for the unleashing of a new world war (...) In practice, the Cold War policy has become clear in the creation of aggressive political–military blocs, In the arms race, in the establishment of military bases in the territory of other States, in the hysteria of war, in the intimidation of peace–loving peoples (...) in the disorganization of peaceful economic relations, in attempts to replace violence and dictatorship generally recognized norms of diplomatic relations between States "

Corresponding to this definition, the conflict originated the United States and is directed against countries that do not share their social system, that is, against the socialist countries, which advocate peaceful coexistence. However, the latter is directly affected by the constant climate of international tension that generates a permanent danger of triggering a third World War.

With the development of the Cold War, the US government authorized the implementation of undercover operations in times of peace, with psychological operations being one of its pillars. So with the National Security Act of 1947, a number of institutions that legalize a state of national security and secrecy (in favor of public safety) in which psychological operations embodied the link between security goals were created, the economic expansionism of transnational corporations and the creation of academic theories and publications justifying spaces confronting the great 'Soviet threat'. The theory of modernization, realism in international relations and the various functionalist–systemic communication theories are part of this plan. But undoubtedly the real objective of the government and part of the US private sector was to ensure the flow of resources, raw materials and access to markets abroad, to expand and ensure the 'American way of life'. Psychological warfare should be directed to 'win the hearts and minds' in favor of this way of life (which succeeded).

RAUL OJEDA

ANATOLI FIÓDOROVICH DOBRYNIN, THE RUSSIAN DIPLOMATIC, WHO EXECUTED AS AMBASSADOR TO THE SIX US PRESIDENTS DURING THE COLD WAR

Anatoli Fyodorovich Dobrynin (Russian: Анатолий Фёдорович Добрынин) arrived in Washington in 1962 and only 42 years was the youngest ambassador in Moscow (Russia), remained as such during the mandates of **Kennedy, Johnson, Nixon, Ford, Carter** and **Reagan,** becoming The main channel of communication between the White House and the Kremlin, leading events such as the Cuban Missile Crisis in 1962. In his book 'In Confidence', he provides details of the circumstances surrounding the major struggles between the United States and the Union Soviet in the period of the Cold War. Dorbryn was a crucial figure in the preparation of all high – level meetings between leaders of the two nations, from first held in 1955, until the last between **Gorbachev** and **Bush** in 1990.

The work established the interest to balance the greater number of elements involved, in order to present a more coherent explanatory structure and detached from the traditional parameters imposed by the official interpretations established by the Soviet Union. However, every man is the son of his circumstance, therefore, it is logical that he also tries to explain the explanation and in many cases justification of the world's operations to which the Soviet Union belonged, and also of his own acts as the first Representative of that world in front of its main enemy, the United States.

It is suggestive appreciation about the Cold War, referring to it as a 'temporary perversion, based on ideology and not in the national interest'. This last one affirms in its interest to emphasize the possibilities of understanding that Russia and United States have after the end of the Cold War, since in the absence of clash of interests between both, and to have moved away of the communist ideology, the future presents / displays Great possibilities of an effective approach and cooperation between both countries. Throughout his work, Anatoli Dorbryn expresses a great critique of the ideological overload with which Soviet–American relations were impregnated.

The major contributions of this book can be compared to those willing to works of **Henry Kissinger** and **George Kennan,** these two last as representatives of the Western bloc, led by the United States. The points in common lie essentially in the fact that these three authors in writing about the Cold War not only do so in response to their interest in a relevant period of the twentieth century, but in turn are attempting to put into historical perspective their own action within Of that period, since all of them were involved in the events that narrate and explain.

WESTERN INTERPRETATION

Expresses the definition established in the **Manual of Military Issues** Federal Republic of Germany in 1963:

"The Cold War is the form of aggressive world-wide communism, of political-spiritual and psychological-propaganda confrontation with the non-communist world. In the Cold War, world communism wants, first of all, to dominate the consciousness of the masses. Therefore, it tries to influence its influence in all vital areas of society in non-communist states. The supreme goal of the cold war lies in the complete domination, discovered or hidden, of the non-communist world. Non-military means are preferably used for this purpose. But from time to time military resources can also be used. Communist successes in the Cold War can lead to revolutionary situation"

According to this, the Cold War is an instrument of world communism, which hopes to achieve the subversion of the masses in Western countries. To achieve their goals, the communist world preferably used non - military means, such as 'political marketing'. However, the use of military means is not ruled out. In this way, US action is explained as part of legitimate defense against the imminent danger posed to the Western world by the aggressive and expansionist pursuits of the communist world. In the West the orthodox interpretation became more and more oriented towards more objective studies that tried to put into perspective the various factors involved in the causes that originated the so-called Cold War.

THE HIDDEN FACE OF GLOBAL GEOPOLITICS

To systematically understand this evolution can be mentioned proposed by Jean Duroselle, in his book **'Europe 1815 to today'** (1967). This book evidences the clear interest in approaching a critical and unorthodox study of the conflict held by the two superpowers. For the author, the conflict between two political-social ideologies was transformed into the most outstanding phenomenon of the postwar period. During the war, the need to remain united had disguised the deep differences between the major components of the coalition, but once the conflagration ended, divergences became insurmountable.

Moreover, because the war had contributed to consolidating both the United States and the Soviet Union in the quality of military superpowers. From this point of view, the conditions for World War III were already generated. But the conflagration was not carried out, due essentially that Duroselle called 'balance of terror', which is explained by the fact that the military technology used by both sides had surpassed for the first time the limits of mass destruction.

Under such conditions, to begin a direct conflict, it would have meant death sentence to the people themselves, question that neither warring factions came to risk. It had been until 1967, which is published for the first time the work cited Duroselle, and so remained until the end of the Cold War.

RAUL OJEDA

BIPOLAR WORLD: US AND THE USSR

The first zone of confrontation between the two superpowers victorious World War II (US and USSR) was precisely the German country. After his surrender in April 1945, Germany was militarily occupied by the Allies. Thereafter, each block area defended his influence against the advance of the opposing block. Washington and Moscow used different mechanisms to achieve these goals. Meanwhile, the new countries born of thedecolonization process tried unsuccessfully to create a movement to escape from this bipolar logic (later will discuss the Movement of Non – Aligned Countries).

Historically I to division of Germany took place from 4 to Nov. 11 February 1945 when they met in the city of Yalta: **Winston Churchill** (UK), **Franklin D. Roosevelt** (United States) and **Joseph Stalin** (Soviet Union). The victors divided the German territory into four occupation zones: the east was controlled by the Soviet Union and the West by France, Britain and the United States. The city of Berlin, located within the Soviet occupation zone, reproduced the same division scheme.

In 1947 the United States and Britain decided an economic union of German territory being created the Bizone (or Bizonia), based in Frankfurt. In April 1949 the French sector would join and calling the Trizone, although France felt great misgivings about promoting German unification.

In June 1948 the Western allies carried out a unilateral currency reform revalued issuing a new, different frame used in the Soviet zone.

On 23 June 1948 the Soviet authorities carried out the closure of all access communication (railways, highways and waterways), as well as supplies of gas and electricity in Berlin. The city was cut off from West Germany.

On 26 June 1948 the Western powers responded to the blockade with an airlift to supply two million people inhabiting West Berlin. Day and night flights were made to transport goods (food, coal and oil). This air traffic tried to avoid the effects of the blockade, which was finally lifted on 12 May 1949.

On May 8, 1949 the Constitution that ratified the creation of West Germany was approved in the **Federal Republic of Germany** (FRG), with its capital in Bonn. The major parties were the Christian Democrat and Social Democrat. A new constitution for Germany, the Basic Law, reflecting the "anti – totalitarian" lessons of the recent past was written. The second German democracy was designed as functional parliamentary democracy, with Federal Chancellor (head of government) and a Federal President with reduced powers.

The foundations of the state were established so that remained safe even favorable to alter the constitutional majority, resulting therefore impossible to abolish democracy via "legal" in order to avoid what happened in 1933 when the

Nazis agreed to the power. That same year in the east, the Soviet occupation zone, was established the **German Democratic Republic** (GDR), which was ruled by a dictatorship and one – party Marxist–Leninist sign. Its capital was Pankow; later he moves to Berlin.

WEST BLOCK

United States to ensure the development of its ambitious foreign policy deployed a broad policy of alliances. First, it reinforced transatlantic ties with Western Europe. The Berlin crisis gotten down the constitution in 1949 of the **Organization of the North Atlantic Treaty** (NATO, the bloodiest since the Second World War), the great military alliance of the Western bloc to the present.

Second, the government contributed decisively to begin the process of European integration that culminated in 1957 with the signing of the way **Treaties of Rome** and the birth of the **European Economic Community**.

Third he began to weave a network of anti – Soviet alliances worldwide. **The Organization of American States** (OAS); the **ANZUS** (acronym from Australia, New Zealand and the United States); **Treaty Organization Southeast Asia** (SEATO for its acronym in English); the **CENTO** (Central Treaty Organization: Central Treaty Organization) and the **Security Treaty** with Japan were the main elements of the network of alliances.

COMMUNIST BLOCK

The first step in the formation of the Soviet bloc was the creation of the **Cominform** (Information Office of the Communist and Workers Parties) in 1947. Its creation was the answer of Stalin's famous Marshall Plan and she sought to group matches Communists in the area under Soviet influence (**Poland, Czechoslovakia, Hungary, Bulgaria and Romania**), her powerful communist parties of France and Italy joined.

At its inaugural meeting, the Soviet representative and member of the Bureau of the Communist Party of the Soviet Union (CPSU), **Andrei Zhdanov**, delivered a speech in which he laid the foundations of Soviet foreign policy doctrine (Doctrine Zhdanov). This is published on 5 October of the same year, in the French Communist newspaper L'Humanite. The basic objective of this report is to define the new Soviet political orientation facing the Western camp, in response to the Truman Doctrine. Abstract:

"The more we move away from the end of the war, the more clearly the two main directions of international politics postwar corresponding to the arrangement in two main fields of political forces operating in the global arena appear: the imperialistic and undemocratic field and anti–imperialist and democratic field. The United States is the main driving force of the imperialist camp. The anti–imperialist and anti–fascist forces form the other field. The USSR and the countries of new democracy are their foundation"

The essential lines of action of the new organization were based on the exchange of information and experience, coordination of actions and mutual assistance between the communist parties. In practice, the Cominform served as an instrument to government orders from Moscow to the Western challenge resulted in the Truman Doctrine and the Marshall Plan. However, the Cominform attended the first great schism in the Communist world: Yugoslavia **Josip Broz Tito** was accused of deviance of the Marxist–Leninist doctrine. It was a statement from the Cominform in June 1948 which proclaimed the condemnation of the regime of Tito.

In 1949, was born the **Council for Mutual Economic Assistance** (Russian: Совет экономической взаимопомощи, Sovet ekonomícheskoy vsaymopómoshchi, СЭВ, SEV; abbreviation for **Comecon**, CMEA or Comecon), an organization grouping the USSR and the "democracies European". This association was aimed at economic coordination and did not work with full until 1960. After the victory of **Mao Zedong** in 1949, the USSR signed military cooperation and agreements with Communist China.

Finally, in response to the entry of the FRG in **NATO**, he was born in 1955 **Warsaw Pact**, the military alliance that joined the USSR with all European communist bloc countries except Yugoslavia.

THE NON-ALIGNED MOVEMENT

The new African and Asian nations that were emerging from decolonization process tried to defend own interests outside the two blocs. To that end was held, the **Asian-African Conference in Bandung** in 1955, where he was born what came to be known as the **Non-Aligned Movement (NAM)**.

This conference was led by the great leaders of what was beginning to be called the "Third World", the undeveloped world: the Hindu **Sri Jawaharla Pandit Nehru**, the **Egyptian Gamal Abdel Nasser** and Indonesia's **Sukarno**.

Figure 1. Leaders founders of the Non-Aligned Movement (NAM).

Economic and political weakness of most of its members and its own internal divisions prevented the movement would serve as a real alternative to the bipolar world of the Cold War.

Undoubtedly the Cold War was a struggle that reached its maximum focus, once both political entities –USA and USSR were installed on top of the international scene, being face to face in the middle of the European continent; there, as far as his armies had managed to get in the onslaught against Nazi troops. From this perspective, World War II only came to be the last step that made the Cold War a conflict of world order. Thus the alliance between the Soviet Union and Western countries from 1941 would have meant only a parenthesis in the history of the Cold War. As the British historian **Eric Hobsbawm**, the Alliance War against Hitler constituted an unusual and temporary fact, while **'a paradoxical process because during most of the century, except for the brief period of anti – fascism, relations between the capitalism and communism were characterized by an irreconcilable antagonism'.**

Indeed, the latter is key to understanding the events that arose after the end of the war. That 'unlikely alliance' did not survive once the common enemy had been defeated. War did not leave a united world, but a bipolar.From 1945 victory had made disappear the only bond between allies. After the war they found themselves facing two opposing systems of organization resources, Socialism and Capitalism.

THE HIDDEN FACE OF GLOBAL GEOPOLITICS

In its early stages of development the Cold War manifested itself in Europe, which saw the first friction between the two superpowers, however, soon each tacitly accepted the sphere of influence of his opponent and thus stabilized, or rather the division of Europe was frozen throughout the period of the Cold War, from 1945 to 1989-1991. This last factor was the cause for the Cold War spread to the periphery, especially to those places where the delimitation of the influences was not yet defined. As crucial example is Asia, with the exception of Japan, who after his defeat became controlled exclusively by the United States.

The Non-Aligned Movement (NAM) was created and founded during the collapse of the colonial system and the independence struggles of the peoples of Africa, Asia, Latin America and other regions of the world and at the height of the Cold War. During the early days of the Movement, its actions were a key factor in the decolonization process, which led later to the attainment of freedom and independence by many countries and peoples and to the founding of tens of new sovereign States. Throughout its history, the Movement of Non-Aligned Countries has played a fundamental role in the preservation of world peace and security.

While some meetings with a third-world perspective were held before 1955, historians consider that the Bandung Asian-African Conference is the most immediate antecedent to the creation of the Non-Aligned Movement. This Conference was held in Bandung on April 18-24, 1955 and gathered 29 Heads of States belonging to the first post-colonial generation of leaders from the two continents with the aim of identifying and assessing world issues at the time and pursuing out joint policies in international relations.

The principles that would govern relations among large and small nations, known as the "Ten Principles of Bandung", were proclaimed at that Conference. Such principles were adopted later as the main goals and objectives of the policy of non-alignment. The fulfillment of those principles became the essential criterion for Non-Aligned Movement membership; it is what was known as the "quintessence of the Movement" until the early 1990s.

In 1960, in the light of the results achieved in Bandung, the creation of the Movement of Non-Aligned Countries was given a decisive boost during the Fifteenth Ordinary Session of the United Nations General Assembly, during which 17 new African and Asian countries were admitted. A key role was played in this process by the then Heads of State and Government Gamal Abdel Nasser of Egypt, Kwame Nkrumah of Ghana, Shri Jawaharlal Nehru of India, Ahmed Sukarno of Indonesia and Josip Broz Tito of Yugoslavia, who later became the founding fathers of the movement and its emblematic leaders.

Six years after Bandung, the Movement of Non-Aligned Countries was founded on a wider geographical basis at the First Summit Conference of Belgrade, which was held on September 1-6, 1961. The Conference was attended by 25 countries: Afghanistan, Algeria, Yemen, Myanmar, Cambodia,

Srilanka, Congo, Cuba, Cyprus, Egypt, Ethiopia, Ghana, Guinea, India, Indonesia, Iraq, Lebanon, Mali, Morocco, Nepal, Saudi Arabia, Somalia, Sudan, Syria, Tunisia, Yugoslavia. The Founders of NAM have preferred to declare it as a movement but not an organization in order to avoid bureaucratic implications of the latter.

The membership criteria formulated during the Preparatory Conference to the Belgrade Summit (Cairo, 1961) show that the Movement was not conceived to play a passive role in international politics but to formulate its own positions in an independent manner so as to reflect the interests of its members.

Thus, the primary of objectives of the non-aligned countries focused on the support of self-determination, national independence and the sovereignty and territorial integrity of States; opposition to apartheid; non-adherence to multilateral military pacts and the independence of non-aligned countries from great power or block influences and rivalries; the struggle against imperialism in all its forms and manifestations; the struggle against colonialism, neocolonialism, racism, foreign occupation and domination; disarmament; non-interference into the internal affairs of States and peaceful coexistence among all nations; rejection of the use or threat of use of force in international relations; the strengthening of the United Nations; the democratization of international relations; socioeconomic development and the restructuring of the international economic system; as well as international cooperation on an equal footing.

Since its inception, the Movement of Non-Aligned Countries has waged a ceaseless battle to ensure that peoples being oppressed by foreign occupation and domination can exercise their inalienable right to self-determination and independence.

During the 1970s and 1980s, the Movement of Non-Aligned Countries played a key role in the struggle for the establishment of a new international economic order that allowed all the peoples of the world to make use of their wealth and natural resources and provided a wide platform for a fundamental change in international economic relations and the economic emancipation of the countries of the South.

During its nearly 50 years of existence, the Movement of Non-Aligned Countries has gathered a growing number of States and liberation movements which, in spite of their ideological, political, economic, social and cultural diversity, have accepted its founding principles and primary objectives and shown their readiness to realize them. Historically, the non-aligned countries have shown their ability to overcome their differences and found a common ground for action that leads to mutual cooperation and the upholding of their shared values.

The ten principles of Bandung

1- Respect of fundamental human rights and of the objectives and principles of the Charter of the United Nations.
Respect of the sovereignty and territorial integrity of all nations.

2- Recognition of the equality among all races and of the equality among all nations, both large and small.

3- Non-intervention or non-interference into the internal affairs of another -country.

4- Respect of the right of every nation to defend itself, either individually or collectively, in conformity with the Charter of the United Nations.

5- Non-use of collective defense pacts to benefit the specific interests of any of the great powers.

6- Non-use of pressures by any country against other countries.

7- Refraining from carrying out or threatening to carry out aggression, or from using force against the territorial integrity or political independence of any country.

8- Peaceful solution of all international conflicts in conformity with the Charter of the United Nations.

9- Promotion of mutual interests and of cooperation.

10- Respect of justice and of international obligations.

Evolution

The creation and strengthening of the socialist block after the defeat of fascism in World War II, the collapse of colonial empires, the emergence of a bipolar world and the formation of two military blocks (NATO and the Warsaw Pact) brought about a new international context that led to the necessity of multilateral coordination fora between the countries of the South.

In this context, the underdeveloped countries, most of them in Asia and Africa, felt the need to join efforts for the common defense of their interests, the strengthening of their independence and sovereignty and the cultural and economic revival or salvation of their peoples, and also to express a strong commitment with peace by declaring themselves as "non-aligned" from either of the two nascent military blocks.

In order to fulfill the aims of debating on and advancing a strategy designed to achieve such objectives, the Bandung Asian-African Conference was held in Indonesia in April 1955. It was attended by 29 Heads of State and Government of the first postcolonial generation of leaders and its expressed goal was to identify and assess world issues at the time and coordinate policies to deal with them.

Although the Asian and African leaders who gathered in Bandung might have had differing political and ideological views or different approaches toward the societies they aspired to build or rebuild, there was a common project that united them and gave sense to a closer coordination of positions. Their shared program included the political decolonization of Asia and Africa. Moreover, they all agreed that the recently attained political independence was just a means to attain the goal of economic, social and cultural independence.

The Bandung meeting has been considered as the most immediate antecedent of the founding of the Movement of Non-Aligned Countries, which finally came into being six years later on a wider geographical basis when the First Summit Conference was held in Belgrade on September 1-6, 1961. This gathering was attended by the Heads of State and Government of 25 countries and observers from another three nations.

This First Summit of the Movement of Non-Aligned Countries was convened by the leaders of India, Indonesia, Egypt, Syria and Yugoslavia. On April 26, 1961, the Presidents of the Arab Republic of Egypt (Nasser) and Yugoslavia (Tito) addressed the Heads of State and Government of 21 "non-Aligned" countries and suggested that, taking recent world events and the rise of international tensions into account, a Conference should be held to promote an improvement in international relations, a resistance to policies of force and a constructive settlement of conflicts and other issues of concern in the world.

The Movement played an important role in the support of nations which were struggling then for their independence in the Third World and showed great solidarity with the most just aspirations of humanity. It contributed indisputably to the triumph in the struggle for national independence and decolonization, thus gaining considerable diplomatic prestige.

As one Summit after another was held in the 1960s and 1970s, "non alignment", turned already into the "Movement of Non-Aligned Countries" that included nearly all Asian and African countries, was becoming a forum of coordination to struggle for the respect of the economic and political rights of the developing world. After the attainment of independence, the Conferences expressed a growing concern over economic and social issues as well as over strictly political matters.

Something that attested to that was the launching at the Algiers Conference in 1973 of the concept of a "new international economic order".

By the end of the 1980s, the Movement was facing the great challenge brought about by the collapse of the socialist block. The end of the clash between the two antagonistic blocks that was the reason for its existence, name and essence was seen by some as the beginning of the end for the Movement of Non-Aligned Countries.

The Movement of Non-Aligned Countries could not spare itself difficulties to act effectively in an adverse international political situation marked by hegemonic positions and unipolarity as well as by internal difficulties and conflicts given the heterogeneity of its membership and, thus, its diverse interests.

Nevertheless, and in spite of such setbacks,the principles and objectives of non-alignment retain their full validity and force at the present international juncture. The primary condition that led to the emergence of the Movement of Non-Aligned Countries, that is, non-alignment from antagonistic blocks, has not lost its validity with the end of the Cold War. The demise of one of the blocks has not done away with the pressing problems of the world. On the contrary, renewed strategic interests bent on domination grow stronger and, even, acquire new and more dangerous dimensions for underdeveloped countries.

During the 14th Summit of the Non-Aligned Movement in Havana, Cuba in September 2006, the Heads of States and Governments of the member countries reaffirmed their commitment to the ideals, principles and purposes upon which the movement was founded and with the principles and purposes enshrined in the United Nations Charter.

The Heads of States and Governments stated their firm belief that the absence of two conflicting blocs in no way reduces the need to strengthen the movement as a mechanism for the political coordination of developing countries. In this regard they acknowledged that it remains imperative to strengthen and revitalize the movement. To do so, they agreed to strengthen concrete action, unity and solidarity between all its members, based on respect for diversity, factors which are essential for the reaffirmation of the identity and capacity of the movement to influence International relations.

They also stressed the need to promote actively a leading role for the movement in the coordination of efforts among member states in tackling global threats.

Inspired by the principles and purposes which were brought to the Non-Aligned Movement by the Bandung principles and during the First NAM Summit in Belgrade in 1961, the Heads of States and Governments of the member countries of the Non-Aligned Movement adopted in their 14th Summit in Havana the following purposes and principles of the movement in the present International juncture:

Purposes

1- To promote and reinforce multilateralism and, in this regard, strengthen the central role that the United Nations must play.

2- To serve as a forum of political coordination of the developing countries to promote and defend their common interests in the system of international relations.

3- To promote unity, solidarity and cooperation between developing countries based on shared values and priorities agreed upon by consensus.

4- To defend international peace and security and settle all international disputes by peaceful means in accordance with the principles and the purposes of the UN Charter and International Law.

5- To encourage relations of friendship and cooperation between all nations based on the principles of International Law, particularly those enshrined in the Charter of the United Nations.

6- To promote and encourage sustainable development through international cooperation and, to that end, jointly coordinate the implementation of political strategies which strengthen and ensure the full participation of all countries, rich and poor, in the international economic relations, under equal conditions and opportunities but with differentiated responsibilities.

7- To encourage the respect, enjoyment and protection of all human rights and fundamental freedoms for all, on the basis of the principles of universality, objectivity, impartiality and non-selectivity, avoiding politicization of human rights issues, thus ensuring that all human rights of individuals and peoples, including the right to development, are promoted and protected in a balanced manner.

8- To promote peaceful coexistence between nations, regardless of their political, social or economic systems.

9- To condemn all manifestations of unilateralism and attempts to exercise hegemonic domination in international relations.

10- To coordinate actions and strategies in order to confront jointly the threats to international peace and security, including the threats of use of force and the acts of aggression, colonialism and foreign occupation, and other breaches of peace caused by any country or group of countries.

11- To promote the strengthening and democratization of the UN, giving the General Assembly the role granted to it in accordance with the functions and powers outlined in the Charter and to promote the comprehensive reform of the United Nations Security Council so that it may fulfill the role granted to it by the Charter, in a transparent and equitable manner, as the body primarily responsible for maintaining international peace and security.

12- To continue pursuing universal and non-discriminatory nuclear disarmament, as well as a general and complete disarmament under strict and effective international control and in this context, to work towards the objective of arriving at an agreement on a phased program for the complete elimination of nuclear weapons within a specified framework of time to eliminate nuclear weapons, to prohibit their development, production, acquisition, testing, stockpiling, transfer, use or threat of use and to provide for their destruction.

13- To oppose and condemn the categorization of countries as good or evil based on unilateral and unjustified criteria, and the adoption of a doctrine of pre-emptive attack, including attack by nuclear weapons, which is inconsistent with international law, in particular, the international legally-binding instruments concerning nuclear disarmament and to further condemn and oppose unilateral military actions, or use of force or threat of use of force against the sovereignty, territorial integrity and independence of Non-Aligned countries.

14- To encourage States to conclude agreements freely arrived at, among the States of the regions concerned, to establish new Nuclear Weapons-Free Zones in regions where these do not exist, in accordance with the provisions of the Final Document of the First Special Session of the General Assembly devoted to disarmament (SSOD.1) and the principles adopted by the 1999 UN Disarmament Commission, including the establishment of a Nuclear Weapons Free Zone in the Middle East. The establishment of Nuclear Weapons-Free Zones is a positive step and important measure towards strengthening global nuclear disarmament and non-proliferation.

15- To promote international cooperation in the peaceful uses of nuclear energy and to facilitate access to nuclear technology, equipment and material for peaceful purposes required by developing countries.

16- To promote concrete initiatives of South-South cooperation and strengthen the role of NAM, in coordination with G.77, in the re-launching of North-South cooperation, ensuring the fulfillment of the right to development of our peoples, through the enhancement of international solidarity.

17- To respond to the challenges and to take advantage of the opportunities arising from globalization and interdependence with creativity and a sense of identity in order to ensure its benefits to all countries, particularly those most affected by underdevelopment and poverty, with a view to gradually reducing the abysmal gap between the developed and developing countries.

18- To enhance the role that civil society, including NGO's, can play at the regional and international levels in order to promote the purposes, principles and objectives of the Movement. The movement has succeeded to create a strong front on the International level, representing countries of the third world in the International organizations on top of which the United Nations.

Current Challenges facing the NAM include the necessity of protecting the principles of International law, eliminating weapons of mass destruction, combating terrorism, defending human rights, working toward making the United Nations more effective in meeting the needs of all its member states in order to preserve International Peace, Security and Stability, as well as realizing justice in the international economic system.

On the other hand, the long-standing goals of the Movement remain to be realized. Peace, development, economic cooperation and the democratization of international relations, to mention just a few, are old goals of the non-aligned countries.

In conclusion, The Non-Aligned Movement, faced with the goals yet to be reached and the many new challenges that are arising, is called upon to maintain a prominent and leading role in the current International relations in defense of the interests and priorities of its member states and for achievement of peace and security for mankind.

The Spanish historian **July Pecharramán**, in his book **"The Cold War, NATO front of the Warsaw Pact, Editorial Siglo XXI, Madrid 1998. Page 8"** states that the main features of this conflict can be noted as follows:

1. An extremely radical bipolar system, in which the intermediate positions, two blocks aligned countries grouped around two imperial powers, the United States and the Soviet Union, that meant one thing was created not allowed: **or you're with them or against! – No intermedias– positions**. The post – war world had been prepared to contemplate the hegemony of the big three, but the exhaustion of the UK and the serious problems that led to its decolonizing process forced him to download gradually its international responsibilities in the US that became the gendarme's western front led by the Soviet bloc.

2. A policy of carefully calculated risks, strategically aimed at the containment of the adversary and then advances to dissuade him from any hostile act, but avoiding a conflict of global character (is set a third world war). This policy led to the continuous emergence of so- called "hot conflict" (Korean War, the Vietnam War, the Berlin Crisis, missile crisis of Cuba, etc.), where the blocks measured their forces, ready to return to negotiations when risks were excessive for both. The great uncertainty about the intentions and the resilience of the adversary forced to a continuous increase in the offensive capability of the blocks.

3. The role assigned to the United Nations Organization (UN) as a forum for discussion between the blocks, the last resort to the crisis and, at the same time, the scene of the propaganda of the opponents. Despite the negative effects of the veto, the World Board representing the permanent members of the Security Council and the increasing role of the General Assembly and the Secretary, turned to the UN in a vital platform for "dialogue" in a few years when the international language seemed laden with military connotations.

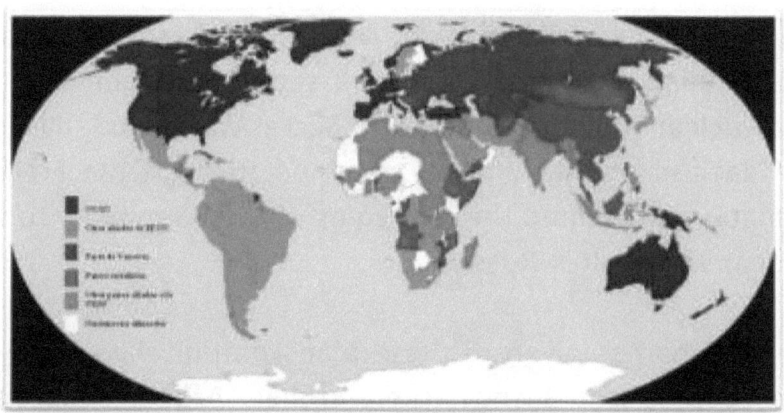

Figure 2. Map of the world in Cold War in 1980, in shades of red allies of the USSR and other countries Communists, and in shades of blue the NATO and its allies capitalists.

THE HIDDEN FACE OF GLOBAL GEOPOLITICS

USA PLANNED TO DESTROY THE UNION SOVIET WITH A MASSIVE NUCLEAR ATTACK

In 2015 the **National Security Archive United States** released a declassified 1950 with a list of sites for nuclear attacks in the territories of the Soviet Union and its allies document. The list contained about twelve hundred cities departing from East Germany in the West to China in the East. Moscow topped the list with Leningrad (now St. Petersburg) and had 179 to continue to atomic attacks in Moscow and St. Petersburg 145 other "designated places". The atomic weapons would fluctuate between 1.7 and 9 megatons (in comparison, the atomic bomb dropped on Hiroshima on August 6, 1945 named little Boy was about 0.013 to 0.018 megatons). The declassified documents comes from the **SAC** (entitled Study on Strategic Nuclear Requirements Strategic Air Command) for 1959 prepared in June 1956

Researchers **Michio Kaku** and **Daniel Axelrod and** n his book **"Winning a nuclear war plans secret Pentagon war – To Win a Nuclear War: The Pentagon's Secret War Plans"** based on these declassified documents obtained through the Freedom Information, presented the strategies of the US military to start a nuclear war against Russia.

The names given to these plans graphically portray his offensive purpose: Bushwhacker, Broiler, Arden, Shakedown, Offtackle, Dropshot, Trojan, Pincher, and Frolic (Guerilla, Grill, Burning, Intimidation, approach, Fling, Troyano, Nip, and Mischief).

According to declassified documents, the SAC had planned to raze the Soviet airpower before it developed means of intercontinental range, indicating the offensive nature of the work that President **Harry Truman** had ordered them to prepare the Pentagon and they strove to name their plans war accordingly. The study contains a list of eleven hundred airfields in the former Soviet bloc. If the USSR refused to surrender, USA continues regularly bombarding urban and industrial areas until a complete destruction. The destruction of the Soviet airpower was the priority US for nuclear attacks. The report notes that the priority given to American airpower (BRAVO) provided the use of thermonuclear weapons high power for the leveling of surfaces with the purpose of destroying high priority targets including air bases in Eastern Europe. Researchers at the National Security Archive show that the plan specified SAC "the systematic destruction of all urban–industrial targets and the Soviet bloc that specifically and explicitly attack the -población- in all cities, including Beijing, Moscow, Leningrad, East Berlin and Warsaw ". East Berlin was listed along with other cities located beyond the Soviet borders and included 91 designated targets. The researchers note that "deliberately civilians were targeted as such, which would be in direct conflict with international standards, which prohibit attacks against populations if (contrary to military installations with civilians in its Area)".

In September 1948, the thirty – third US President **Harry S. Truman** approved a document of the National Security Council (NSC-30) on **"The Politics of Nuclear War"**, which declared that the United States should be prepared to "use

THE HIDDEN FACE OF GLOBAL GEOPOLITICS

with promptly and effectively all appropriate means available, including nuclear weapons, in the interests of national security and should plan accordingly. At that time, US generals desperately needed information about the location of Soviet military centers and industrial centers.

They launched thousands of flights flying over Russia and photographing Soviet territory, triggering concerns about a potential Western invasion of the USSR among Kremlin officials.

That did nothing to force the Soviets to rush to strengthen its defensive capabilities, while military and political leaders of the West precisely used this military growth accelerated his rival as justification for building more weapons. Meanwhile, in order to support their offensive plans, Washington sent its B-29 bombers to Europe for the first Berlin crisis in 1948.

In 1949, it created the **North Atlantic Treaty Organization** (NATO), led by the United States six years before the USSR and its allies in Eastern Europe to respond defensively to establish the **Warsaw Pact, called the Treaty of Friendship, cooperation and Mutual Assistance.**

General **Curtis LeMay Emerson** as SAC commander ordered the preparation of **Operation Dropshot** in 1949, which provided that the US attack the USSR and its allies, stating that throw at least 300 nuclear bombs and 29,000 high explosives on 200 targets in a hundred cities and towns (including

58

Moscow and Leningrad), in order to raze 85% of the industrial potential of the Union Soviet with a single attack. 75 or 100 of the 300 nuclear devices were directed towards the destruction of Soviet ground combat aviation.

It noted that the **Operation Dropshot** was not the only planned by the Pentagon, also created the **Totality Plan**, which initially contemplated a nuclear attack on the USSR with about 30 atomic bombs. He scored 20 Soviet cities for its complete destruction in a first strike: Moscow, Leningrad, Kiev, Stalino (Donetsk), Kuibyshev, Baku and others.

The directors of the National Security Council meeting on August 18, 1948 raised two basic objectives for the USSR:

1- Reduce the power and influence of the USSR so that never again pose a threat to peace and stability in the world.
2- Produce a radical change in the theory and practice of international relations maintained by the Russian government.

The fulfillment of these two objectives would allow the USSR and the USA possible to maintain normal international relations. But it is not questionable that the real intention of the US raze was the main political and economic potential military targets using conventional weapons, long-range and high precision. In adherence, planners offered to begin a ground campaign against the USSR for a 'complete victory' over the Soviet Union together with European allies. According to the plan of Washington, the war would begin on January 1, 1957.

And so for an extended period of time, the only obstacle to start this massive nuclear attack was that the Pentagon did not have enough atomic bombs (in 1948 Washington boasted of possessing an arsenal of 50 bombs), or dispose of aircraft to carry out the attack. For example, in 1948 the US Air Force had only thirty-two B-29 bombers modified to throw nuclear bombs.

Elnök úr, tárgyalhatunk!
Angol karikatúra, 1962.
Forrás: Schmid 110. o.

Figure 3. Graphical representation of the rivalry between the leaders of the two great powers of the Cold War (Nikita Khrushchev and JF Kennedy).

In Figure **No. 3** leaders of the great powers are reflected, (Nikita Khrushchev and JF Kennedy), facing each other, measuring forces and next to blow themselves each other to smithereens, because each of them is sitting nuclear missiles whose control depends on the opponent. With the latter referring to US missiles in Turkey since 1957 and installed in Cuba in October 1962. In the cartoon looks to each of the characters with your finger on the button.

PROJECT A119 ULTRA-SECRET: THAT WAS HOW US THOUGHT OFF A NUCLEAR BOMB ON THE MOON

In 1958 an ultra – secret plan carried out by the US Air Force (charted whose existence has been denied for a long time until recently when declassified documents on this project were published). Under the name of "**A Study of Lunar Research Flights**", the project was intended to detonate a nuclear bomb on the lunar surface. A project developed under the context of the Cold War where the US sought to prove their superiority over the Soviet Union and the rest of the world, and scientifically speaking, this event was also designed to answer many questions in planetary astronomy and astrogeology.

It happened a few years before the man on the moon and the goal was not to blow up the satellite, the project was a "complaint" facing the population that the detonation of the bomb would help in answering some of the mysteries astronomy and Planetary Geology.

Project leader was **Dr. Leonard Reiffel**, a physicist who carried out studies in 1958 to a foundation for research funded by the US Army. **Carl Sagan** (astronomer, astrophysicist, cosmologist, writer and science popularizer) a genius, who stood out among all partners Reiffel, joined the research team responsible for investigating the effects of a nuclear explosion on a site (like the moon) with low gravity as well as the subsequent effects causing that on Earth.

The reality is that the detonation of the bomb, similar to the one that was dropped on Hiroshima City a few years earlier, it would be addressed on the lunar limb when the satellite submit the full moon phase. Thus a staging of film, a nuclear mushroom that would be illuminated by the Sun and from the Earth could make out like a real show, Dantesque and terrifying, but above all and from the point of view American, propagandistic be achieved and demonstration of force.

Unquestionably neither this nor the Russian project were carried out and were canceled in 1959 for fear of a negative reaction of the world population, changing later the target for the arrival to the moon, certainly more popular.

On August 5, 1963 signed the **Partial Nuclear Test Ban Treaty** (PTBT) and 27 January 1967 the **Outer Space Treaty** (OST), which would lay the groundwork for preventing future exploration under the concept of the detonation of a nuclear device on the moon.

The Soviet counterpart, according to these reports, after US develop its project to detonate a nuclear bomb on the moon; the Soviets had developed a similar project. It started in January 1958; it was part of a series of proposals under the codename "E". **The E-1 project** demanded plans to reach the moon while projects **E-2 and E-3** would allow sending a probe to the hidden side of the Moon to take a series of photographs of its surface. Most of the documents relating to the plan, which was revealed only in 2000, has been destroyed and

Washington has not officially confirmed the existence of such a program (or stupid they were).

AFSWC-TR-59-39

SWC
TR
59-39
Vol I

HEADQUARTERS

AIR FORCE SPECIAL WEAPONS CENTER

AIR RESEARCH AND DEVELOPMENT COMMAND

KIRTLAND AIR FORCE BASE, NEW MEXICO

CATALOGED BY DDC 425380
AS AD No.____

A STUDY OF LUNAR RESEARCH FLIGHTS
Vol I

by

L. Reiffel

ARMOUR RESEARCH FOUNDATION
of
Illinois Institute of Technology
19 June 1959

Figure 4. Cover the declassified document evidencing the existence of a secret project to detonate a nuclear bomb on the moon.

THE HIDDEN FACE OF GLOBAL GEOPOLITICS

US SECRET KEY MISSILES TO LAUNCH WAS '00000000'

Between 1960 and 1977, the secret password that allowed US presidents launch nuclear missiles was **'00000000'**. The code, or PAL-for their stands for **Permissive Action Link** (safety device arms) was introduced by President **John F. Kennedy** in 1960 to prevent an unauthorized launch of nuclear missiles.

Interestingly people who were in the underground reservoirs missile also had a dual key system to ensure a joint decision, so that no one could throw them alone and without authorization.

This protection was implemented for long-range missiles thousand Minuteman which were introduced during the missile crisis in Cuba in 1960, which remained the backbone of the US strategic deterrent until the early 70s.

But think of something interesting: nobody told neither the president nor his Secretary of Defense, **Robert McNamara**, the generals **Strategic Air Command** in **Omaha** (city in the state of Nebraska the United States) had decided that the risk of forgotten passwords was greater than that of an unauthorized launch. So they chose one that everyone would remember.

The codes "secrets" were finally improved in 1977, but only after a long campaign of a former employee of the Air Force and congressman, who highlighted the threat that meant leaving so open procedure. **McNamara**only learned of the deception in 2004, when he told a former member of the team responsible for firing the Minuteman (US nuclear missile) and said: – **"I am in absolute shock and outraged, who authorized that?"** And if the British think they can make fun of Americans, should take into account that the government in London had no password protection.

Unveiled documents and made available to the public in 2007 show that the **nuclear warhead WE 177** (was a nuclear bomb freefall or nuclear depth charge deployed respectively by the Royal Air Force and Royal Navy), with which they trained the Tornado aircraft crews and previous V-bomber, was assembled using a simple device that resembled safe to prevent theft of a bicycle.

To launch an atomic missile, it had to remove two screws from a similar panel to the cover of a television remote control. That revealed a sequence of dials and a standard Allen key is how he selected would deploy the weapon: high or low power, bursting in air or land, etc. To complete the process, a bicycle key is inserted and turned ninety degrees: no password, no dual key system, a nuclear missile is fired.

THE HIDDEN FACE OF GLOBAL GEOPOLITICS

USA SPENT THE SUM OF EIGHT BILLIONS DOLLARS IN THE COLD WAR

Military expenditures have had an amazing growth in the last seventy years. Before the Second World War these expenses worldwide were estimated at about 48 billion dollars, but in 1972 they had grown to 240 billion and reached $ 1.4 trillion in 1990 (Sivard, 1974, SIPRI, 2010).

Walter LaFeber historian of Foreign Affairs has estimated that US disbursed during the Cold War about 8 trillion, taking into account the money that the US spent in the Korean War and Vietnam, the intervention in Afghanistan, Nicaragua, Cuba, Chile, Dominican Republic and Granada, the operations of the CIA and weapons development.

Most initial escalation of these costs occurred between 1939 and 1945, when the United States spent $ 3.2 trillion at constant 2002 prices, while the USSR erogó 582 billion rubles (48 billion dollars) to current prices of those years and the cost of the war for Germany is estimated to have reached the equivalent of 68 billion dollars at current prices also (Morss, 2010; Podkolzin s / f; Exordio, 2004).

During the Cold War that can be placed in the period between 1946 and 1990, military expenditures were maintained in a growth process especially associated with the rise of new nuclear weapons and the development of military alliances such as NATO and the Warsaw Pact. Additionally, these expenses increased promptly with the Korean War (1950–53) and the Vietnam War (1965–1975).

In terms of its weight in the economy, military spending accounted for a strong outlay for the top contenders of the Cold War, both the United States and the Soviet Union. Indeed, these expenses came to represent 9.3% of gross domestic product (GDP) US in 1960, 8.1% in 1970, 4.9% in 1980 and 5.2% in 1990. In the USSR is estimated that reached 11.1% of GDP in 1960, 12.0% in 1970, 12.8% in 1980 and 14.3% in 1990 (US Government, 2010; Rand, 1989).

SYMBOLIC MEDALS

In 2007 the US Congress It approved a bill to establish a new award for participation in the Cold War. It is a medal without official status that the US Army He does not recognize. Any soldier who served in the US Armed Forcesduring this period, you can get this medal. Only Louisiana, Texas and Alaska consider it an official medal.

In U.S.A. there is an association of veterans of the Cold War that demands to be recognized by the authorities but has only managed the Department of Defense give them certificates confirming their participation in the Cold War.

Figure 5. Symbolic Medal given to veterans who participated in the Cold War.

CRISIS AND COLLAPSE OF THE USSR: END OF THE COLD WAR

The process that led to the end of this conflict was led by **Ronald Reagan** and **Mikhail Gorbachev**. A **George Bush** only corresponded to him to witness the final blow of the Cold War. At the beginning of his mandate communism collapsed in Eastern Europe (1989) and the Soviet Union (1991) disintegrated, these two facts undeniably confirmed the end of the Cold War. **Henry Kissinger** said that both leaders were convinced of victory own side. But the first understood well the sources of their society, while Gorbachev precipitated the fall of his system by requiring a reform for which he was unprepared.

The Cold War came to an end for two main reasons: on the one hand can be considered as an important factor of economic pressure from rearming sponsored during the first period of **Ronald Reagan** and other internal changes experienced by the Soviet Union during the process of reforms undertaken by **Mikhail Gorbachev**. But the fundamental factor was given by the concrete effects that caused the reforms in the USSR during the eighties: they failed to revive the ailing Soviet economy and also helped to destroy the political and ideological support of the Soviet regime.

The long period of sustained clashes between US and the USSR caused by the mid-1980s, the Soviet Union saw facing the wear and suffocation raised by an arms race that had consumed its economic resources for decades.In this situation, the last of the Soviet leaders, Mijael Gorbachev undertook a deep reform program known as **perestroika** and **Glasnost**. But the USSR did not survive the reform plans. Perestroika and Glasnost expected to respond to the many problems afflicting the Soviet system, but the more the reform process lasted more proved its ineffectiveness.

In 1987 it begins to become a reality the need for a radical reform of the economy. At the plenary meeting of the Central Committee of the CPSU in June 1987 the "principles of radical restructuring of economic management" were adopted.

Depending on this, they created mechanisms that gave management autonomy to Soviet enterprises, and circuit productivity incentives, thereby "Perestroika" tried to make the group of state companies efficient and competitive. Since that time it was expected that the companies were directed by the principle that production should cover costs, together with the fact that companies should finance its activities without government subsidies.Moreover, one of the first legislative steps of perestroika was also given by the law on individual work (November 1986), aimed at stimulating the initiative of individuals to make a series of linked to small service sector economic activities. As noted by **Rafael Aracil**, it was expected that these changes will encourage Soviet enterprises to turn them competitive and thus reach the objectives proposed by the Perestroika. From the political point of view, perestroika envisaged a restructuring aimed at democratizing the Soviet Union. On this point, in his book Perestroika, Gorbachev said:

"We are firmly convinced that only through constant development intrinsic to socialism democratic forms and through the expansion of self – government, we can make progress in production, science and technology, culture and art and in all social spheres (...) perestroika itself can only be achieved through democracy (...) to gain democratic freedoms, the working masses come to power (...) the radical and comprehensive restructuring must also develop the full potential of democracy".

Perestroika contemplated the full opening to the West, through the adoption of a new foreign policy that sought understanding and to tensions. Realizing the impossibility of combining the Cold War and the solution of the serious problems afflicting the economy and Soviet society, the Soviet leader, proclaimed at the XXVII Congress of the Communist Party of the Soviet Union (CPSU) in 1986 what he called a "new" political thought: "the new world was characterized by" global interdependence "henceforth had to forget about the logic of the Cold War and seek cooperation and consensus on the direction of international relations it was to seek" a reciprocal, constructive and creative action at the same time to prevent nuclear catastrophe and that civilization can survive" This idea is clearly expressed in his book Perestroika (1987):

"Of course, there will still distinctions. But should we engage in a duel for their cause? Would not it be better to spend on the things that divide us, on behalf of the interest of all humanity, in the name of life on earth? We have made our choice, affirmed our political vision, both through statements and through actions and specific facts. People are tired of so much tension and confrontation. Prefers to seek a safer and reliable world, a world in which everyone keeps his own philosophical, political and ideological opinions and way of life"

The USSR was preparing for a great retreat, both in its competition with the US and the international commitments that had been acquired during the Cold War. Finding the reality of the Soviet situation, Gorbachev realized the need to reduce the obligations in the Third World and to avoid new commitments. He decided to cut Soviet aid to Marxist forces in Nicaragua, Cambodia, Angola and Ethiopia, as well as ending the costly military intervention in Afghanistan. Indeed, in late

1988, the USSR Mikhail Gorbachev had largely got rid of the conflicts that held on different continents.

Mikhail Gorbachev tried to overcome the problems implementing a comprehensive reform program known as Glasnost and Perestrika. However, Soviet leader did not achieve its objectives because, as Henry Kissinger points out, the more lasting the **Perestroika** and **Glasnost**, more isolated and more confidence was lost. Each reform was a half – measure that accelerated the Soviet decline. In an attempt to reform communism and in particular its efforts to establish a limited democracy in both Eastern Europe and the Soviet Union, allowed critics of communism deny its legitimacy. From this perspective, once was abandoned communism, which was the glue that held the Soviet empire, both countries of Eastern Europe and the republics that formed the Soviet Union took the opportunity to go their own way.

US pressure adds to all the internal problems of the Soviet Union, but is not itself the primary cause of the collapse of the USSR. At this point we must note that the stated goals of the Reagan administration were using the arms race to subdue the Soviet economy at a pressure that would lead to bankruptcy. In his memoirs Ronald Reagan said: "I intended to let the Soviets were going to spend what they have to spend to stay ahead in the arms race".

Hobsbawm points out, was not the crusade by Reagan, against what he called **"Evil Empire"**, which produced the Soviet collapse, were the American propagandists who claimed that his fall was due to an active campaign of harassment and demolition. "But there is no sign that the government of the United States contemplated the imminent collapse of the USSR or that he was prepared for this time. While they hoped to embarrass the Soviet economy, the US government he had been informed wrongly by their own intelligence services that the USSR was in good shape and able to maintain the arms race. In the early eighties, still believed that the USSR was waging a strong overall offensive.

THE "FAILUR" OF GORBACHEV'S REFORMS AND THE END OF THE COMMUNIST BLOCK

Gorbachev project involved the inability to maintain by force regimes "popular democracies" as had been set after the successive Soviet interventions.

The **Perestroika** and **Glasnost** had an immediate effect in the satellite states of Eastern Europe. The way Gorbachev launched the collapse of the "Soviet empire" was simple: do nothing to defend the regimes of Eastern Europe. Without the Soviet intervention, these governments were swept with extraordinary ease in the short term of a few months. Finally, as noted by **Henry Kissinger**, Gorbachev's attitude was the explicit renunciation of the "**Brezhnev Doctrine**", according to which the USSR had the right and duty to quell uprisings and insurrections in the Eastern Europe. Gorbachev did not apply the Brezhnev doctrine and liberalization proved to be incompatible with communist governments.

THE HIDDEN FACE OF GLOBAL GEOPOLITICS

By September 1988, Gorbachev had closed the Liaison Committee with the socialist countries in the CPSU, a sign that the Kremlin abandoning the **Brezhnev Doctrine** (this political doctrine introduced by Leonid Brezhnev in 1968, determined that when there were forces hostile to socialism try to turn the development of some socialist country towards capitalism, they would become not only a problem of the country concerned but also on a problem common to all communist countries). In December of that year he announced solemnly in the General Assembly of the UN a unilateral cut of more than half a million soldiers, of which half would retire with more than five thousand tanks from Eastern Europe. Moscow's attitude was more and more clearly conciliatory towards reform in the "popular democracies".

1989 revolutions in Eastern Europe had been a historic event of multiple resonances. On the one hand, they were the collapse of communist systems built after 1945, on the other, meant the loss of the zone of influence that the USSR had built after his victory against Nazism. With this you can see that attempts to reform communism in Eastern Europe, eventually causing it to fall and eventually own disintegration of the Soviet Union. As Robert Service points out, the outcome was spectacular. In early 1989 the Communists ruled all the East European countries Elbe River. At the end of the year, the only Communist state remained west of the USSR was Albania, and Albania had been hostile to the USSR from the government of Khrushchev.

The Cold War confrontation that had marked international relations since the end of World War II, will end by the collapse and disintegration of one of the contenders. The end of the Cold War and the demise of the Soviet Union are two parallel phenomena that radically change the world. For the British historian **Eric Hobsbawm**, the Cold War ended before the Soviet Union disintegrated, but the end of the conflict became apparent only when the latter had ceased to exist:

"The Cold War ended when one of the superpowers, or both, recognize the sinister and absurd race of atomic weapons, and when one or both accepted that the other sincerely wanted to end this race (...) The real Cold War, as it is easy to see from our perspective today, ended with the Washington summit in 1987, but it was not possible to recognize that was over until the USSR left a superpower be, or plain power (...) but the gears of the war machine continued turning on both sides. The professionals paranoia, secret services continued to suspect that any movement on the other side was no more than a cunning trick to guard down the enemy and defeat him better. The collapse of the Soviet empire in 1989, the disintegration and dissolution of the USSR itself in 1989–1991, made it impossible to pretend that nothing had changed, and even less believes".

Henry Kissinger said that the end of the Cold War occurred at the time when the Soviet Union launched the internal transformation of his regime. This process was developed throughout the period led by Gorbachev, that is, from 1985, however, the most concrete manifestation, according to Kissinger, occurred in the XXVII Congress of the Communist Party of the Soviet Union (1986). This time was completely abandoned the theory of the inevitable class struggle and coexistence was proclaimed as an end in itself. From the perspective of analysis of Henry Kissinger, this fact came to ratify the theory proposed by Kennan in 1946, about the need for the United States show an attitude of containment against the communist forces and against the USSR until it any experienced a radical change in their internal structures. With this in mind, we can say that the Cold War ends during the administrations of **Ronald Reagan** and **Mikhail Gorbachev**, as between 1985 and 1989 the atmosphere of tension and intermittent crises, characteristic of the Cold War, giving way to a kind of international relations based on the search for understanding.

In conclusion, it was the failure of Gorbachev's reforms and the democratic revolutions in Eastern Europe that led to the collapse of the Soviet bloc, which, in turn, also disintegrated intestinally since the separatist aspirations of the Republics had begun to manifest through the demands of "democracy" and "national self – determination". As the Russian historian **Robert Service**, in some cases as in the Baltic countries (Estonia, Latvia and Lithuania), these demands were responding to a commitment to these values, but in most of the other republics, those claims were nothing more than the attempt by local Communist Party elite to maintain power. Declaring independence expected isolate their respective republics of daily interference from Moscow.

The Cold War ended before the USSR knew his purpose. However, it was only evident when one of the contestants had ceased to exist. The Cold War ended by successive strokes. The gears were stopping and what began with a pacifist rhetoric continued with concrete announcements as the speech Gorbachev at the UN, announcing the unilateral reduction of his army and the removal thereof from Eastern Europe, he continued with a series diplomats from which gestures westward approach was being in evidence. The death sentence of the Cold War was declared by Gorbachev and Bush.

On December 8, 1991 in agreements Minsk (Belarus Capital) death of one of the contenders of the Cold War was declared, solemnly declaring that "We the Republics of Belarus, the Russian Federation (RSFSR) and Ukraine as founding states the USSR signed the treaty of the Union of 1922, hereinafter referred to as high contracting parties, we find that the USSR as a subject of international law and a geopolitical reality ceases to exist".After the Soviet collapse left standing only the huge American empire. From this point of view it is legitimate to say that the winner of this peculiar War was US.

The Cold War was over. In an extremely fast process the USSR and the US ended the long conflict that had begun after the end of World War II. Now in the process of finalizing the Cold War, one of the actors he failed and disintegrated, left his opponent as one great superpower. This is the theme developed by the British historian **Eric Hobsbawm**, in his article published in "Le Monde Diplomatique" "After Winning the War", which states: "Indeed, the collapse of the Soviet Union left the United States as the only superpower, which no other power could or wanted to challenge".

With the disintegration of the Soviet Union the end of the Cold War was confirmed. Thus, the peculiar conflict that characterized the development of international relations for 45 years played an end with the fall of one of its contenders. The collapse of one of its protagonists, gave way to a world indisputably led by the United States as economic and military superpower. Below is a synopsis of the successive revolutions that shook Europe presents.

This, which produced an end to the Soviet sphere of influence (1989):

– POLAND

Poland was the country that started the revolutionary process. After a series of strikes in the summer of 1988, the communist government, led by **General Jaruselzski**, had to sit down and negotiate with the union Solidarity.Agreements April 1989 meant the legal recognition of the union and the opening of a process of democratic transition. With this fact a historic agreement occurred, because for the first time since 1946, free elections were organized in Eastern Europe, but from a practical point of view freedom would be controlled and limited (the Union Solidarity undertook to grant 65 % of the 460 minutes of the Diet the Communist Party, while the minutes of the Senate would be objects of real competition, but this only had the power to reject laws passed by the Diet). Poland thus entered a transition process whose duration was scheduled in four years, after which, the choice of the two chambers would be free. In the elections of June 1989, the Communist Party was severely beaten (99 of the 100 seats in the Senate were occupied by Solidarity; the remaining occupied an independent candidate). Faced with this situation, the Communist Party proposed the establishment of a national unity government with the participation of Solidarity, an issue rejected by the union. At the end General Jaruzelski saw no other solution than to allow the formation of a government, who's Prime Minister would Mazowiecki, leader of Solidarity. The first non – communist government in Eastern Europe thus formed since 1945. The rapid decomposition of the communist regime, allowed **Lech Walesa** (leader of the labor movement Solidarity), was elected president in 1990.

A concrete example of the changes experienced in the Soviet Union was the refusal of Gorbachev to use Soviet troops to annul the election results in Poland, thereby demonstrating concretely that the Brezhnev doctrine, which had been formulated to justify intervention in Czechoslovakia 1968, there was really dead.

THE HIDDEN FACE OF GLOBAL GEOPOLITICS

– HUNGARY

The Hungarian Communist Party tried to emulate Gorbachev's reform program, with the same order to save communism, but to no avail. On 11 January 1989 the Hungarian Parliament, which was dominated by the Communists, legalized freedom of assembly and association for non – communists, a month later groups legalized independent political parties. On April 8 **Janos Kadar**, who had assumed the leadership of the Communist Party after the 1956 revolution, was ousted from power.

On May 2 Hungary became the first country in the Soviet bloc to open the border with Western Europe. In September the communist government and the newly created opposition parties agreed to participate in free elections, which were scheduled for March 1990, which allowed the democratic opposition party establish a non – communist government under the leadership of **Jozef Antall**. (The Communist Party, which by then had adopted the name Socialist Party won only 9% of the votes). In short, the Communists reformers themselves were the ones who abolished the system very quickly. In 1989, the multiparty system and later this year the Communist Party was falling apart, establishing a democratic constitution was established. Then in 1990 they came to power anticommunist.

RAUL OJEDA

– GERMAN DEMOCRATIC REPUBLIC (GDR)

The decision of the authorities in Budapest (capital of Hungary), to open its border with Austria in September 1989 opened a "gap" in the 'iron curtain' by the tens of thousands of people of the Democratic Republic of Germany fled to the Federal Republic of Germany through Czechoslovakia, Hungary and Austria. The exodus of the population would soon join a wave of demonstrations throughout East Germany.

The leader of the GDR, **Eric Honecker**, who had just publicly congratulate the Chinese ambassador repression in Tiananamen Square, was convinced that the reforms would lead to the collapse of the regime. From here the events were precipitated, Honecker was replaced by a reformist communist, Egon Krenz, who took the historic decision to open the Berlin Wall on November 9, 1989 and the holding of free elections. At first the new leader of the GDR, tried to stop the exodus of East Germans ending restrictions that prevented travel to the West, but the move only served to encourage the flight of East Germans more. In view of this situation, the 9 November event occurred which it will become a symbol of the end of the Cold War, that day saw the opening of the Berlin Wall. Thousands of East Germans immediately went to West Berlin.

The rapid collapse of the GDR opened a negotiation process between the four victorious powers of World War II and the FRG, led by a chancellor, Helmut Kohl, who was well aware of the historic opportunity that opened to Germany. At first, the Soviets tried to prevent unification by proposing to revive the institutions of German occupation by the four victorious powers, however, the Soviet goal then went on to try to prevent a future unified Germany be a member of NATO. Before this situation the Western Allies proposed to hold talks "Two Plus Four", the two German states, plus the United States, Britain, France and the Soviet Union.

Finally on July 14, 1990 Gorbachev accepted the unification of Germany and its membership in NATO. In return, the West German chancellor, Helmut Col promised to grant large loans and other forms of economic aid to the Soviet Union. He also agreed to limit the military forces of united Germany to 370,000 people and assured Gorbachev that there would be biological, nuclear or chemical weapons in the German arsenal. He also promised to provide 8,000 million for maintenance and withdrawal of Soviet forces from Germany.

A Ronald Powaski point, with the realization of the agreements of German unification, was taking out the last treaty pending the Second World War in Europe. On 23 August the East German parliament set October 3 as the date for the merger with the Federal Republic. On 12 September 1990 the four Allied powers of World War II and the two Germanys signed the "Treaty on the Final Determination with Respect to Germany". On October 1 the victors of World War II officially renounced their rights and responsibilities over Germany and Berlin. On October 3 Germany was reunified.

RAUL OJEDA

– CZECHOSLOVAKIA

On November 17, 1989, thousands of young people gathered in the main square in Prague to demand recognition of their rights. Two days later, about 200,000 people demonstrated in the capital to demand free elections and the resignation of Communist leaders. On November 24 resigned General Secretary of the Communist Party, **Milos Jakes**. After 4 days, after a general strike, the government allowed non – Communist parties to organize. On December 10 a new cabinet, in which the majority were not comunitas was sworn in. On 29 December 1989 an interim government with Vaclav Havel as president was created. The new government called free elections byJune 1990 and opened the border with Austria. In the elections the Communist party won 14% of the votes, 12% Democrat and Civic Forum (led by Havel), and 47%. The latter proceeded to create a coalition government with the new Democratic party and the new government was no room for any Communist.

– BULGARIA

I was also affected by the events of the rest of Eastern Europe. On November 9, 1989, the day saw the opening of the Berlin Wall; the Communist Politburo ousted Bulgaria **Todor Zhikov**, who had been party leader since 1961. In his place was **Petar Toshev Mladenov**, with greater propensity to carry out the reforms, however, after a year communism it was also defeated at the polls.

THE HIDDEN FACE OF GLOBAL GEOPOLITICS

– ROMANIA

In this country the transition from communism to democracy was more violent. On 21 December 1989 the security forces of the state (the **Securitate**, the secret police of the regime) killed in the city of Timisoara hundreds of Romanians demonstrated against the government's attempt to evict a dissident priest. The killing provoked even more demonstrations. On December 22 the Romanian communist leader or **Conducator** (title that it had been granted), **Nicolae Ceausescu** tried to flee the country to realize that military units began to support the demonstrators. However, he was captured and summarily executed by the army on December 25. In **1990 Ion Iliescu**, he won the presidential elections.

– THE MIDDLE EAST GULF WAR (1990–1991)

When **Saddam Hussein** invaded August 2, 1990 the small and wealthy state of Kuwait to try to alleviate the enormous losses caused by the war that had confronted Iraq with Iran did not take into account the new situation created by the end of the Cold War. This war was also called by the Iraqi leader as "the Mother of all battles".

UN, following the proposed US He condemned the assault, economic sanctions and decided finally authorized military intervention. The USSR, traditional ally of Iraq, was not enough to veto in the Security Council the guidelines of the American political force. So President George Bush could articulate a large international coalition. In addition to its traditional allies in NATO, the USSR and the new regimes of Eastern Europe, Egypt and most Arab countries, Japan and the newly industrialized Asian countries they sought the alliance and friendship with the superpower.

The war outcome was predictable. Hussein could just throw a Scud missile on Israel, mostly American missile intercepted by Patriot missiles. After an intense bombardment started on 15 January 1991 when it concluded the ultimatum issued by the UN, coalition troops liberated easily Kuwaiti territory. To the surprise of many, not US troops continued their way to Baghdad and allowed Saddam to continue in power. On February 28 a cease – fire agreed in an unfinished conflict would not end here.

– THE PROCESS OF "PEACE" ARAB–ISRAELI

After the outbreak of the **Intifada** (Palestinian uprising against the Israeli Zionist occupation) in 1987 in Gaza and the West Bank, the Organization for the Liberation of Palestine (LOP) and its leader **Yasir Arafat** managed toconsolidate in the direction of the Palestinian resistance. In this context, the Palestinian National Council (met PNC) in Algiers in 1988 and agreed to the proclamation of the independence of the Palestinian state, accepting the UN agreement of November 1947 that decided the partition of Palestine into two states, which implied recognition of the State of Israel. **Mikhail Gorbachev** had received Arafat in April 1988 and had asked him to take into account "the interests of the security of Israel".

THE HIDDEN FACE OF GLOBAL GEOPOLITICS

The end of the cold war provided the US and the USSR convene a Conference on Peace in the Middle East in Madrid in October 1991. In the capital of Spain a difficult peace process based on the principle of "land for peace" opened. After arduous secret negotiations in Oslo in September 1993 was signed in Washington the "Declaration of Principles on interim autonomy arrangements" that gave the go -ahead to a peace process that unfortunately ended in failure. This topic will be expanded later.

CREATION AND IMPLEMENTATION OF A NEW ORDER POST– WAR COLD

In the past, the new international orders were established as a result of major wars – by the **Treaty of Westphalia**, which was two agreements reached in the cities of Osnabrück and Münster in 1648, one on 15 maypole and the other on 24 October. According to these treaties, end the war he got between the belligerent states in Germany, Protestants on one side and the Holy Roman Empire and Catholics on the other princes, and the confrontation that for eighty years faced also concluded Spain with the Republic of the Seven Countries Netherlands. It was, in short, the treaty that ended the Thirty Years' War, which began in 1618 with the Defenestration of Prague; by the **Congress of Vienna** "Restoration" after the final defeat of Napoleon, the absolute monarchs of Europe sought to return to the stage before the French Revolution, which meant the elimination of social measures, political and economic dictated by the revolutionary ideals of the eighteenth century, mainly those concerning the constitutions and the postulate of national sovereignty, giving way again to the unlimited power of kings, return to the nobility and clergy privileges, reconstruct the map of Europe that had It has been defaced by the conquests and annexations caused by war, and rethink international life based on a system of joint and balanced security not to allow more revolutions or attempts by any country to achieve continental hegemony); by the **Treaty of Versailles** after the First World War, in Yalta (Crimea) and Potsdam (a German city, capital of the federal state of Brandenburg) after World War II.

Continuing the passage of history, a new world order should be established after the Cold War. Among contemporary politicians who referred to the need for a new world order was for example the first President **George Bush**. Since the summer of 1990 until March 1991, he used the term **"new world order" 43 times**.

The end of the Cold War only created more instability, more security challenges and sources of international conflict. On the other hand, it also created extraordinary to solve many problems resulting from the inherent tension of a bipolar world system opportunities.

The American political scientist **Francis Fukuyama** in the early nineties, called the end of the Cold War "end of history", some thought to challenge that idea. It was soon clear, however, that instead of "end of history" were actually against "a return of history", ie, a revival of traditional sources, historical tension and international conflict. The course is ironically called the "back to the future". This is the general diagnosis. The long – term therapy would be the creation and implementation of a new world order.

It should define the trends of economic, technological, military and sociopolitical would decide the future of international relations. This includes all the dramatic transformations that are taking place as a result of the end of the Cold War– the disintegration of the bipolar world system and cooperation, rather than confrontation, between recent ideological adversaries. The term **"New World Order"** also covers the emerging international system and the need to create a new balance of power as well as new structures.

An important role in the new global order should be played by the United Nations –reformada and adapted to the new global balance of power, and new challenges and threats. The new world order must be equipped with an effective instrument in the form of an international military force. That force should be constituted to address any potential aggressor you plan to use the army as a tool to pursue political goals.

The new world order also means a more important role of diplomacy and diplomatic techniques to resolve international conflicts. It means shifting the emphasis from military to diplomatic methods. Arms reduction will remain an important component of the new world order agenda.

The first President Bush often expressed the importance of the International Monetary Fund and the World Bank in shaping the new global order. Meetings of the Group of Eight most industrialized countries have replaced the old conference of heads of state.

The new world order is often seen as a way to provide the world's stability and security. But democratization and the growing struggle for sovereignty in various parts of the world have helped to create more internal than international (tensions and conflicts, as in Yugoslavia, the former Soviet Union and Africa), to stabilize the situation.

And from the "**New World Order**", the US government has long experience of toppling governments adversaries – however legitimate they are– by promoting civil wars; direct invasions or others; military, parliamentary or financial shocks; assassinations and other variants known and secretas– constantly incorporated into its interventionist repertoire. Radically US It has become a super power macabre and interventionist.

Therefore, it is necessary to know the many similarities of different countries in the actions and procedures of the US armed forces aimed at destabilizing governments that are not like to cause the overthrow of the legitimate authorities and related leaders to promote imperial domination. – All this, in order to implement the New World Order.

It is amazing to compare these characteristics with the tactics used for the preparation and implementation of – efectivos or fallidos– blows in many countries in the western hemisphere and the world. For example, in Chile against Salvador Allende, against the Sandinista Nicaragua, against the **Farabundo Martí National Liberation Front** (FMLN) in El Salvador, Ecuador, Honduras and Venezuela, the methods practiced by the United States have much in common. And the same can be said about the similarities of these so used in Afghanistan, Iraq, Egypt, Pakistan, Libya and Syria recently.

The systematic review of "Manual **Training Special Forces US Army Unconventional Warfare"** ("US Army Special Forces Unconventional Warfare Training Manual") published in November 2010 places exposed the real reason for these "strange "matches in the origin and purpose of such actions. This shameful document is available on the website:

https://info.publicintelligence.net/USArmy–UW.pdf

In his ninety-seven pages explains the actions that have been or are being implemented by these US forces in those countries. In the first chapter of the US Army Manual activities are they oriented defined **Special Operations Command US** and support given to the **United States Special Operations Command** (English its acronym "USSOCOM"), to promote movement of resistance or insurgency calls to coerce, disrupt or overthrow a legitimate government operating through clandestine, auxiliaries and guerrilla forces.

It describes the concepts of generalized war, guerrilla war, limited war, insurgency, subversion and resistance movements are defined. The role of unconventional warfare (is based **fourth generation warfare**) in the US national strategy and the viability of American sponsorship.

The manual orients create conditions to divide or weaken the organizational mechanisms available to the government that aims to overthrow to maintain its control over the civilian population and how to organize a minimum core of leadership of the clandestine resistance activities.

The US genocidal Manual is to "use all means available both involving the use of armed force as those that do not involve, as well as means involving casualties and acarreenmeans not to impose the enemy own interests. This includes the emergence of "non-state actors who have knowledge and high-level technologies that can perform asymmetric attacks with the intent to promote individual or group interests".

This is war without limits attacks on all areas of vulnerability: **War Cultural**, influencing the cultural views of the opposing nation; **Drug War**, invading the opposing nation with illegal drugs; **War economic aid**, using the dependence on financial aid to control the adversary; **Environmental warfare**, destroying the environmental resources of the opposing nation; **Financial War**, subverting or dominating the adversary banking system and stock market; **International Legal War**, subverting or policies dominating international or multinational organizations and exerting a strong boycott against a nation; **Media war**, manipulating foreign media; **War on the Internet and social networks** through the domain or destruction of transnational computer systems; **Psychological Warfare**, dominating the perception of the capabilities of the opposing nation; **Resource War**, controlling access to scarce natural resources or manipulating its market value; **Contraband war**, invading the market with illegal goods adversary; **Technology War**, gaining an advantage in controlling key civilian and military technologies, and the**terrorist war** against the civilian population.

A true manual for genocide is the one running the US government against those who do not sympathize with its foreign policy.

Dear Reader: Are you prepared the War of Fifth Generation?

RAUL OJEDA

NEW WORLD ORDER

"We are on the verge of a global transformation. All we need is a major crisis and the nations will accept the New World Order "David Rockefeller

DEFINITION

The first appearance of this term as autártico occurred in 1920 in the book "The New World Order " of **Frederick C. Hicks**, but mistakenly believed that the first antecedent was the book of the same name written by **HG Wells**in 1940. Previously, phrase had been used by **Nicholas Murray Butler** (politician, philosopher and Nobel Peace Prize in 1931) in his book "a World in Ferment" (1917). It was also mentioned in a 1940 essay written by the practitioner of esotericism and English writer **Alice Bailey**, which included in the posthumous compilation book "The Externalisation of the Hierarchy" (1957). **Hicks, Wells and Bailey** referred to a "New World Order" a peaceful democratic socialist utopia, they hoped, would soon emerge as a natural reaction to the barbarity of Western society (Capitalism), while Butler was referring to the First War World then was raging. However, believers in this alleged conspiracy claim that the term has its origin in **Cecil Rhodes and Lionel Curtis**, in 1909.

The phrase "New World Order" entered the conspiranoico lexicon in 1972 with the publication of the book "None Dare Call It Conspiracy" written by the American ultra - right organization **John Birch Society**. According to the book, "New World Order" was the "keyword" that would use the communist movement to initiate it's a conspiracy between the Soviets and the world's billionaires whose aim was to control humanity and impose a socialism in which the "super -rich" they would have absolute power.

The first time a high - profile politician used the phrase on Wednesday January 30, 1991, during a speech that the US president **George Herbert Walker Bush** spoke before Congress after the end of the Cold War. In this speech, Bush referred to "The **New World Order is coming before our eyes**". [Key Appointments Text State of the Union by President Bush in January 1991]:

"Mr. President of the Senate, Mr. Speaker of the House of Representatives, members of the United States Congress. I come to this house of the people to speak to you and all Americans with the certainty of being in a time definition. On the other side of the world we are engaged in a great struggle in the skies, at sea and in the sand. We know why we are there. We are Americans: part of something larger than ourselves. For two centuries we have worked for freedom. Tonight we are leading the world when faced with a threat to decency and humanity. What is at stake is more than a small country, it's a great idea: a New World Order – where diverse nations unite in common cause to achieve the universal aspirations of mankind: peace and security, freedom and the government the law. Such is the world worthy of our struggle and worthy of our children's future. The community of nations has come together to condemn and resolutely repel any illegal aggression. Unprovoked invasion of Saddam Hussein – his impious and systematic rape of a peaceful neighbor – violated everything the community of nations more esteem. The world has said that this aggression can not be maintained – and will not be maintained. Together we resisted the trap of conciliation, cynicism and isolation that causes temptation to tyrants. The world has responded to the invasion of Saddam with 12 resolutions of the United Nations, beginning with the demand that Iraq withdraw immediately and unconditionally – supported by forces from 28 countries on six continents. Except for a few, the world is unified. Triumph in the Gulf. And when we do, the world community will have sent him a lasting message to every dictator and despot present or future to think to carry out an illegal aggression. The world can then take this opportunity to make the old promise of a New World Order – where brutality and lack of reward aggression will find collective resistance"

THE HIDDEN FACE OF GLOBAL GEOPOLITICS

The new order as they conceive it is not a reordering of the world in terms of achieving social, political and economic balances, on the contrary it is intended to establish new mechanisms to maintain the hegemony of the current global power structures through intensive psychological control, permanent war and military threat to everything that opposes its geostrategic and economic interests. Because of these plans the **US Department of Defense** and the **NSA** (National Security Agency) outlined strategies for managing the challenges they would face as the dominant power in the world, a part of these strategies is proposed that one of the main objectives of the United States will avoid at all costs the rise of any emerging superpower in Asia, Europe, the Middle East or any part of the territory of the former Soviet Union. They designed for this the development of a comprehensive and sophisticated military power as an essential element to ensure perpetual supremacy and as a mechanism to deter any nation or group of nations if they defy their economic, technological and military dominance.

The ideologue of this policy was **Paul Wolfowitz**, Undersecretary of Defense (2001–2005) administration of George W. Bush, acknowledged member of the Bilderberg Group and the Trilateral Commission, including Wolfowitz was the tenth President of the World Bank, and was forced to resign from this institution in June 2007, after a scandal of nepotism.

Under the approval of **General Henry H. Shelton** (Chairman of the Joint Command Headquarters), the **Policy and Strategic Plans US Army**, J5 **Division Strategy** in June 2000 (Defense Technical Information Center) developed a document called [Joint **vision 2020**], where it is established that this vision is firmly anchored in the idea that the US army It should be a joint force capable of achieving full spectrum dominance. It is based on four pillars: the global interests of the United States and the continued existence of a broad spectrum of potential threats to those interests; the centrality of information technology for evolution, not only of our own army, but also to the capabilities of other actors around the world; the emphasis that a broad spectrum of military operations continued to put on the successful integration of multinational and interagency partners and the interoperability of processes, organizations and systems; and our reliance on the joint force as the foundation of future US military operations.

Joint Vision 2020 is built on that foundation and maintains the set time with Joint Vision 2010. It confirms the direction of the ongoing transformation of operational capabilities, and emphasizes the importance of further experimentation, exercises, analysis and conceptual thinking, especially in the areas of informational operations, command and joint control, and multinational operations and international agencies.

At the same time, it emphasizes that technological innovation must be accompanied by intellectual innovation that leads to changes in the organization and doctrine. Only then can we achieve the full potential of the joint force – decisive capabilities across the spectrum of military operations. This vision depends on the skills, experience and training of the people who make up the Total Force and its leaders.

The major innovations needed to operate in the environment described here can only be achieved through recruitment, development and retention of men and women with courage, determination and strength to ensure that we are persuasive in peace, decisive in the war and superior in any form of conflict.

TRANSNATIONAL ELITE AND THE NEW WORLD ORDER

The transnational elite (TE by its acronym in English) is defined as an interconnected network that control every major field of social life (political, economic, social, ideological, etc.) and its function is similar to that of the national elite the pre-globalization "nation–state" era (the nation–state is a historically specific form of global social organization that is in the process of being transcended by capitalist globalization). It is shown that an economy of transnational market needs its own political and economic elites transnational to control exactly the same way as when the market economy was mainly due "national", when the function of enforcing market rules was assigned to " Nation-State "– through its monopoly of violence – and the political and economic elites that control. In conclusion it is that, contrary to the systemic propaganda, the conception of the transnational elite (as well as the NWO) has nothing to do with "conspiracies" of any kind.

In recent days, thousands of citizens across Europe have participated in demonstrations against the NWO (New World Order) of neoliberal globalization and transnational elite (TE), primarily the network of transnational elites based in the countries of the Group of Seven (numeronym G7 or G-7), which executes it. The reason was the last TE plan for a transatlantic trade agreement called **"Transatlantic Trade and Investment Partnership"** (TTIP). The negotiations of this new agreement are actually very advanced and have taken place between representatives of the political and economic elites US and the European Union (EU). **On October 5, 2015 a similar agreement called the Trans-Pacific Treaty (signed TTP) among the nations of the Pacific Rim (Canada, USA, Japan, Australia, New Zealand, Chile, Vietnam, Peru, Mexico, Singapore, South Korea, Malaysia, Taiwan and Brunei).**

"The TTP is a huge trade agreement; a sort of super free trade agreement. And when I say "free" I mean no rules, regulations zero in it all possible. Neither more nor less than the market rate always dreamed big capitalists and oligarchs is that that does not limit them nothing and gives all the guarantees to do business with virtually everything you can think of, but as in the United States and ransacked to the invisible, then they go for resources of other countries "- Whoops that chutzpah, come with full freedom to rob the people!

Russia and **China** (emerging economies, members of the so – called BRICS) are deliberately excluded from these negotiations, which instead are carried out exclusively among the members of the ET, and fully integrated into the **New World Order** as an associate or members subordinates it. As has been attempted to show in an article in Pravda (in Russian : Правда, the truth), Russia is not fully integrated into the New World Order, despite its recent accession to the World Trade Organization (WTO), which aims it is to fully integrate the new neoliberal order many countries as possible, as long as they agree fully liberalizing their markets for commodities, so that **transnational corporations** (hereafter TNCs) have no fee or other barriers that restrict their activities.

Please note that the Neoliberal Project accelerated further in 1995 with the establishment of the **World Trade Organization** (WTO), replacing the **General Agreement on Tariffs and Trade** (GATT).

WTO promptly launched a systematic campaign to increase the power of corporations, through treaties of "free trade" that are mandatory for all WTO members, including of course the European Union. The total effect of Neoliberal Project has been decreasing living standards, undermine national sovereignty, destabilize the national finances and, in general, destroy everything that the Bretton Woods system was meant to protect.

Although the World Trade Organization had a supposed great success in the market opening and liberalization of goods, it was not so successful in opening services markets, **since many countries are still trying to protect basic needs services such as health, education, transport and communication**, are still characterized as social services and are not, therefore, it is free to become easy prey for transnational corporations and their lucrative activities. This is unlike the case of the United States, where the satisfaction of these basic needs depends on market forces (ie, the thickness of the portfolio citizen) and not in collective social decisions taken democratically.

In addition to this, the World Trade Organization was not particularly successful in opening and liberalization of some sectors of production in the "South" (eg agriculture), which remains the main production sectors (at least in terms of job creation) many of these countries.

The World Trade Organization has not proved to be tremendously popular. Even, **the organization has been mainly used as a vehicle to force vulnerable economies and thus make the rich richer and the poor poorer worldwide** – simply are responsible for the siege of the working people.

Again, as expected, the talks on further liberalization in the global framework of the World Trade Organization have stalled. One of the most concerning ways to do this is by searching for the institutionalization of what is known as **the arbitration of investor–state differences** (ISDS English Investor-state dispute settlement) within the framework of the agreements.

THE HIDDEN FACE OF GLOBAL GEOPOLITICS

Without any discussion, these agreements are part of the same process that began with the emergence of the **New World Order** following the massive expansion of transnational corporations in the last thirty years or so – which is a new phenomenon in history of the capitalist market economy – and the collapse of the Soviet bloc. As a result of the massive expansion of transnational corporations, which, for 2009, had more than 80,000, representing about two thirds of world trade, experts in the area and talk about hyper globalization. A study by the British magazine **New Scientist** has shown that currently only 1,318 TNCs, through ownerships locking, own 80% of global revenues and 147 companies outside (ie, less than 1% network) form an "entity" that control 40% of the wealth of the entire network. This vast expansion of transnational companies would have been impossible without open and liberalized markets of commodities and capital; they have been established around the world in the last thirty years or so by governments of all persuasions: Christian Democrats, Social Democrats, liberal and any combination thereof. This was not the result of a conspiracy by economists and politicians in power, exploiting any kind of crisis, according to suggest by some authors. Instead, this was just the inevitable effect, following the collapse of the social and democratic model in which the model was based domestic markets, and that was not compatible with most of the growing internationalization of the market economy. Finally, governments in the new framework had to follow neoliberal policies that their economies were competitive and capable of continuous growth and expansion of the consumer society.

However, a transnational economy needs its own political and economic elites to control it. Although the state monopoly of violence still remains in the internationalized market economy, it is now complemented by a transnational form of violence, which applies not only in a state – even if it happens to be the last "empire" in the classic sense of the word (US) – but by the major military powers in the G7 ie France, United Kingdom, United States (powers "FUKUS").

Therefore, despite the economic power extends today between a few hundred transnational corporations, which originated mainly in the G7 countries (ie FUKUS plus Germany, Japan, Canada and Italy), the USA; because of its clear military superiority, he has a leading position – but not the emperor. In other words, the New World Order is an "empire" in the sense of a unipolar world, but without an emperor – except deemed as "emperor" to all ET.

According to this you can perfectly define the " transnational elite " as that which obtains its vast power (economic, political and social) to operate transnationally – a fact which means that does not express, solely or even primarily, the interests of a particular state. It consists of a network of interconnected elites who control every important field of life (economic, political, ideological, etc.). Therefore, the following elites are the main components of the transnational elite:

THE HIDDEN FACE OF GLOBAL GEOPOLITICS

1. Transnational economic in charge of economic globalization elite control the main ETN (corporate directors, executive directors and major shareholders of the largest TNCs) and addresses the major international economic organizations (IMF, World Bank and the Organisation for Economic Co-operation and Development).

2. Transnational political elites responsible for political globalization control the clear political–military dimension of NOM and consist of the globalization of bureaucrats and professional politicians who operate either within major international organizations or the state machines the major market economies (mainly the G7 countries).

3. transnational elites responsible propaganda promoting the ideology of the New World Order, through its control of transnational media (eg CNN, BBC, ABC News, NBC, FOX, ABC) and elite involved in the implementation of this ideology in the treatment of human rights protection, etc. (The leading cadres of international non – governmental organizations funded by transnational economic elites, such as Human Rights Watch, Amnesty International, etc.). Transnational media and international non – governmental organizations and "social networking" (Facebook, Twitter, Instagram, etc.) have played a crucial role in making "news" (and legitimacy of "insurgents"), and have created a magnificent propaganda about the supposed progressive role of criminal organizations such as NATO.

Now it is known, for example, that the **Projects Agency Defense Advanced Research** (DARPA, an agency of the US Defense Department) has revealed to the magazine "Scientific

American" some details about Memex, an advanced search engine that allows disclose information flowing through the "Deep web" hidden Internet segment.

The system has been developed for the needs of intelligence agencies in order to identify those individuals involved in drug trafficking, weapons, people and other illegal services. The search has advanced features that reveal customer data, track users on the dark network and analyze the information collected.

To create Memex, DARPA has worked with about 17 research groups from private companies and universities. The search engine will not be accessible to the average user and most of the information about it remains classified.

4. Transnational academic elites, ie, prominent systemic scholars in various transnational organizations (foundations, institutes, research centers and others) in charge of the creation / enhancement of the ideology of the New World Order and globalization, "scientifically" which **justifies the need for globalization, and create in people a supreme confusion about the real causes of the current multidimensional crisis.**
5. Cultural transnational elites, namely the film industry (mainly controlled by transnational and Zionist elites who run the powerful Hollywood film industry), which plays a crucial role in the spread of the values of globalization and how "normal" life (which "coincidentally" becomes one mode bourgeois, consumerist life) and the music industry (especially the pop industry also is controlled by TNCs) and so on.

THE HIDDEN FACE OF GLOBAL GEOPOLITICS

Undoubtedly the globalization process led by the ET has already led to an unprecedented concentration of wealth and income, and according to the report **Credit Swisse** (financial services company, headquartered in the city of Zurich, Switzerland) shows that 1% of the elite now owns 48.2% of the world's wealth, up from 46% reported in 2015, while the lower half of the world population owns less than 1% of total wealth.

The twin objective of ET from the implementation of the New World Order has been:

First, to expand globalization in countries that have not yet lost national and economic sovereignty in the process of globalization, mainly Russia and countries still controlled by governments that came to power through the national liberation movements (Syria and Iran, after the destruction of the same ET in countries like Iraq and Libya) or alternatively through the socialist and progressive movements in Latin America (Cuba, Bolivia, Ecuador, Venezuela and others). The means used to achieve this goal were economic violence, such as with respect to the peripheral countries of the EU or physical violence, exercised directly by the ET (such as in the hotbed of the Middle East), or any combination of the two forms of violence.

Second, to deepen the process of globalization in areas not yet covered by the WTO rounds and in particular the movement of capital, the complete freedom to move, until now, has only been established within the**European Union** and the **North American Free Trade** agreement, NAFTA by its acronym in English, signed in 1994 by the US, Canada and Mexico) and with regard to other countries primarily through bilateral agreements. **It is important to stress that the FTA weakened economies and sovereignty of all three nations. His pretext of "free trade" was truly empower corporations at the expense of nations, ie, the Reagan-Thatcher revolution on steroids. According to such treaties, corporations have the right to sue governments if regulations weaken corporate profits.** The new agreements (TTIP and TTP) propose clauses that create universal mechanisms to resolve conflicts between transnational corporations and states. Therefore, unlike individual deals on the development of specific natural resources, TTIP and TTP they cover a wide range of what are considered investments in the states. So, "incorporating these clauses mean that if a country later makes a law that contravenes the terms of TTIP or PTT, for example, for the protection of public health, a company that is damaged (for example, because they have been making a product that is contrary to the new rule) **may sue the state for compliance with the treaty, without going through the normal judicial system of that country.** In other words, foreign companies are placed above the law of the host country through these agreements".

Therefore, transnational corporations with a stake in the health service in the UK, for example, could sue the government if it decided to follow a program of nationalization. It is no wonder that **Gail Cartmail,** Assistant Secretary General of "Unite" (Britain's biggest union with 1.4 million members) urged conference delegates in the latest UK

Trade Union Confederation (TUC) to oppose support TTIP and proposed a manifestation among people in the UK to claim the former prime minister, David Cameron, to maintain health services in Britain outside the TTIP agreement. And so he said:

"It is clear that this government thought they could do this secret agreement – an agreement that would mean the massive sale of our National Health Service (NHS) in the United States", Cartmail said. "Wall Street financiers as Blackrock and Invesco are already heavily investing in the NHS – over 70% of new contracts are now in private hands Over 11 million of our money in the hands of capitalists casino". he added.

It's no wonder that once this agreement to the EU legislation is sent and then will open the doors to national parliaments (as is known, **at least 75% of the legislation of each EU country has its origin in the European Commission**), then it could open the way to privatization of any social service still available after the onslaught of the New World Order of neoliberal globalization and the massive neoliberal legislation adopted in the last 30 years by both Democrats and conservative parties, social democrats in power. Environmentalists are also worried that the dispute settlement procedure could be used by transnational corporations to block measures to protect the environment. The development of the negotiations is also debatable. Activists say they are secretive and undemocratic, as of course you would expect, are in fact (although procedures) carried out between**unelected bureaucrats US and** the EU, which owe their positions to political elites and economic transnational, and representatives of TNCs.

For example, in Britain (characterized as "the capital of job creation in western economies"), it hides the fact that **"unemployment is low largely because the British workers have been willing to bear the greatest real wage reduction since the Victorian era"** – all this as a result of globalization. It is not surprising, therefore, that even the conservative daily **Times** of London had to recognize this fact to explain the reasons why the nationalist right under the leadership of **Nigel Farage,** the UK Independence Party (in English, United Kingdom Independence Party or UKIP) is increasing rapidly.

The emergence and rapid expansion of multinational companies (a new phenomenon in the history of the capitalist market economy), initially led to an informal opening and liberalization of markets that was later institutionalized Thatcherism and Reaganomics by. It was this development which, **together with the change in the subjective conditions, ie, the decline of the labor and socialist movements in the aftermath of deindustrialization in the West, marked the collapse of social democracy and increasing neoliberal globalization. Considerations:** This article is based on excerpts from the forthcoming book author subjugate the Middle East: integration into the new world order, Vol.1: The Pseudo democratization (Progressive Press, 2014).

THE HIDDEN FACE OF GLOBAL GEOPOLITICS

ELITE PLAN FOR A NEW TRANSNATIONAL SOCIAL WORLD ORDER

Richard K. Moore worked for 30 years in major software companies in Silicon Valley (it being apparently an engineer with a doctorate), and then in 1994 (at retirement) moved to Ireland to continue their "real work". Since then he has been studying the problems that humanity is facing, and exploring ways to their solution. He is a prolific writer with a great blog (cyberjournal.org) created to try to understand how the world works and how we can improve it. Many years of research and writing culminated in his widely acclaimed book "**Escaping the Matrix: How We the People Can Change the World**" (2005).

This article was first published in the bimonthly magazine New Dawn (www.newdawnmagazine.com) on September 2014. Let us thinking about:

In the Industrial Revolution in Britain, in the late 1700s, you could generate big business investing in factories and industries, opening new markets and gaining control of sources of raw materials. It is interesting that those with more capital to invest were not in Britain but rather in the Netherlands. The latter had been the largest Western power in the 1600s, and their bankers were the major capitalist. In search of profits, the Dutch Capital flowed to the British stock market, and so the Dutch financed the rise of Britain, which then overshadowed economic Holland and geopolitically.

So British industrialization became dominated by wealthy investors, and capitalism became the dominant economic system. Britain had essentially been an aristocratic society, dominated by landowning families. As capitalism was becoming dominant economically, capitalists became dominant in politics. Tax structures and import–export policies were gradually modified to favor investors over landowners.

Round capitalist business is investment management, and that control is usually handled through the mediation of banks and brokerage houses. It would not be surprising that investment bankers came to occupy the top of the hierarchy of wealth and power. And in fact, there are a handful of banking families, including **Rothschild** and **Rockefeller**, which has come to dominate the economic and political affairs in the Western world.

Unlike aristocrats, capitalists are not linked to a site, or maintenance of a place. Capital is unfair and mobile – flowing where you can find the greatest growth, as it flowed from Holland to Britain, then Britain to the US, and recently from all over China. As a copper mine can be exploited and then abandoned under capitalism a whole nation can be exploited and then abandoned, and that is observed in industrial areas damaged US and Britain.

A capitalist causes a war to make profits, and in fact our elite banking families have financed both sides of most military conflicts since at least World War. Why historians have trouble 'explain' the First World War in terms of motivation and objectives. And without going too far, the defense industry is one of the most lucrative in the world (according to SIPRI annually about 1.5 billion dollars are spent).

In pre-capitalist days warfare was like chess: each side was winning. Under capitalism war it is more like a casino where players participate as they can get money for more chips and the winner is always be the banking bankers who finance the war and decide who will be the last to resist. Wars are not only the most profitable of all capitalist enterprises, but to choose the winners, and manage reconstruction, banking elite families succeed, with the passage of time, adapt the geopolitical configuration to serve their own interests. Millions die in wars, infrastructures are destroyed, and while the world laments, bankers count their profits and make plans for their investments in post-war reconstruction.

From his position of power, as financiers of governments, banking elites have perfected over time their methods of control. Always staying between racks, pulling the strings that control the media, political parties, intelligence agencies, stock markets and government offices. And perhaps the greatest lever of power is their control over the coins. Through its thymus central banks, causing booms and ruin, print money from nothing and then loan with interest to governments. The power of the banking elite (the 'banksters') is absolute.

"Some of the most important men in the US. They are afraid of something. They know that there is a power somewhere so organized, so subtle, so watchful, so interlocked, so complete, so pervasive that it is better not to talk aloud when they do to condemn " President Woodrow Wilson.

The banksters against capitalism

It is presumed that **Ferdinand Pecora** was who coined Americanism "**bankster**", a term that includes the word banker and gangster. Pecora, born in Sicily, Italy, ended the career of lawyer and worked as an assistant in the Office of New York. In 1933, the Senate sought an incorruptible professional and appointed him chief counsel Banking Committee to question the most important bankers. The causes of the crash of 1929 on Wall Street, anteroom of the Great Depression were investigated.

The Great Recession or Great Financial Crisis of 2008 catapulted the term **banksters** to the pages of newspapers and magazines. Recently, following the manipulation of one of the most important types of interest of the world, the so – called Libor London, the word banksters was associated with the practices supported by Barclays and made with UBS, Deutsche Bank, Societe Generale, Royal Bank of Scotland, JPMorgan, Citigroup and brokerRP Martin.

Constantly was inevitable on a finite planet that would be a limit to economic growth. Allowed industrialization has accelerated precipitously toward that limit over the past two centuries. Production has become increasingly efficient markets increasingly global, and finally the paradigm of perpetual growth has reached the point of diminishing returns.

Since 1970 the capital has not sought growth through increased production, but rather by extracting higher yields of relatively limited production levels. Hence globalization, which transferred production to low-wage areas, ensures higher profit margins. Why is privatization, which transfers revenue streams investors, previously reached national treasures? Hence derivative and currency markets, which create the electronic illusion of economic growth, without actually producing anything in the real world.

In almost forty years, the capitalist system was maintained by these various mechanisms, none of which was productive in any real sense. And then, in September 2008, the house of cards collapsed suddenly on his knees putting the global financial system.

If the collapse of civilizations is evaluated, it is learned that this inability to adapt is fatal. Two centuries of real growth were taken, in which the growth dynamics of capitalism was in harmony with the reality of industrial growth. Then there were four decades of artificial growth of capitalism supported by a house of cards. And now, after the collapse of the house of cards, it seems that every effort is made to produce 'recovery' growth. It is very easy to get the impression that our civilization is in a process of collapse, based on the principle of the inability to adapt.

The capitalist system has passed its expiration date, the bankster elite is well aware of that fact and is adapting. Capitalism is a vehicle that has helped bring the banksters to absolute power, and have no loyalty to that system to place or anything or anyone.

He was not allowed to capitalism a natural death. Instead it was brought down by a controlled strategy. To do this, first he was placed in a global system based on privatization and foreign exchange markets. Then they injected a euthanasia solution, in the form of real estate bubbles and toxic derivatives. Finally, the **Bank for International Settlements** (the leading bank of central banks) canceled the life support system: declared rule 'mark to market', which led to instant insolvency of all banks in possession of risks, although it took a while before it was apparent.

The end of economic sovereignty

As was directed strategically financial collapse, so it was the post–collapse scenario, with their suicidal rescue programs. National budgets were already put to the limit; there were certainly no reserves available to save insolvent banks. Therefore bailout commitments were nothing but exorbitant acceptance of new debts by governments. In conclusion: It had to borrow capital to the same financial system that was rescued!

Not that the banks were too big to fail, rather the banksters were too powerful to fail "**did politicians an offer**

they could not refuse". In U.S.A. Congress that no ransom would be martial law the next morning he told himself. In Ireland, the ministers who have financial chaos and riots in the streets said. In fact, while Iceland manifested itself, the sensible way to deal with insolvent banks was an orderly bankruptcy process.

The effect of the rescue was under pressure to transfer the insolvency of banks to national treasuries. Bank debts were transformed into sovereign debt and budget deficits. Now, quite predictably, are the nations which seek bailouts and these bailouts come with conditions. Instead of the bankruptcy of banks, they take place the nations.

In his book **Confessions of an Economic mobster** (The hidden face of American imperialism), **John Perkins** explains how it has coerced the Third World in recent decades – through pressure and various types– tricks to accept perpetual bondage of indebtedness, in particularly in sub – Saharan Africa, the ravages of neoliberal project have been extended still further by the actions of the International Monetary Fund and by other means.Intentionally, debts can never be paid. Instead, debts must be periodically refinanced, and each turn of refinancing buried deeper into the nation into debt – and takes her to submit to draconian IMF conditions: governments are forced to cut social assistance, and are required corporations selling national assets – like water rights – at bargain prices. With the orchestrated financial collapse, and thymus of 'too big to fail', the banksters have created a situation in which there is no turning back: hitman plans now operate here in the first world.

In the EU, the first round of nations to fall will be the so – called **PIGS** pejorative acronym with which Anglo – Saxon financial media refer to the group of countries in the European Union: **Portugal, Ireland, Greece and Spain**. The fiction that the PIGS may face redemptions is based on the assumption that the era of unlimited growth will resume. As fully aware of banksters, just not going to happen. Finally the PIGS will be forced to default, and then the rest of the EU too, all part of a controlled demolition project will collapse.

When a nation succumbs to debt bondage, it ceases to be a sovereign nation, governed by some kind of internal political process. Instead it falls under the control of IMF dictates. What we have seen in the Third World, and is happening now in Europe, those dictates have to do with austerity and privatization. Government functions are eliminated or privatized, and national assets are sold. Gradually –again a demolition controlada– the nation state is dismantled. Finally, the primary functions that remain the government are police repression of its own population, and tax collection for delivery to the banksters.

In fact, the dismantling of the nation state began long before the financial collapse of 2008. In US and Britain began in 1980 with Reagan and Thatcher. In Europe, he began in 1988 with the Treaty of Maastricht.Globalization accelerated the process of dismantling, through the export of jobs and industries, privatization programs, agreements 'free trade' and the establishment of the World Trade Organization (WTO) regulations shredder.Events since 2008 have enabled the rapid acceleration of a process that was already well under way.

With the collapse, bailouts, and the fact that it has not initiated any effective program and recovery, the signs are very clear: they let the system completely collapse, paving the way for a 'solution' previously designed. As the nation state is dismantled, a new regime to replace global authority is established. As seen in the case of the WTO, IMF, World Bank, and other parts of the embryonic global governance, the new global system will not display claims of popular representation or democratic process. The government will take place through autocratic global bureaucracies, who receive their orders directly or indirectly from the bankster clique.

In his book **[The globalization of poverty]**, **Michel Chossudovsky** explains how globalization and IMF actions, created a massive extreme poverty around the so – called Third World during the last decades (they were responsible for looting the great wealth of these countries). According to that seen with the dramatic emphasis on austerity, after the collapse and the bailouts, this project of creating poverty no longer be reversed. In this new world system there will be no prosperous middle class. By the way, the new regime will look like in the old days a lot of royalty and serfdom (the old regime). The banksters are the new royal family, and everyone will be his domain. The technocrats who run the global bureaucracies, and the mandarins who present themselves as politicians in waste nations, are the privileged upper class.

"Today, Americans would be outraged if UN troops entered Los Angeles to restore order; tomorrow will thank you. It especially if they are told that there is an outside threat from beyond, whether real or promulgated, that threaten our very existence. Then all the peoples of the world will plead with world leaders to release them from this evil. The one thing every man fears is the unknown. When presented with this scenario, voluntarily waive individual rights in exchange for the guarantee of their well being granted by their world government " Henry Kissinger, speaking in Evian, France, May 21, 1992, meeting of the Bilderberg.

The end of freedom

Over the past four decades, since about 1970, it has undergone a process of regime change, global system from an old to a new global system. In the old system, the first world nations were relatively democratic and prosperous, while the Third World suffering under the tyranny of police states, mass poverty, and imperialism (exploitation by foreign powers).

During that time the movement against globalization dominated the international news pages, and opposition to globalization reached massive proportions. The visible movement was only the tip of an iceberg anti systemic.In a very real sense, the general popular sentiment in the developed world began to take a radical turn. The leaders of the movement now thought in terms of an anti-capitalist movement. There was political volatility in the air, in the sense that possibly illustrated popular sentiment could bring about a change in the course of events.

That all changed on September 11, 2001, the day when the twin towers fell. The anti-globalization movement, along with globalization itself, disappeared almost entirely from public consciousness on that fateful day.Suddenly there was a global whole new stage, a whole new media circus - with a new enemy - a new kind of war, a war without end, a war against ghosts, a war against "terrorism".

The orchestrated financial collapse of September 2008 allowed certain existing projects were quickly accelerated, such as the dismantling of sovereignty, and the imposition of austerity. Similarly, the events of September 2001 made it possible for other existing projects were accelerated considerably, such as the abandonment of civil liberties and international law.

Before 11-S, they had already drafted the "Patriot Act", which states very clearly that this was the police state (to the US) with all its strength and to stay - the Bill of Rights lost its legal force.

Before long, "anti - terrorist" legislation had been adopted similar throughout the developed world. If any anti - systemic movement raise its head again in the first world (as did, for example, recently in Greece), they could be implemented arbitrary police powers -so as necessary- to crush the resistance. Do not allow any popular movement max out the designs of regime change the banksters. The anti - globalization movement had been shouting: "this is the true democracy". With 11-S, the banksters replied, "this is the true oppression".

The events of 11-S led directly to the invasions of Iraq and Afghanistan, and in general helped create a climate in which they could easily justify the invasions of sovereign nations, with one excuse or another. International law was abandoned as comprehensively as they were civil liberties. As any restriction of internal police action was removed, any restriction of military interventions geopolitical removed. Nothing should get in the way of plans for regime change the banksters.

"The era technetronic involves more controlled gradual emergence of a society (...) dominated by an elite, not limited by traditional values (...) this elite would not hesitate to achieve its political goals using the latest modern techniques for influencing public behavior (...) The persistence of the crisis social, the emergence of a charismatic personality, and exploitation of mass media to obtain public confidence would be the steps in the transformation of a little US in a highly controlled society (...) In addition, it might be possible-tempter exploited for strategic political purposes the fruits of research on the brain and human behavior" Zbigniew Brzezinski, The Age technetronic, 1970.

Zionism Isreali

"Since 1948, Palestinians live condemned to perpetual humiliation. They can not even breathe without permission. They have lost their country, their land, their water, their freedom, their everything. They not even have the right to choose their rulers" Eduardo Galeano

WHAT ARE THE ZIONISTS?

The Zionists form a founded by Austro – Hungarian journalist and writer of Jewish origin movement **Theodore Herzl** (Hebrew: בנימין זאב הרצל, Binyamin Ze'evHerzl; in Hungarian Tivadar Herzl) in 1896. The goal of this movement is to achieve the return of the Jews Eretz Yisrael or Zion, Jews to define synonyms to the land of Israel and Jerusalem. All those who support the idea of the Jewish state outlined by Theodor Herzl in 1896 and the return of Jews to the Land of Israel are called Zionists. But not all Jews are Zionists, contrary to what one might think, there is a strong movement among the Jews rather is opposed to Zionism and the very idea of the state of Israel.

On the other hand, the Israeli state was created unilaterally by the Zionist organizations. Is known as its existence is closely related to the economic interests of the Northern power.

Zionism is the Jewish nationalist movement and colonialist that, since the late nineteenth century, the creation of the State of Israel was proposed and promoted and promotes migration of Jews to Palestine, the ancestral "promised land", rooted feeling that their "destiny historic "is in that land. This movement took on political significance thanks to Teodor Herzl, an Austrian journalist who thought that European powers would support the Zionist ideal for: get rid of the Jews and anti-Semitism (avoiding the influx of Jewish immigrants from Eastern Europe) and use the Jewish influence organized to fight revolutionary movements and other internal factors. Herzl explained that Palestine should be colonized and occupied a strategic position and Europe soon allows the settlement of the Jews".

Unquestionably, Zionism is an imperialist ideology because it selected the most suitable for installation place of the Jewish state, no matter who inhabited the area, displacing a people and seizing their property, their land, their identity, etc.

THE HIDDEN FACE OF GLOBAL GEOPOLITICS

In 1897, **Theodor Herzl** organized the first Zionist Congress in Basel, Switzerland, the program said: "Zionism wants to create a home for the Jews in Palestine under public law". When the Ottoman government rejected Herzl's proposal to grant autonomy to Palestine, Zionists sought the support of Britain. In 1903 the British government offered Jews uninhabited 6,000 square miles in Uganda to be established, but the Zionists rejected this offer and insisted Palestine.

With the outbreak of the First World War the Zionists promoted the Balfour Declaration, which promised British support Jews in the creation of a Jewish national state in Palestine. This statement was included in the British Mandate of the League of Nations Palestine (1922). Thus, over time, they were getting the support of the UN who handed Palestinian land in 1947.

"When we occupy the territory, we must provide immediate benefits to the state to receive us. We must expropriate gently the private property in the state that we have been assigned. We try to displace the poor that is along the border, seeking employment for it in transit countries, while denying it employment in our country. The owners will come to our side. Both the process of expropriation and the elimination of poverty must be carried out discreetly and wisely. Let the owners believe that they are deceiving us, selling us things more expensive than they actually are worth. But we are not going to resell anything (...) We sell only to Jews, or any exchange of real estate should be done only among Jews. Needless to say we respectfully tolerate people of other religions and protect their property, their honor and their freedom with the most severe coercive measures. This is another area where we must show the world a magnificent example (...) There must be many unmovable owners in individual areas (who will not sell their property), we should just leave them there and develop our trade towards other areas we belong to us" -**quotes Theodor Herzl noted in his diaries in 1895, as dispossession and displacement,** notes the historian revisionist Israeli **Benny Morris.**

The Zionist movement within the Jewish congregation itself is confirming us our position against the decisions of the Zionists (hawks) now, from the Pentagon, and under false political-religious precepts they are leading the world into a global confrontation which he linked to a kind of "self – fulfilling prophecy" is simply the mask of the same Zionist debauchery that through recent history, has done nothing but misrepresenting the sake of perverse interests, the true morality of the people Jewish.

Surprisingly, a protest of more than 10,000 Orthodox Jews on 28-04-05 at the gates of the Israeli Consulate in New York, shouting slogans and showed 110 saying, "**Israel has no right to rule over the holy land", Jews regret the 56 years of Israel's existence, the Zionists do not represent the Jews, the true Jews will never recognize Israel, the Zionists purposes will never be successful, the Zionist state of Israel must be dissolved.**

In a publication of **Lenni Brenner**, under the title: "Zionism in the Age of the Dictators" was published on 7/17/2004 in the magazine electronic publication "Jews Against Zionism" not only the treacherous character noted the Zionists to misinterpret the scriptures of the Torah (in Hebrew, תּוֹרָה [Torah], "instruction, teaching" is the text containing the law and identity heritage of the people of Israel, it is the basis and foundation of Judaism) but they accuse them of being responsible for the suffering of the Jewish people by anti – Semitism which have suffered precisely because of the positions taken by the Zionists throughout the twentieth century. Many of us have wondered why the persecution and extermination of Jews during World War II. Some answers lead to an explanation based on the monopolistic character on the German economy came upholding the Jews as opposed to theinterest of Hitler to achieve full control of the country, but we never imagined is that there was another reason, other than the political –economic, which also explain why the holocaust.

According to this article, the Zionists have encouraged anti – Semitism and persecution of the Jewish people to justify the need for the creation of a Jewish state. Under a kind of high Machiavellianism its greatest exponent, the Zionists have sponsored fear, hatred, persecution and destruction of their own fellow Jews to justify the creation of a savior status. In the pursuit of this perverse goal, the apostate maximum of Zionism **Theodore Herzl** wrote:

"It is essential That the Sufferings of Jews (...) Become worse (...) this will assist in realization of our plans (...) I have an excellent idea to (...) I Shall induce anti-Semites to liquidate Jewish wealth (...) The anti-Semites will assist us thereby in That They will Strengthen the persecution and oppression of Jews". (From His Diary Part 1, pp. 16).

The consequences of this perverse position of the father of Zionism did not wait and already by 1920, a hostile language the Jews began to speak at the German University of Heidelberg. An array of opinion was created to blame the Jews for Germany's defeat in World War I (1914-1918) "The Jews of Germany have nothing in common with the Germans, have no loyalty to the country where you are born, They behave like foreigners "were some of the comments that were made. But, surprise! these statements did not come from Adolf Hitler, they were outlined by prominent Zionist Jews as Nahum Goldman, who later became President of the "World Zionist Organization", or Jacob Klatzkin who was the great ideologist of Zionism in Germany for the time in which (1921) the Jews enjoyed all their political and civil rights in that country. During the years before World War II, the decadent British Empire gave a great boost to the Zionist movement, Theodor Herzl. Anglican Chaplain William Hetchler, one of the most important figures of Christian Zionism in England, met in Vienna the Zionist project of Herzl and became not only his best friend but also one of the biggest promoters of the project in Europe.

Hetchler Herzl made available its contacts with the British government to support the leader of Zionism in their quest for political patronage – economic development of their project. It was Hetchler who arranged meetings with the Ottoman Sultan Herzl and the Kaiser of Germany. His contacts with the British social elite served to fix the historic 1905 meeting between Theodor Herzl and political Arthur Balfour. Later this meeting, emerge the Balfour Declaration in 1917. This declaration was given the first international legitimacy to the Jewish people's right to possession of a state. The backing of Prime Minister David Lloyd–George Herzl Zionist project demonstrated that the interests of the British Empire in its colonialist policy were the main reason to support the draft Herzl. The fascist nature of British colonialism and its unflagging intention subjugate the Arab people, laconically became apparent in the famous speech of Balfour in 1919 when he said, "about Palestine we do not propose to ascertain the wishes of the present inhabitants of that country. the four great powers are willing to support Zionism (...) and Zionism, be it right or wrong, good or bad, is rooted in a historical tradition which, we believe that the present needs and aspirations of the future are much more important than the desires and prejudices of the 700,000 Arabs who now inhabit these ancient lands" (refers to Palestinians, as seen, were sentenced to destruction by Western powers since the early twentieth century) the conclusion to which arrive editors of the items discussed is that Zionism, in general, coincided with Nazism and fascism long before its advent. They always argued that Jews can not live in harmony with any society in the world; they should be removed for the benefit of society itself which coexisted. Herzl Zionist followers in pursuit of its objectives did not care about such coincidence and promoted these ideas well before the arrival of Hitler to power in Germany.

But what the Zionists hawks fly over the world?

The Basque internationalist **Jesus Valencia** explains this discriminatory and racist ideology born in the cradle of colonialism, when Europe interpreted the wider world was available who got appropriate it. The great powers took over large areas and allowed the other Zionism both the small Palestine. Since its inception, Zionism and capitalism have become very good friends; the first mastiff fattened as protecting the interests of the latter. Warmongering Zionist cancer soon spilled over Palestinian borders and spread across the globe. Wherever there was a tyrant, there were Israeli agents to defend him. Al-Hasan ibn Muhammad Hassan II of Morocco or commissioned them toorganize the Praetorian Guard that should protect him; Israeli counterinsurgency was next to Somoza until the Sandinista Front shooed both. Uribe, former Colombian president known for belligerent and drug dealer, Israeli Foreign Minister praised him as "a **great friend**".

When Hassan II wanted to get rid of former leader of the Moroccan independence, he knew where to turn; Israeli agents convinced **Ben Barka** for him to come on a date from which he never returned. When Turkey tried to arrest Ocalan had the invaluable assistance of the Israeli Mossad; this delved into the heart of Africa and did not relent to arrest the Kurdish leader and deliver it to the Government of Ankara. The Government of Colombia appealed to Israel when he managed not eliminates the FARC leader Raul Reyes. The Zionist counterinsurgency planned the night assault, killed almost all members of the border camp and seized the computer of Reyes; opportunely manipulated, that contraption has been providing all the information that will be useful to the Colombian government.

Today, Zionism has set up a macro arms market and advice to anyone trying to smother the popular movements. Wendi Avila was a Honduran student who denounced the coup against Manuel Zelaya; He died asphyxiated by toxic gases that Israel facilitated the coup. The Mapuches counted from now with added enemy small drones that Israel has provided the Chilean government. Until Zionism is not defeated, Palestine will not know peace. And the world, either. The boycott of Israel is a democratizing therapy that even Jewish and Israeli demand sectors.

RAUL OJEDA

THE ESTABLISHMENT OF THE STATE OF ISRAEL

Since its inception, the Israel–Palestinian conflict as a phenomenon tried to explain two different and irreconcilable religions: Jewish and Muslim. The establishment of the State of Israel (better known as Al Nakba) was the ultimate expression of the problem and at the same time was the highlight where surfaced hidden truths and the real causes of the differences between the two nations.

"Killing a man is a crime, destroy a whole people, it is a matter to discuss" Tuqam Ibrahim, a Palestinian poet.

Since its inception, the Israel–Palestinian conflict as a phenomenon tried to explain two different and irreconcilable religions: Jewish and Muslim. The establishment of the State of Israel (better known as Al Nakba) was the ultimate expression of the problem and at the same time was the highlight where they surfaced hidden truths and the real causes of the differences between the two nations: the State Israel is nothing more than an imperialist policy in the Middle East.

The main justifications for this assertion is the fact that Israel was formed colonizing a people and a land (Palestine), immediate and close relationship of the Jews with the United States, and current methods of maintenance and support of the state leading to by the Israeli government.

PALESTINE COLONIZATION

The main argument of the occupation of Palestine by the Jews, wandering people throughout history, it is certain that his divinity (Yahweh) promised by the patriarch Abraham a promised land and he was right there: on Palestinian land. **Robert Allen Warrior** compares this occupation with colonization of America by Europeans, explaining how Yahweh commands the annihilation of the indigenous population of the area: the Canaanites, whose descendants are the Palestinians. In the Old Testament narratives, with respect to lands that were promised to the Jewish people (...) it recounted when Yahweh, your God, delivers them, and you defeat them, destroy them and not make any covenant with them and not have mercy with them (Deuteronomy 7: 1-2). God's promises are already said, what remains is to enter the land and expel those who live there.

Palestine is a land invaded throughout its history. In 1516 were the Ottomans, in 1914 enters the British occupation. At that time the Arab population consisted of 604,000 people, while the Jews were only 85,000. When Britain decides to leave Palestine, the international community leaves the decision. On 29 November 1947 the General Assembly of the UN through **Resolution 181**, approved the following points: the termination of the British Mandate, the progressive withdrawal of the British army, setting the borders between the Palestinian state, the Israeli state and Jerusalem no later than October 1, 1948. It recommended the partition of Palestine into a Jewish state, an Arab state and a particular international zone under regime. 14,000 sq. Km, with 558,000 Jews and 405,000 Arabs to the Jewish state, 11,500 sq. Km, with 804,000 Arabs and 10,000 Jews to the Arab state, 106,000 Arabs and 100,000 Jews to the area under international control comprising the Holy Land, Jerusalem and Bethlehem. Between the two states should establish an economic, customs and monetary union.

The Plenary Assembly of the **UN** voted for the partition plan recommended by the **UNSCOP**, the final result of 33 votes in favor, 13 against and 10 abstentions, while made adjustments to the proposed boundaries between the two states. The partition would take effect from the withdrawal of the British. The resolution did not include any provision to implement the Plan, which had consequences in the long run, as it was not possible toapply. The United States and the Soviet Union were among those who voted in favor of the resolution.

The Jewish state alongside an international conspiracy was the replacement of one people by another, becoming an alleged British decolonization in a new qualitatively different colonization, through the emergence of a state based on Jewish immigration, old aspiration of Zionist origin. Shimon Peres, Israeli political leader said that "When Theodor Herzl, founder of Zionism, referred to a people without land to a land without people looking forwas not aware of the existence of an Arab population in Palestine". To maintain colonization force and due to the small Jewish population on Palestinian land, the State of Israel had to establish in 1950 the Law of Return which allows all Jews in the world can obtain citizenship being based in the country and conscription creating tables combative defend the invaded land, transforming Israeli society into a militarized society. The Palestinians want torecover their territory and will not terminate their fight to get it. Israel became an area of imminent danger, dispute, where among Israeli citizens only thing that survives is fear. **Is the fear of conflict or fear of Palestinian retaliation?** Anyone who invades a land never going to be quiet living in it and the feeling in Israel is truly remarkable.

AMERICAN ISRAELI PUBLIC AFFAIRS COMMITTEE

Few outside US They have heard of him, even in that country unnoticed if not in the upper echelons of politics and the economy. However, it has enormous power over the foreign policy of the leading world power. **AIPAC** stands for Affairs Committee United States–Israel one of the most important lobbies in the world.

Figure 6. American Israeli Public Affairs Committee (AIPAC)

Founded in 1951 by **Isaiah L. "Si" Kenen**, original member of the American Zionist Committee and former employee of the Ministry of Foreign Affairs of Israel, this had no real lobby both financial and political power to influence the forefront of American politics to early 70s of last century. Becoming one of the lobbyists who opens the doors of the House of Representatives (Congress and Senate) to which self – respecting to meet their demands.

The official target of **AIPAC** is to lobby the United States Congress on issues and legislation related to Israel, because it has more than 100,000 members (150 of which are dedicated exclusively to pressure Congress, the White House and all administrative agencies in making policy decisions that may affect the interests of the State of Israel). This lobby meets regularly with members of Congress and Senate sharing through various events, the point of view of the Jewish community in North America.

Not being a political action committee in the strict sense, not directly donate money to election campaigns, but makes contributions through other interest groups or personal contributions directly to federal candidates. It is estimated that since 1990 has allocated 56.8 million dollars to finance the two big American parties.

No doubt the great staging of this lobby is its annual convention, in which brings together leading political figures of the country. Usually it has the assistance of two thirds of the members of the House of Representatives, including the President.

Moreover, although the Jewish population in the United States does not reach six million are active voters (abstention rates in the US are high uniform) and. Although traditionally Democratic voters, in fact, the Jewish electorate is mobilized en masse to vote for the political option that puts more emphasis on defending the interests of Israel. Their motto makes clear: "**Protect the Jews – Who is not with us, is against us**".

AIPAC also promotes the introduction of Jewish influence on senior government officials, some of the most active are: Eric Cantor, Republican Congressman from Virginia, Dianne Feinstein, Democratic senator from California, and **Dov Zakheim**, undersecretary of defense with **GW Bush**.

Worth noting that during the second term of President Barack Obama, was the staging of a "misunderstanding in relations" Israeli–US. due to the prevailing geopolitical concept in the Obama Administration and whose brain would be the former National Security Advisor to President Carter, **Zbigniew Brzezinski**. Thus Brzezinski in a speech to the National Iranian–American Council (NIAC), said: "I do not think there is an implicit obligation of the United States to follow that stupid mule, Israel does because I believe that the US. have the right to decide their own national security policy "because since the assassination of John F. Kennedy, (who fought a secret war to **Ben Gurion** in a futile effort to stop the Israeli nuclear weapons program), the US geopolitics Middle and the Middle East would have been conditioned by the interests of Israel in its march towards the dream of Greater Israel.In addition, Brzezinski, would be faced with the Republican neocon US lobbyists (Technocrats – come mainly from the Zionist lobby in Israel, the Christian right, think tanks, foundations and large consortia and television media diaries and radiales– chains that integrate business loggia contractor Military Industrial Complex) and with his usual pointedly would have discredited the geostrategic myopia of both lobbyists saying that "are so obsessed with Israel, the Persian Gulf, Iraq and Iran have lost sight of the overall picture: the real power in the world is Russia and China, the only countries with a real ability to resist the United States and England and which would have to fix their attention".

However, after the election by Republican presidential candidate Donald Trump Indiana Governor Mike Pence as his running mate, there will undoubtedly be a considerable increase in the pressure of pro–Israeli lobby US (AIPAC) to proceed to the destabilization of Syria and Iran for expeditious methods in the post–Obama stage. This war will be a new local episode that would fall in recurring endemism return to Cold War US–Russian and involve both superpowers having as necessary collaborators regional powers (Israel, Egypt, Saudi Arabia and Iran) covering the geographical area extending from the Mediterranean area (Lebanon, Libya and Syria) and to Yemen and Somalia, having Iraq as epicenter (recalling the Vietnam War with Lindon B. Johnson from 1963 to 1969), and whose outcome could have side effects such as designing a new favorable geopolitical interests of the US, Britain and Israel with the implementation of the Greater Israel ("Eretz Israel").

In conclusion, the existence and activity of **AIPAC** pose a continued US support of various governments the State of Israel, so their activity is vital to the survival of Zionism as we know it today.

ISRAEL AND THE UNITED STATES: A PROFOUND AFFAIR

United States and the Zionist State of Israel are the only superpower, which because of its military power, have global control, and have already implemented a World Military Dictatorship aimed at enslaving Terrorist all the normal countries.

The support of the United States to Israel leads us directly to a double strategic interest of the two countries, leading to a chain of favors that are summed up in the complex formula of protection-Israeli security, and destruction of foci of Arab conflict (world called terrorists). There should stagger the world-imperialist power of the power of the North, Israel being a bulwark against Islamic fundamentalist terrorism, neutralizing oil sellers Arab countries and also providing advanced technology. In return the US government it offers financial aid to its ally for growth thereof, to hide his deceptions and ambiguities; and arming military and warlike manner, making it the sixth world power in this matter, matched in number and quality with British, French and Chinese. Washington continues to provide 3,000 million dollars in aid Israel despite the Symington Agreement, which prevents granting aid to countries developing nuclear weapons outside the control and international treaties. It is not difficult to understand that both the US as Israel want to keep this secret, with which the first problem to justify its military and economic aid to Israel avoided, and the latter can still comfortably receiving US assistance. Thus, in a Pentagon report 2001, Israel did not appear in the list of states with nuclear weapons, despite the evidence and reports from the Central Intelligence Agency US (CIA) who claim otherwise, as a document 1968 which concluded that the country had begun to produce nuclear weapons, but not critical discovery while chasing for these reasons other Middle Eastern nations such as Iraq, Iran and Syria.

The Israeli government does not recognize or deny the existence of nuclear weapons, and in parliament, the Knesset ('The Assembly' is the parliament of Israel, consisting of a single chamber of 120 seats, elected in asingle constituency, for a term of four years, by the system of proportional representation for lists of party) had never discussed the issue in open session until 2 February 2002 Issam Makhoul called a congressman broke the silence and was ejected from the courtroom. Then Makhoul said: "Today the so – called nuclear ambiguity applies only to the citizens of Israel can not participate as democratic critics of his government because it hides the truth about a subject of which their lives depend".

Moreover, Israel never signed the **Treaty on the Non-Proliferation of Nuclear** Weapons (as if they did Iran and North

Korea) set to prevent the spread of nuclear weapons globally. Because of this, the Israelis have not been subject to inspections and the threat of sanctions by the **International Atomic Energy Agency** at (IAEA) under the United Nations Organization.

A clear example of this state secret is the case of Israeli scientist **Mordechai Vanunu**, who spent 18 years imprisoned in solitary confinement for having revealed to a British newspaper related to the nuclear power of Israel many secrets. Vanunu worked at the top secret Dimona nuclear plant in the Negev desert and being fired revealed that Israel is a nuclear power with 200 atomic bombs. The Israeli secret service, Mossad, was framed by an agent scientist named Cindy, who served as bait to stop him and bring him to Justice Israeli. **Is not it too coincidental that this agent, whose real name is Sheryl Bentov, alive today just in Florida, United States?**

Vanunu after his release from prison said on television: you do not need any Jewish state; there must be a Palestinian state and Jews can live anywhere in the world. Vanunu was born in a Sephardic Jewish working class family in the arid Negev and had witnessed the persecution of the indigenous Palestinians, feeling compassion for them.

Finally, it is of interest to note that only shortly after its creation, the State of Israel was interested in acquiring nuclear weapons. **Was he trying to show power to summon people to whom he submitted, knowing that it was (in the near future) try to recover their land?**

Currently there US powerful pro-Israeli and Zionist groups who have power over the most influential media communication on strategic sectors of the US economy, political parties, members of Congress and the Executive. They determine who unfailingly access the presidency of the United States. In the words of American intellectual James Petras: "These lobbyists have considerable influence on the media, the White House and among opinion leaders in other words. Is not the Jewish vote, which represents only 5% in across the country, but the economic and political power of the Jews aligned with Israel which explains why the main presidential candidates are reluctant to condemn the Israeli killing of Palestinians? In an article in 2001, Petras analyzes hegemonic Israeli position in the United States, which has endured under Democratic and Republican presidencies, a relationship that is not based on personalities or transitional configurations party politics. The second administration of President George W. Bush was fully controlled by the neo-conservative-Zionist extremists.

In addition, these influential Zionists US reached high positions in the Pentagon and the State Department and from there promote wars against Arab countries, demonizing them and fabricating stories of imminent threats such as weapons of mass destruction (paradoxically being Israel the sixth power of the world in that category) terrorism and Muslim fundamentalism. A key example of these policies is the US invasion of Iraq, where the only other country that is beneficiary is the State of Israel (the only one in the Middle

East who supported the occupation) and war destroyed a major human contingent of the Palestinian Intifada, lifting-resistance struggle of the Palestinian people. The State of Israel has repressive methods of maintenance and support. **Perhaps another reason would be to put an imperialist state prisons and unacknowledged legalized torture, a wall that isolates similar to the South African apartheid, programs and talks to promote Jewish immigration and visit everyone Palestinians**? Some of these defense policies (they argue Israelis) are:

PRISONS

Israel has more than 7,500 Palestinian prisoners being held without charge and suffering terrible conditions such as indiscriminate beatings, launching tear gas, isolation for long periods of time, ban the right to visit, retention medicines and medical treatment to sick detainees, strict diets and child sexual abuse by prison guards. During interrogations using practices torture has been legalized in the Israeli and permitted judicial system in individual cases deemed a detainee a threat to state security in some cases detainees have died while in custody as a result of torture.

There is also a clandestine jail in central Israel called **Establishment 1391**, built on a hill overlooking a kibbutz, completely hidden by high walls and rows of pine trees. It not on the maps was erased from aerial photos and poster indicating their number was eliminated. The censors removed the Israeli media any reference to its geographical location in the name of secrecy that (according to the government) is essential to prevent that conspires against the country's security. The own internal security of Israel, Shim Bet, acknowledged in June 2003 have Secret Detention Centers. Despite the efforts of the Israeli government to block this information, horrible deeds committed there began to surface. According to the Syrian Cultural Association: what happens behind the walls of the establishment flagrant violation of international law. This prison can be likened in horror to which built the Americans in Guantanamo, Cuba.

HATE AND APARTHEID WALL

The construction of this wall has a primarily political dimension, not linked to security, as argued by the Israeli government. If for security reasons they had built on the border line marking and not six kilometers inside Palestinian territory explains current Mayor autonomous Palestinian town of Qalqilya, Maa'rouf Zahran. The wall is intended solely to serve to unilaterally annexing a large part of the West Bank and strengthen military control in Palestinian cities, keeping their inhabitants locked. **Or it is understandable that a security wall is fortified with reinforced concrete walls 8 meters thick, control towers every 300 meters, pits 2 meters deep, barbed wire and bypass routes?**

Once the wall is completed, the Jewish state will be annexed 7% of the West Bank, including 39 settlements and some 290,000 Palestinians, 70,000 of whom have no right to reside in Israel or traveling, or social services, suffering extreme vulnerability as it surely will be forced to emigrate.

The greatest losses suffered with this wall isolating the Palestinian people is the most important groundwater wells, as well as connections to electricity grids, destruction of olive fields, closing factories, businesses and shops. It has also increased the distance between the city and the people. Each time the wall is crossed there to face military checkpoints called cheek points where the arbitrariness of the soldiers turn decides the possibility of passage or not. With that is running the human and business interaction was between the Palestinians and Israelis tell the Administrative City of Qalqilia, Sheikah Nidal Ahmed.

PROGRAM VISIT TO THE COUNTRY

A free educational program of visit to Israel for 20 days, for young people from 18 to 26 years from different countries promotes Jews. This aims to revitalize a nationalism that never existed and which depends on the maintenance of the State of Israel. The trips are fully funded (stay, food, activities, transfers, excursions and other) by the government of Israel, Jewish communities (the Union of Jewish Communities, Keren Hayesod, the Jewish Agency) and a group of philanthropists. In Argentina, one of the contingents perform this type of travel is Birthright (BRIA), who announced the program from its website (addressing Argentine Jews) as: Your adventure. Your birthright. Our gift.

RAUL OJEDA

LAW OF RETURN

False name (fallacy) if any return call to a law that promotes the entry of Jews from around the world to a land appropriated in 1948. This law gives automatic citizenship to every Jewish immigrant to Israel, example clearly the need to populate a land with people who never had the same parallelism conversion Act, with which any converted to Judaism and have loving relationships with the State of Israel person may obtain citizenship. Torture the Palestinian people. Not only denounced by the Israeli Palestinian people, but also by the newspaper Ha'aretz, who said that the Israel Defense Forces (IDF) have been studying the tactics that the Nazi SS troops used in 1943 against Jewish resistance in the Warsaw ghetto, and that currently apply against Palestinians in the West Bank and the Gaza Strip.

Former Minister Ariel Sharon (who died on January 11, 2014), a member of a right – wing party, openly acknowledged admiration for the practices executed by the Nazis, by stating in an interview with **Amos Oz**, (journalist and Israeli leftist writer, published in the Israeli newspaper Davar on December 17, 1982): all reproach me to be a Nazi, well, I vindicate loud and clear voice, because that is the only true and right there in this world and this method it has proved effective since Hitler. Then Sharon declared his intention to apply to the Palestinians what Hitler did to the Jews during World War II. **Is it not a contradiction made these statements by the Israeli prime minister, who was responsible for the construction of a security wall, the same person who is accused of massacres,** torture, rape and disappearances, one of more than 3,000 civilians (including children, elderly and women) who were between 16 and 18 September 1982, in the Palestinian refugee camps of Sabra and Shatila?

"Here we will die. Here, in the last passage. Here or there (...) our blood will plant its olive trees "Mahmud Darwish, the Palestinian poet

Currently, the State of Israel is recognized by many countries, organizations and public figures. On the other hand, the Palestinians, dispossessed of their land and also increasingly stripped of their identity, they are agglomerated under the terrorists term by the mere fact of using scarce and poor methods of defense of his people (immolations, small stones, hunger strikes, intifadas and others), while the Israeli state with their tanks and war planes murderers and their magnitude are seen worldwide as the Jewish people always oppressed and victim of anti – Semitism. The latter term is used excessively by the Jewish people, whom he accuses of anti – Semitic anyone who is proclaimed in favor of the struggle of the Palestinian people, as owner of the land where today the State of Israel stands.

It also paradoxical, since the resolution 3070 of the UN, November 30, 1973 also reaffirmed the legitimacy of the struggle of peoples for liberation from foreign colonial domination and alien subjugation by all available means including armed struggle. No example that illustrates this situation more than said the Palestinian ambassador to

Argentina Suhail Hani Daher Akel: (...) a Palestinian village resisting stones against Apache helicopters and warplanes F-16.

In turn, this case serves as an example to see how a power like the United States uses Israel-Palestinian conflict (among many others, along with the invasion of Iraq, and others) to get him benefits, as control of the nation Arab obtaining mineral and energy resources such as oil, that are vital to himself.

The media supporting this idea, trying to warn of global terrorism plaguing the world, when they could transmit documentaries and reports that explain under what circumstances are the nations in conflict and explain the origin of each of the positions.

CONSTRUCTION OF A MYTH AS TRUTH

Foucault argues that power is exercised only through the production of a truth, but it is also necessary that truth is accepted by others as truth. The Zionist movement not only built a truth, but which in turn had strategies that allowed him to build a speech with which it was possible to legitimize their claims to Palestine and turn the inhabitant of that land into a non – person and then in enemy.

Why was Palestine the place chosen to settle there the state of Israel? – Herzl announces: "Palestine is our unforgettable historic homeland". The Jews claimed ancestral rights over Palestine; his speeches are based on biblical

147

stories: Palestine was the land God had given His people, Israel; this was the "promised land".

He not only built right on land, but stripped of rights to the inhabitants of Palestine denying existence: "For a quarter century the policy of the State of Israel is to simulate the Palestinians are Jordanians, Egyptians, Syrians or Lebanese who they have gone mad, who say they are Palestinians. " The option that was chosen was to make the Palestinian an invisible being, well reflected it is this reflected in the words of **Golda Mair**, "Palestinian, I do not know what that is". This can be understood more clearly if we compare it with the phrase: "a land without a people for a people without land"; It was necessary condition to deny existence to the Arab people. However, the Arabs existed and were reluctant to leave their land. Every fight, every resistance he interprets it as a product of "Arab terrorism", because these Arabs were violent nature.

RAUL OJEDA

ZIONISM AND POLICY IMPLICATIONS OF THE STATE OF ISRAEL

The year 1948 not only marks the year of the creation of the State of Israel but also the beginning of the Arab-Israeli war and the exodus of Palestinians. Although the partition of Palestine into two states: an Arab state and a Jewish state, the state of Israel received 60% of the land was not satisfied with this, and continued its expansion. "The result was the occupation of Haifa, Jaffa, Beisan, and Acre, Palestinian suburb of Jerusalem and other smaller towns and purification of Galilee. Before Ben Gurion proclaimed the State of Israel had already 400,000 fugitives Palestinians".

The problem, which has proved to be the cruelest side of the Arab-Israeli conflict, is the Palestinian refugees. In 1949, the United Nations General Assembly creates Relief and Works Agency United Nations (English, UNRWW); it was providing basic services such as housing, healthcare and education. These were mostly peasant's expropriated refugees, a product of the Zionist occupation.

The Zionists argue that the refugee problem was caused by the Arab leaders themselves, not abide by the resolution of the United Nations to establish two states in Palestine. Ben Gurion argued that the Arabs were not expelled, but was exiled by his own decision. The truth is that in the Zionist conception, the State of Israel could not think of integrating Arab, so they are a minority; the idea was to move the Palestinian population to other Arab states.

THE HIDDEN FACE OF GLOBAL GEOPOLITICS

The Arabs could not accept being dispossessed of the land they had occupied since forever, which initiated the Palestinian Revolution. She is not the product of "Arab terrorism", but represents the struggle of a people to recover their land and their rights. This revolution would give the pattern to Ben Gurion, and Arab leaders that the Palestinians do not peacefully accept the installation of the Jewish state. Another major problem, which was raised to the state of Israel established, was that the principles of democracy that arose were contradictory with the Zionists postulates. Theoretically, the state should be for all citizens, they should have equal rights. However, the state was conceived by the Zionists as a Jewish state for Jews. As a brand Diner, this was also due to the base state identity was not to be the "nation of Israel" but Jewishness.

ALWAYS TO REMEMBER

Eric John Ernest Hobsbawm states that "nationalism comes before nations". States do not build nations and nationalities but the other way around. This is the basis in the case of Zionism. The Zionist movement is a nationalist movement that aims to be a "Jewish nation". However, despite that Zionism is coated Jewish identity, you can not say that all Jews support the movement and Zionism has more points of contact with the ideas of European nationalism of the nineteenth century, with the own traditional ideas of Judaism.

What becomes of Judaism Zionism is the idea of the return to Zion. To settle a nation a territory was necessary, and

Palestine could, using the Bible, claim rights to that land. The problem is that Palestine was not a "land without people". Everyone knows that the Arab peoples inhabited forever. So the solution became Zionists was to drive them out, expropriate their land, deny their existence and commit against them the greatest crimes against humanity. However, the Palestinians did not give up and started the revolution, a struggle to regain their land, Zionism cataloged worldwide in terms of terrorism.

Free Palestine!

THINK TANK

"Currently the" sovereign people "think about all depending on how television and induces says. And in fact lead opinion, the power of the image is placed in the centrote all processes of contemporary politics "Giovanni Sartori

Think tanks is the name given in English what could be described as a center, institute or institution dedicated to spreading the civil society –of disimulada– means a ideological propaganda (usually political) form of dissemination of ideas or constructive, necessary and innovative thoughts, useful for ordinary, for students citizen, the country's leaders, intellectuals and others leaders. His appearance dates back to 1831 when the **Royal United Services Institute** (RUSI) was created in the City of London by the Duke of Wellington. It is recorded that RUSI's original mission was "to study the naval and military science". At that time the military domination of the seas was essential for the spread of colonialism, empire building, exploitation, theft, suffering and murder. The final award of the crown was the transformation of China into a source of income for opium from British elites.

With the advent of the research institution, the elites could now leave behind the castle walls and openly operate, the popular defense, while planning their selfish policies. All under the guise of uniting the brightest minds from academia to solve the problems of society.

The common public perception of the think tank is being centers or foundations independent research, but most are linked to power groups or lobbies that are even branches of superstructures linked to multinationals, intelligence agencies or imperialist countries who are finally those who finance and manipulate these think-tanks. The mission of think-tanks is therefore to instill and enforce in a population, a civil society, a way of thinking, to accept the values and ideas that certain key groups want to impose or to prevail – according to their interests, enjoining them discreetly, without being apperceived who is behind all this. For that reason the "think tanks" have the financial means to recruit personalities, artists, prestigious intellectuals to work for them and propagate ideas or beliefs of these think tanks.

In the case of the United States, the oldest think tank is the **Carnegie Endowment for International Peace** founded in 1910. Today, the high elite of globalization and the defender of the agenda of Rockefeller, **Jessica Tuchman Mathews** He has been president of the think tank Carnegie located in

Washington DC since 1997 while at the same time, a member of the Bilderberg Steering Committee. The president of the Carnegie Foundation's work, "try a voluntary agreement to achieve world peace that persists over time" -In addition facilitates the transition to a new world order.

In 1947, the **Tavistock Institute of Human Relations** was created in London by **Henry Dicks** to focus on the psychological and psychiatric aspects of crowd control on a global scale (psychoanalytically oriented). Heavily influenced by the works of avant – garde psychoanalysts Sigmund Freud and Carl Jung, Tavistock is credited to give "guidance" to the Institute for Social Research, Research Institute of Stanford (SRI), the Brookings Institute, Wharton School of Economics, RAND, the Club of Rome and intelligence agencies as the OSS (the predecessor of the CIA), and others. In the book of **John Coleman**, **Conspirators Hierarchy – The Committee of 300 (1992)**, the Tavistock Institute is established as part of a global conspiracy that will lead to a New World Order, psychologically manipulating the population, especially through television and music.

In the United States currently the most publicized think tanks regularly host seminars and televised presented as representatives of a certain socio-political ideology. For example, the Heritage Foundation, founded on February 16, 1973 by **Paul Weyrich** and **Edwin Feulner** with funding from **Joseph Coors**, who also founded the **Moral Majority** and the **Domestic Policy Council**, is the largest and most influential think maybe tank "conservative" who rose to fame in 1981 with the Reagan administration. These thoughts tanks have defended and promoted the devaluation of conservative economic and social policies increased funding for defense and military interference abroad. Finally, it is presented as an advisory institution for what is perceived as the policies of the Republican Party.

In contrast to the **Heritage Foundation** is the **Center for American Progress** (CAP). The center pretends to be dedicated to improving the lives of Americans through progressive ideas and actions. In fact it is now a front for the political machinery of Clinton / Obama, which is nothing more than the left arm of the Rothschild global financial system that currently governs the United States.

The CATO Institute was founded in 1977 in San Francisco, California by Edward H. Crane and initially funded by Charles Koch. It was in these years related to the beginning of the Libertarian Party. The name refers to the letters of Cato and was proposed by Murray Rothbard founder and board member who then went by internal problems with the organization in 1981. This is defined as a think tank "libertarian" dedicated to spreading and increase understanding of public policies based on the principles of individual liberty, limited government, free markets and peace. The institute is dedicated to establishing presidencies of the Republican Party and legislatures promote policies that directly benefit the Koch brothers, their industries and their political ideologies, under the pretext of promoting individual freedoms, the government non-intrusive, peace and prosperity for all.

It is important to mention that there are other organizations declared as philanthropic foundations, designed to create a humanistic perception empathize and hide the cold psychopath powerful machinery. From 1913, the same year that this psychopath machinery usurped the money supply of the United States through the insidious Federal Reserve Act, the Rockefeller Foundation was created. This philanthropic institution is defined as a non-profit organization, non - governmental organization (NGO) dedicated to health and education for all. By controlling education and health. Under the guise of charity and good heart, the Rockefeller Foundation has been instrumental in the control of the curriculum in schools of all levels in order to mold the young minds to think in a same way. The Rockefeller Foundation is an important part in medical research and development, largely driven by the benefits and loaded with biological engineering and psychiatry.

To reinforce all the above, it is mentioned that the website of the New York Times published a series of documents collected during the conduct of an investigation called "Foreign Powers Buy Influence at Think Tanks" by Eric Lipton, Brooke Williams and Nicholas Confessore, The New York Times, September 6, 2014.

According to this research the newspaper New York Times, 64 foreign governments have come subsidizing 28 "think tanks" or "think tank" major US since 2011, which constitutes a violation of the Foreign Agents Registration Act of 1938. According to the US newspaper precise, these governments have prevented these think tanks publish works that may impair their interests and, in some cases, have even managed to impose analysis that favor their own concerns and even use them in lobbying operations.

This newspaper mentions directly to Japan, Qatar, the United Arab Emirates, Norway and Azerbaijan Emirates as countries using this way to influence while the Atlantic Council, the Brookings Institution, the Center for Global Development and the Center for Strategic and International Studies are among the think tanks that accept such bribes.

TELL ME WHAT 'THINK TANK' APPOINTMENTS AND TELL YOU WHO MANIPULATES YOU

Those days **Stephen Hadley** (former national security adviser of President George W. Bush) was very busy. United States thought whether or not to bomb the Syrian government for allegedly using chemical weapons.Hadley, **appeared on CNN, Fox News and Bloomberg TV as an independent expert**. He believed he had to attack. What the audience did not know, because nobody had told, it is that Hadley was director of Raytheon, **one of the manufacturers Tomahawk missile** that would eventually be used in the attacks. Raytheon shares rose to a record high. **The piece of cake Hadley in the company rose to nearly $ 900,000,** all according to a study by the Public Accountability Initiative (Public Accountability Initiative). At least another **22 fellow members in proposing the means to attack Syria were related to the military industry**, according to the nonprofit entity.Only 13 of the 111 media appearances presented these conflicts of interest.

In Washington, the capital more power concentrated in the world (the government of the first power, and institutions such as the IMF or the World Bank), study centers in the hundreds, and up I to propaganda has evolved dramatically in recent decades, especially with the advent of television continuous information and Internet welter. **Lobbyists** no longer flying banners or launch newsletters with an explicit agenda. **They disguise themselves as independent scholars** and confused between the mass of fellow members and experts quoted by journalists. And in this form of media manipulation, the US is a true master.

"**The boom energy will bring Pennies from Heaven for American families – IHS** ". This headline news agency Reuters (**of September 4, 2012**) was a real treat for economic journalists. According to the latest report from consultancy IHS-CER, he told the agency in full out of recession **every American family will earn $ 2,500 more per year** through increased oil production in the country, amid one of the worst crises job reminiscent United States. In addition, according to the note, they would have added 2.1 million jobs to the economy in 2012, direct and indirect, and the figure would rise to 3.3 million in 2020. An idyllic setting, impossible to resist the siren.The teletype was replicated by dozens of media.

But something did not smell good on that note: the report extolled the controversial fracking and oil from tar sands very blatant way, making it almost an emotional blackmail that manna could be reduced by falling 67% in production if "concerns they end restricting production environment. " This correspondent contacted the consultant.

STUDIES PAID BY 'LOBBIES' OIL

It is right to know: **What is a Lobby** – A "lobby" is a specialist in political pressure and funded by multinationals that influence to influence the decisions of local, state and regional governments team. The most powerful are the industrial "lobbies" of large multinational financial or large banks. Over the past two decades, decision-making within the European Union has been spectacularly kidnapped by these large corporations through their sectoral lobbies.

In Brussels there are over 500 lobbyists, mainly industrial or financial, which employ an army of lobbyists (it is estimated to be about 10,000) to influence economic policies formulated in Brussels, which increasingly affects us more at the local level.

"IHS maintains complete editorial independence", said the company, 8,000 employees and specializes in the sale of strategic information. But at the same time **it acknowledges that the study was paid for by the** America's Natural Gas Alliance, the American Petroleum Institute (API), the Chemical

Council of the United States, and the Institute for Energy XXI Century Chamber of Commerce, among others. Hardly lacked any industry lobbyist.

None of this implies that the report is false or that its estimate of future data will not be met. But there is an obvious conflict of interest that should have figured prominently on information from Reuters. A "full disclosure" as it is called in this country, would have been right. Other organizations such as the Association for the Study of Maximum Oil and Gas in the USA (ASPO–USA), ensure that the report of the IHS–CERA has a "credibility problem" and that "alters the markets". In addition, **the estimate of job positions mixture indirect jobs**, difficult to prove, **to direct**. In fact, workers in the industry of oil exploration and drilling in the United States are counted rather by tens of thousands, according to the Bureau of Statistics. The think tanks are increasingly cited by the media (over 4,000 mentions in 2012 only for the Brookings Institution and the Heritage Foundation). That means ability to influence public opinion. Therefore, **in Washington**, the capital that concentrates more power in the world (the Government of the first power, and international institutions such as the IMF or the World Bank), **study centers in the hundreds, and rising.** Typically they produce thousands of complex reports, with hundreds of pages, which few journalists read in full. So normally they send a synopsis with catchy headlines that then played in the mass media.

"HISPANICS DO NOT REACH THE IQS WHITE"

An example of this is: **"Immigration reform will cost 6.3 billion US dollars, according to the Heritage Foundation"**. It seemed the perfect harmony that seemed to leave the Senate in May of that year (2015) on the new immigration law counterpoint. The report of the Heritage appeared to be legit (legitimate) with serious head ("The Fiscal Cost of Unlawful Immigrants and Amnesty to the US Taxpayer Special Report"), its executive summary, and its prestigious signature, Dr. Jason Richwine. However, Richwine was, as destaparía later, an activist against immigration responsible for lectures like this: "No **one knows whether Hispanics will ever to IQ (IQ) of white**, but predicting that new Hispanic immigrants they will have children with low IQ is difficult to discuss. **At least 23 of the coterie that proposed in the media attack Syria were related to the military industry. Only 13 of his 111 appearances these conflicts of interest were exposed**: The Heritage is the most conservative faction of the Republican Party what the Ideas Foundation was the PSOE or the PP FAES **Aznar**. It has two branches: the well – known think tank and activist organization Heritage Action. The latter was a key element in the **revolution of the Tea Party** that led the US government to close early October. **He threatened to lower the note in one of its prestigious lists congressmen to vote in favor** of the proposal to reopen the government had just introduced the Republican Speaker John Boehner. After learning of the threat, many congressmen backed down and the vote was canceled.

"The Heritage Foundation remains a center of studies even if the Heritage Action as lobby", says to The Confidencial anonymously a representative of the group Think Tank Watch. "Other think tanks have the same scheme, such as the Center for American Progress (Center for American Progress, CAP) linked to the Obama Administration".

OBAMA'S THINK TANK'S SECRET DONORS

The magazine **The Nation** (an American leftist weekly published in the United States, founded on July 6, 1865 and is published by The Nation Company, LP at 33 Irving Place in New York) published a report entitled "Secrets donors **Center for American Progress**". In it he suggested that the CAP had supported Barack Obama's energy policy and companies like First Solar because it was part of the Business Alliance, "a secret group of corporate donors". The CAP denied that "would shape their stories by corporate interests". Contributions to think tanks are anonymous, but are reflected in the statements of income. Based on these data, **FAIR** has determined that, of those 25, **two – thirds receive money from at least one oil – related company**. More than half are funded in part by **ExxonMobil**, and nine **Chevron**. The Koch of Koch Industries, brothers paid seven. **Shell** (five), and **Conoco-Phillips** and **BP** (three). In addition, these companies call "Big Energy" have several of its business in the boardrooms of study centers such as Brookings, CSIS or Aspen Institute. Conclusion: energy issues are particularly sensitive.

Bilderbergers

"The general population does not know what is happening, and does not even know he does not know" Noam Chomsky

DEFINITION

The Bilderberg Club is a private annual meeting attended by important personalities of the most developed countries in the world and representatives of major international organizations. It was founded by the Jewish emigrant and Polish political adviser **Jozef Retinger**, concerned about the growing anti Americanism in Europe Oosterbeek, Netherlands, from 29 to 31 May 1954.

Joseph Retinger, the founder of the Bilderberg Group, was also one of the original architects of the European Common Market and a leading intellectual champion of European integration. In 1946, he told the Royal Institute of International

Affairs (the British counterpart and sister organization of the Council on Foreign Relations), that Europe needed to create a federal union for European countries to "relinquish part of their sovereignty", Retinger was a founder of European movement, a lobbyist organization dedicated to creating a federal Europe. Retinger secured financial support for the European Movement from powerful US financial interests as the CFR and the Rockefellers. However it is difficult to distinguish between the CFR and the Rockefellers, especially after World War II, the main financing CFR came from the Carnegie Corporation, Ford Foundation and especially the Rockefeller Foundation.

The Bilderberg Group acts as a "think-thank secret global" whose original function was "to link governments and economies in Europe and North America during the Cold War". One of the main goals of the Bilderberg Group was to unify Europe in a European Union. Apart from Retinger, the founder of the Bilderberg and the European Movement, another ideological founder of European integration was Jean Monnet, who founded the Action Committee for a United States of Europe, an organization dedicated to promoting European integration, and was also the major promoter and first president of the European Coal and Steel Community (ECSC English or ECSC), the precursor to the European Common Market (ECM-ECM in English).

An invitation from Prince Bernhard to the 1957 Bilderberg Group meeting

Soestdijk Palace, December 1956

Dear Mr. Henge

I have the honour to invite you to the next Bilderberg Conference which will take place on the 15th, 16th and 17th February 1957 at St. Simon's Island, Georgia, in the United States of America.

The object of this conference will be to study common and divergent elements in the policies of the Western World.

Prince of the Netherlands

R.S.V.P.: Dr. J. H. Retinger
27, The Vale, LONDON S. W. 3

Figure 7. Creating the Bilderberg Club in 1956.

Declassified documents (released in 2001) showed that "the US intelligence community conducted a campaign in the 60s and 70s to build a time for a united Europe; he founded and directed the European federalist movement". The documents revealed that "America was working aggressively behind the scenes to push Britain into a European state, a memorandum, dated on July 26, 1950, gives instructions for a campaign to promote a European Parliament own right, it is signed by **General William J Donovan**, head of the Office of Strategic Services (OSSOffice of Strategic Services for its acronym in English, in wartime), forerunner of the CIA, "later" the greatest tool of Washington to shape the European agenda was the American Committee for a United Europe, created in 1948. The governor was Donovan, ostensibly a private lawyer by then. And the Vice-governor was Allen Dulles, the CIA director in 50. The table (of directors) included **Walter Bedell Smith**, the first director of the CIA, and a row of figures and former officials OSS they moved in and out of the CIA. The document shows that ACUE financed the European Movement, the most important federalist organization in the post – war years; curiously, the leaders of the European Movement – Retinger, the visionary Robert Schuman and the former Belgian Prime Minister Paul–Henri Spaak –were treated as hands rented by their American sponsores. US paper It was handled as a covert operation. Funds ACUE came from the Ford and Rockefeller foundations also of business groups with close connections to the US Government.

Figure 8. William J. Donovan General reviews the members of an Operations Group of the OSS in Bethesda (Maryland) before traveling to China, in 1945.

The European Coal and Steel Community (ECSC) was founded in 1951 and was signed by France, West Germany, Italy, Belgium, Luxembourg and the Netherlands. Recently released from the session of 1955, documents show that a main topic of discussion was "European Unity" and the "discussion affirmed complete support for the idea of integration and unification of the representatives of the six nations of the ECSC present in the conference". In addition, "A European speaker expressed concern about the need to make a common currency, and indicated that from their point of view this necessarily implied the creation of a central political authority selfishly", A US participant confirmed that his country he had not bent his enthusiastic support for the idea of integration, however there was considerable strains in America on how to carry out a practical way that enthusiasm. Another US participant urged his European friends to advance the unification of Europe less emphasis on ideological considerations and, above all, be practical and work fast". In addition, at the meeting of the Bilderberg Group 1955, they created a first schedule, the creation of the European Common Market.

Figure 9. The founding members of the ECSC: West Germany, Belgium, France, Italy, Luxembourg and the Netherlands (The French Algeria was an integral part of the French Republic).

In 1957, two years later, the Treaty of Rome, which created the European Economic Community (was signed EEC), also known as the European Community. For decades, various other treaties were signed, and more countries joined the European Community. In 1992, the Maastricht Treaty, which created the European Union and led to the creation of the euro, was signed. The European Monetary Institute was created in 1994, the European Central Bank was founded in 1998, and the euro was launched in 1999. Etienne D'Avignon, Chairman of the Bilderberg Group and former EU Commissioner, revealed in March 2009 that the Euro it was debated and planned at Bilderberg conferences. This was an example of regionalism, integration of an entire region of the world, a continent, in a supranational structure. This was one of the main functions of the Bilderberg Group, which would also come to play an important role in other international affairs.

For several days fixing a number of issues for discussion on which ideas, proposals and viewpoints you exchange. The Club met in Spain on two occasions. Club Bilderberg conferences are scheduled as informal discussions on major issues facing the world. Participants can make use of what was said at the conference, but with the condition never identify the speaker. In Spain he has met on two occasions: between 12 and 14 May 1989 in La Toja; and between 3 and 6 June 2010 in Sitges.

In 2015 it was held between May 29 and June 1 at the Marriot hotel in Copenhagen, where some 140 participants from 22 countries met. Of these 35 guests came from the United States, 13 from Britain and other major European countries, Canada and China. Among the participants include former US Secretary of State Henry A. Kissinger; the general director of the International Monetary Fund (IMF), Christine Lagarde; the editor of The Economist, John Micklethwait; Italian former Prime Minister Mariano Monti; Princess Beatrice of the Netherlands; Secretary General of NATO, Anders Fogh Rasmussen; Swedish Foreign Minister Carl Bildt and President of Airbus, Thomas Enders, among others. At that time there were four Spanish participants, three of them regulars at the forum, such as the Queen Sofía; the president of Prisa, Juan Luis Cebrián; and the CEO of La Caixa, Juan Maria Nin, who has joined this year the Minister of Foreign Affairs, and Cooperation, José Manuel García-Margallo. Since its inception, almost every year was attended by members of powerful families like Rockefeller or Rothchild. Representatives of Coca Cola, American Express, British Petroleum, JP Morgan and Microsoft companies are also regulars at the meetings. Since the presidency of Dwight Eisenhower, all US presidents have attended a meeting of the Bilderberg Club: John F. Kennedy, Lyndon B. Johnson, Richard Nixon, Gerald Ford, Jimmy Carter, Ronald Reagan, George Bush father and son, Bill Clinton and Barack Obama.

MEETING 2016

In **Dresden** in Germany the Dark World Government concentrated. From Thursday June 9 to Sunday 12, kings, aristocrats, politicians, leaders and government officials, bankers, millionaires, owners and CEOs of global conglomerates and so some 120–150 people gathered to "breathe together" to plot and decide the future of the rest of humanity. Despite the high level of the participants to the summit, the traditional press does not delve into the subject and tiptoes through the news.

The summit 64th Bilderberg Club was held this year at the Hotel Taschenbergpalais Dresden Kenpinski among very strong security measures. The topics discussed this year covered, among others, **the economic crisis in China, the problem of refugees in Europe, Russia**, Middle East, cybersecurity, technology, geopolitics, precariat and middle class (...) The agenda was different. One of the most important issues was the papers of Panama, as stated by The Digital Confidential. **Henry Kissinger and David Rockefeller, two of the founding members discussed the proposal that the United States remains as the only tax haven in the world.**These defend at this summit that most territories with bank secrecy and are considered tax havens are used by criminal organizations to launder money, and therefore in this fight against tax evasion, **should eliminate all tax havens world, including Switzerland, Panama, the Cayman or Bermuda** to make US is the main country to which the wealthy around the world take their money, no bank secrecy.

But who they are part of the Bilderberg Club?

The Bilderberg Club is a pyramidal hierarchical organization of three levels. From bottom to top these levels are:

– **Innocent**: It is the largest group, the lower layer of the pyramid. The innocent are invited to Bilderberg possible. Usually powerful, influential, rich people, who want to know their world view and if they would be willing to breathe together (conspire) with the ideals of the organization. Many of these innocent people do not know the true intentions of Bilderberg, and some defrauded out of the meeting, as happened in 2012 to the Spanish vice president, Soraya Saenz de Santamaria. Others, such as Esperanza Aguirre, leave delighted. And others, like Pujol, not like the hard core of the Club.

– **The Steering Commitee or Steering Committee**: Composed of 33 permanent members. The current President is Henri de Castries, CEO of AXA Group. It is the heavyweight of Bilderberg and are responsible for drawing up the list of meeting attendees based on the subjects to be treated. The components of the Steering Commitee have their own agenda and discuss the most discrete subjects (one of his favorite words, instead of secrets) without the rest of the attendees, with which meet to discuss broader issues, know this particular. As I mentioned above, Spain has a representative in the steering committee: Juan Luis Cebrián.

– **The hard core**: The real architects of the globalist agenda. Exactly just the name of David Rockefeller is known. Beside him, we must not forget such important names as Henry Kissinger and the Rothschild Family.

THE CREATORS OF CLUB BILDERBERG

– **Jozef Retinger**: The ideologist of the Club; Polish financial and Freemason. He had such influence and contacts which said that only had to pick up a phone to have a direct line to the White House.

– **Bernhard of Lippe-Biesterfeld**: The public relations club. Sagacious, captivating and hard at the same time man. The Club takes its name from Prince Hotel, the Bilderberg Hotel, where the first meeting took place in 1954. Only in 1976 the annual meeting was not held due to the Lockheed scandal that spattered himself to Bernhard of the Netherlands.

– **David Rockefeller** : He has been and remains its 101 years, the soul of the Club.

TOPICS COVERED IN THE HIDDEN AGENDA OF 2016

To get an idea of the topics discussed and decisions taken at the meeting of the Bilderberg, an article published on 14.06.2015 on the website of the chain- mentioned RT (- Russia Today, based in Moscow, whose owner it is theGovernment of Russia, ANO TV-Novosti) reported: "remember that this meeting come experts with key

173

information that may even be wrong because intelligence is not always as illustrious as evidenced in Ukraine, although always party pulls out or Syria which had to retreat despite the projected invasion". Indeed, six themes were discussed:

One, the degree of cohesion of the elite, that is, establish how strong is the conjunction of interests, personalities who attended and their importance, confront the allies with doubts and establish new contacts showing an impregnable fortress. This is a fundamental topic.

Two, to consider whether the goals set in the New World Order (NWO) are insured and thus ensured continuity continue to receive his riches smoothly through the development of profit and geostrategic power. The creation of a multipolar world that is gradually creating a national and international legislation to root windfall profits of such mega – corporations, such as the law of inheritance tax Correa, which has been supported by the Ecuadorian bourgeoisie, is considered disturbing symptom and should be "held" soon. The hermetic "TIIP Agreement" will be continued hard to be an emblem of extraterritorial legislation that gives authority and jurisdiction over the nations.

Three define which actors will star, laborers, servants governments, to establish the functions they have to play in this plan already scheduled defining the scope and extent of their participation, assessing the concentration of political-military powers and those who have impaired ability critical to a large majority participation, and therefore whether it has distorted the very purpose for which these structures were created. The Mistral case has to Hollande, French president, as a classic reference of subordination.

Four, identify obstacles and degree of force. A nontradable objective is to investigate the most appropriate mechanisms at this time to remove the countries and leaders with divergent conceptions; leaders and nations like Putin, Maduro, Iran, China, will be white. Please confirm that this is not Club overestimates its strength nor the power of the enemy is minimized since they do understand, regardless of the tools they have, and that there are difficult obstacles to overcome and must be eliminated somehow. It is not unreasonable, then, more than six hundred assassination attempts on Fidel Castro and Hugo Chavez's death by a sudden "cancer".

Five, plan the next steps and nodes of conflict which will be Syria that will try to invade through the Islamic State and preparation of the Free Syrian-faction "moderate" Army, weakening the Iraqi army to provoke a "new Libya "threats to Iran with the aim of breaking its global influence, raw destruction of Yemen to allow new settlement of al Qaeda, the intensification of the war in Ukraine, the gaunt attack IMF-ECB to Greece and its government left, strong media pressure and accusations Podemos in Spain, the innocuous attack coalition against terrorism led by the United States, the intervention momentum in Latin America, among others, without neglecting Africa and Asia expanding collisions.

Six, establish new methods of political armed or "peaceful" action and ongoing evaluation to see how the project materializes.

Meeting the following considerations:

– To inform the world of their meeting they are confirming that possess high power and they occupy. In this context becomes evident certainty the statement of Vladimir Putin on the course that took these mega powers after the collapse of the Soviet Union because he felt there was no one opposed his path began to colonize new territories rather than devote his "desire freedom "to build relations with the new countries. The fact is that have gathered to assess what developed and then send basic to a power group that does not need the Bilderbergers but only as a symbol or table pawns to study, conclusions as decisions are taken in other instances and domains. It is a careful thought process as required all corporate management in both conclave to restudy decisions and pre–established plans, coordinate actions, execute instructions and serve as a facade.

– With high probability it was decided to continue with the aim of undermining the sovereignist's countries concentrating their efforts, in the case of Latin America, in Venezuela, Ecuador, Bolivia and Argentina, in order to destabilize the region. Brazil is the subject of a particular study because of their alleged changes can stem the debacle of the separatist's countries. Chile, Peru, Colombia and Mexico, remain the most powerful allies of the continent-except the paternal relationship with Canada. In Central America and it begins to set the extermination opposition Plan and exemplary violence through permissive legislation, military bases and "help" tactic. It not without reason is understood that in Guatemala the impeachment against President Otto Perez Molina, loyal menestral Washington suspended.

In this line, it will avoid conflict with Chile, in crisis by the level of corruption comes to light; it is an important prop for the neoliberal functionality. Colombia, no effective peace process with great achievements, it is appropriate in these circumstances for the democratic forces can not advance. Peru, in a general chaos, is well coordinated and Mexico in the violent escalation will continue until a massive electoral project or organization can lead down a path of peace.

– Islamic State aid or Daesh through the most refined forms, especially with weapons, logistics, funding will be encouraged. France will support these criminal organizations thanks to Hollande commitment to contribute to the crisis of the real left in the world. Naturally, the anti El Coalition will continue its "neutral" possible role in preventing the advance of the liberating forces in Syria and Iraq. It will hinder, as far as possible, the formation of a government in Libya, encouraging the dispersion in order to achieve a strengthening of takfiríes groups. The alliance with countries that support terrorism will be even closer since, despite the alleged serious frictions, the bolt with Saudi Arabia, Turkey and Qatar will build more.

THE HIDDEN FACE OF GLOBAL GEOPOLITICS

– Regarding electoral processes, such as the case of the US, establish a screen that prevents see the shadows behind the nomination and will support Hillary Clinton as puppet, through agreements already acquired. However, they also played two bands as always done "rationally". In all eleccionaria situation will extend its comprehensive networks to drive safely "fidelity" of likely winners.

– According serious analysts, the Bilderbergers have as role controlled organization to continue usufructuando of power (...) disorder which is consistent with its fundamentalist purpose. Thus, contemporary forms of struggle will be increased, approving and renewing experienced since the planet has changed. In this direction means the declaration of Philippa Malmgren (formerly of the White House), confirming last December that the Pentagon is already in a war with China and Russia (...) "in cyberspace", forgetting that the sanctions to Russia or other countries are true acts of economic warfare. You can not forget that the Bilderberg Club was founded by Prince Bernhard in 1957 (Dutch Nazi party member), with John Foster Dulles, an American who actively worked to return confiscated Nazi leaders companies. They are responsible for the creation of the European Union and its expansion to 28 countries, breaking all existing peace agreements with Russia. It is a theoretical center for concrete action on the global geopolitical game, representing the international elite. Therefore, its principles are focused on the business of war, trade, exploitation and territorial domination of the world.

– Despite this incalculable power, mega-corporations will have to take into account the current reality: while know that a war would spread immediately to the United States, as the main target, even though Europe is committed, the discussion abruptly change as national security and family will be at stake effectively; the existence of a firm determination and courage on the part of many peoples and nations creates a worrying detente to expansive interests and defeat are the chances of anyone attempting certain attacks; changing power relations indicates that the multipolar world is already a fact and determines the terms of the agreements or disagreements, forcing diplomacy.

– It can be argued that there is still a great global dominance of mega – corporations, although according to the time when wars in the Middle East are definitively settled at much (at least in Syria and Iraq), will be powerful new situation as force a geographical rethinking of terrorist organizations that would be targeted to Europe itself. The European Union can break starting with Greece, Spain, and nationalist movements, which does not ensure the continuity of the process. If you join the boomerang unleashed in Saudi Arabia for its latest aggression to countries in the region such as Yemen, then begins to increase opposition to the monarchy, it is possible to believe that interventions always bring serious consequences for the invader modifying territories and causing fractures.

– Between the odds, the dialogue between Russia and Saudi Arabia and Turkey can add notes of uncertainty to the unwritten alliances as unalterable, and the possibilities on the

Trans–Adriatic agreements such as the Turkish Stream are accurate shots international impact (...) what could be an incentive for the European Union itself subject to external opinion. To the extent that the German government to understand that war can affect its territory and much of Europe first, and how far apart its proponents (United States, Australia, Canada and New Zealand), the unit will fragmenting and that a task of alternative media.

– The creation of an independent market for mega corporations, as is being designed with the binational exchange local currencies or new that are not dependent on the artificial manipulation of prices, as the case of oil or the power of banks, provided with a robust policy of trust and stimulating the true development of peoples, greatly weaken the colonialist and war at the same time bring a period of social peace with hope in this trend.

Finally, know the reality that involves the Club possible to have a prism to make decisions in the present with the future character, given the arguments provided. The history of this globe continues, its evolution and allows dialectic contrast these definitions and their degree of approach to truth. The opportunity to build a global architecture at the service of man becomes humanized close.

THE MOST EVIL FIFTEEN APPOINTMENTS OF MEMBERS OF CLUB BILDERBERG

1. "Finding a new enemy against which to recover the unity of action, we came up with the idea that pollution, the threat of global warming, water shortage, hunger and so fulfill that work very well". (Club of Rome).

2. "No matter what is true. Just realize what people think is the truth". (Paul Watson, co-founder of Greenpeace).

3. "The current window of opportunity to perhaps an interdependent and truly peaceful world order is built; it will not be open for long. We are on the verge of a global transformation. All we need is a major crisis and the nations will accept the New world order". (David Rockefeller, during a dinner UN ambassadors).

4. "In politics, nothing happens by accident. If it happens, you can bet it was planned that well". (Franklin Delano Roosevelt).

5. "Any kind of complex technology is an attack on human dignity. It would be a catastrophe for us if a source of rich, clean and cheap energy was discovered, if we think about what the man would do with it". (Amory Lovins, founder of the Rocky Mountain Institute, a think-tank Eco).

6. "My three main goals would be to reduce the world population to about 100 million people, destroying the industrial fabric and ensure that wildlife, with all its species, Rallies worldwide". (Dave Foreman, founder of Earth First).

7. "We need broad support to stimulate the imagination of the public (...) For this we offer horrific scenarios, perform dramatic and simple statements and not allow too many doubts (...) Each of us must decide where the balance between

effectiveness and honesty is". (Stephen Schneider, Stanford Professor of Climatology, author of many IPCC reports).

8. "When you become president of a country no other person who makes the decisions, and one notices that can be a virtual minister". (Bill Clinton, 1998).

9. "The Technotronic Era is gradually designing increasingly controlled society. That society will be dominated by an elite of free people, traditional values, do not hesitate to achieve its objectives by refined techniques that influence the behavior of the people, and monitor and monitor in detail to society, to the point that it will become possible to establish an almost permanent monitoring on each of the citizens of the planet. " (Excerpted from the book "The Technotronic Era" by Zbigniew Brezinsky, chief consultant of the Rockefeller Group and architect of the NWO).

10. "Those who make and issue the money and credit are precisely those who run government policies and have in their hands the destiny of the people". (Reginald McKenna, president of The Midlands Bank of England).

11. "The CFR (Council on Foreign Relations, fundamental branch of the NWO) is a central part of American society which originated in England. The CFR, along with the Movement of Atlantic Union and the Council of Atlantic States States believes that national borders should be eliminated and that a single world government should be established what the Trilateral (. concerning the Trilateral Commission: United States, Europe and Japan) really try is to create an economic power of global proportions superior political power of any nation or state involved as leaders and creators of this system, they will rule the world from my point of view, the Trilateral

Commission represents a coordinated effort to seize control and consolidate the four centers of power political, monetary, intellectual and ecclesiastical". (Senator Barry Goldwater – "With No Apologies", 197, 128 and 284 pp.).

12. "The only way to get really change society is to frighten people with the possibility of a catastrophe". (Daniel Botkin, Emeritus Professor).

13. "Capitalism, now triumphant ideology, is the most powerful weapon of conquest: the money. The history of the current domination was perfectly planned long since the US became independent, global economic fraternities were installed in that country to take economic control and thus political. Using expansion policies, old powerful "families" of Europe expanded to new lands their domains. Secret societies established their new empires, from which would leave its financial and political strategies. Johanes Rockefeller immigrated to America and its descendant, John D. Rockefeller, became the leader of the oil monopoly Eventually, allied to European interests, enacted the creation of many global entities his purpose:.. the installation of its power in. everyone for slow and gradual through the infiltration of economic power conquest They planned the establishment of various organizations of international power: the Federal Reserve, the Council on Foreign Relations, the Trilateral Commission, the Bilderberg Group and the United Nations itself. The ultimate goal: the creation of a New World Order "(William Cooper, former member of the American Intelligence –murderer– Extract from the report on the New World Order.)..

14. "We are grateful to the Washington Post, the New York Times, Time Magazine and other great publications whose directors have attended our meetings and respected their promises of discretion for almost 40 years. It would have been impossible for us to be developed our plan for the world if we had been advertised over the years". (A statement from David Rockefeller in 1991, during a secret meeting of the Bilderberg Group).

15. "Economic officers of the largest countries must begin to think in terms of managing a single world economy, together with the management of international economic relations between the countries". (The Reform of International Institutions: A Report of the Trilateral Task Force on International Institutions for the Trilateral Commission, New York: "The Trilateral Commission", 1976, p. 22).

INVITATION FROM HUGO CHAVEZ TO THE BILDERBERG CLUB

In 2007 the King of Spain sends silence Chavez and leaves the closing ceremony of the Ibero – American Summit in Chile. The situation is unprecedented. The King has left the closing ceremony of the Ibero –American Summit tired of attacks on Spain and after broach Chavez "why do not you shut up !" when the Venezuelan again lash out at Aznar. Zapatero, who then intervened in the room, interrupted the monarch – "a moment", he said and just try to appease Chavez. The president did not accompany the monarch and neither did Moratinos, who in 2004 accused Aznar, like Chavez, of masterminding the coup in Venezuela. The minister said that the departure of the King was agreed with Zapatero.

Commander Hugo Chavez had asked for the floor to reply to the intervention of Spanish Prime Minister Jose Luis Rodriguez Zapatero, focused in emphasizing that a country can never progress if seeking justifications for someone from outside impedes their progress. The president had asked the speaking time to refer to Spanish companies.

Venezuelan President disagreed with the arguments of Rodriguez Zapatero and said "can not minimize" the impact of external factors, prior to a long speech in which he again attacked harshly Aznar. "Aznar not only supported the coup (April 2002), but as acting president of the European Union (EU) promoted the adoption of a statement against him", he said.

In his attack on Aznar, Chavez revealed the alleged conversation with the then Spanish prime minister in July 1999. According to Chavez, Aznar said, "I come to invite you to join our club, you have oil, you have to merge the first world, just what you decide, because you have a strong popular and political support".

"But I had to stop relations with Cuba, Aznar told me not suit me friendship with Castro, Fidel Castro, which for me is like a father, a revolutionary father, an example of dignity, of struggle, of resistance to a empire" told Hugo Chavez.

"Those guys are screwed"

"Then, I made you a little question. **Look, Aznar, you who think of Haiti, Central America and Africa?** I apologize for what I have to say, Aznar I said, '**Those guys are screwed**'. That was the whole face terrible fascism and racism. "A snake is more human than a fascist or a racist, a tiger is more human than a fascist or a racist, he said.

Before these accusations Rodriguez Zapatero took the floor to criticize Chavez attacks Aznar. "You can be at odds with the ideological position, not I who is close to Aznar", said President Chavez, before reminding him that "was chosen by the Spanish". Chavez insisted continue talking and King made a feint to intervene in the discussion.

Among the replicas of Chavez, Zapatero insisted on demanding "that respect" for the former president. At that time, the King sat in his chair to address Chavez and blurt, visibly upset: "Why do not you shut up?"

Zapatero then continued telling Chavez that "there is an essence and a principle in dialogue" that "to respect and to be respected can not fall in disqualification", a word very similar to what was said during a public appearance in which he asked "respect" the Venezuelan.

At that time, he intervened in the controversy Daniel Ortega of Nicaragua in support of the thesis Chavez, which in turn criticized the actions in their country of the Spanish electricity company Union Fenosa. Before this intervention, the

King got up from the table and left the act, which he returned a few minutes later.

"An agreed output, according to official sources"

Don Juan Carlos rose from his seat while Ortega intervened, whom Chilean President Michelle Bachelet gave the floor with the proviso that adjust their presentation to three minutes and not to go to replicate.

Official sources explained that the King agreed with Zapatero in absence to demonstrate the "disgust" of the Spanish delegation to the attacks he was receiving Spain.

Ortega denounced the intervention of some presidents do not match interrupted when "certain positions" and complained that Spain had had today a "second intervention" and he only one. "Freedom of expression is a principle. If we will not give the right to speak, no sense these summits", he said. Then Ortega gave the floor to Chavez, who responded to Zapatero "with all my affection" that "the truth I neither offend nor fear". Chavez said Venezuela's government "reserves the right to respond to any aggression, anywhere, in any space and in any tone". Then again he intervenes Ortega, who referred to the "responsibility" for the Latin American left "blackmailed by the Yankees and European". Ortega accused Spain of having a "political, economic and military alliance" with the United States and they upbraided US planes refuel in Spain before bombing the residence of Libyan leader Muammar Gaddafi in 1986 that killed daughter thereof.

COUNCIL ON FOREIGN

"We shall have world government, this like it or not. The only question is whether it will be formed by conquest or consent "Paul Warburg, a member of the CFR

Council of Foreign Relations (CFR) is one of the tanks thoughts (think tank) most influential in the world of American political lobbying. It is the lobbying organization representing the interests of financial monopoly capital of the North American country. Have more than 3600 members of which highlight personalities financial, industrial and industry prominent former government officials. It is a center of analysis that articulates the vision of US imperialism, related various aspects of foreign policy and proposing solutions that extend the geopolitical vision of its dominance in the world. It is a center that proposes concrete policy agendas status, fueling its vision and mission internationally. Monitoring the movement of US foreign policy, it makes reprimands and proposes guidelines to be followed by the political class to respond to US business interests. Founded in 1921, today is one of the most important in generating agreements and consensus among diplomats, businessmen, journalists and academic institutions spaces. Through forums, interviews, research, publications, databases and work teams, the CFR maintains a permanent lobbying activity deeply connected with the exercise of US foreign policies.

In this way, it brings together senior executives from financial institutions, industrial giants and media; researchers and academics; military officer's highest ranking; and politicians, public officials and deans of universities, colleges and research centers.

THE EARLY DAYS OF THE CFR

The **Council on Foreign Relations** (CFR), which is the American branch of the round table groups originated in the secret society of Cecil Rhodes, Carroll Quigley argued that it was planning to America entered the war. The CFR, firmly in the grips of the banking elite, had essentially captured US foreign policy.

The establishment of the Federal Reserve (1913) said the United States would become indebted to and owned by international banking interests, and therefore act in their interests. The EDF (in English, Federal Reserve System, also known as Federal Reserve) funded the US role in World War II, always giving credit for speculation, which led to the Great

Depression, and massive consolidation of interests which owns the Federal Reserve System. Subsequently, he financed the US entry into World War II.

The CFR, established six years after the Federal Reserve was created, worked to promote an internationalist agenda behalf of the international banking elite. It was to alter the conceptualization of its place in the world of the United States – from isolationist industrial nation to an engine of empire working for international banking and corporate American interests. When the Fed took control of money and debt, the CFR took control of the ideological foundations of such an empire – encompassing business, banking, foreign policy, military, media, and academic elite nation in a global world in general a cohesive view. Altering the ideology to that of promoting such an internationalist schedule, the great capital that was behind it would ensure that agenda own rise through government, industry, academia and the media. The other major think tanks and political institutions in the United States are also represented in the CFR. They are constitutive of divisions within the elite, however, these divisions are based on the basis of how to use American imperial power, where to use it, on what basis to justify it, and other various methodological differences. The division between the elites was never on the questions of: **should we use American imperial power? Why America has become an empire, or should not even be an empire?** If one takes these considerations to heart and questions these concepts, either in foreign policy, military intelligence, academia, finance, business, or the media; it is likely that such person is not a member of the CFR.

It was the month of May 1919 when a compact group of influential bankers, lawyers, politicians and academics – all participants of the talks between the victorious Allies and the Central Powers defeated on the battlefields of Europe – meeting at the Hotel Majestic Paris took a momentous decision: to form two "brain banks" or lodges to defend Anglo American global interests.

Since these institutions have now grown into the center of geopolitical planning and world's most important geoeconomic, it has been designing over eighty years a new world order that will accommodate the Anglo–American colonial interests and their allies then and now.

The strategy was to establish two entities: one in London that would be called the Royal Institute of International Affairs (RIIA – Royal Institute for International Relations), and one in the United States that would take the name of the Council on Foreign Relations (CFR), based in New York city.

Both organizations carried the clear ideological stamp of gradual socialism as collective axis control and the late nineteenth century was advocated by the Fabian Society financed by the Round Table Group of the South African magnate Cecil Rhodes and the family of cosmopolitan financiers Rothschild. CFR will also give its support and funding the wealthy and powerful American families such as

Rockefeller, Morgan, Mellon, Harriman, Aldrich, Schiff, Kahn, Warburg, Lamont, Ford and Carnegie (the latter, particularly through a pioneering organization CFR, the Carnegie Endowment for International Peace).

Since its inception, the CFR had a major spokesman who, even today, remains the most prestigious and influential publication in the United States on geopolitical analysis: Foreign Affairs, of which it is said that "what today is published in" foreign Affairs "becomes tomorrow at the official foreign policy of the United States".

Among the founders and first directors of the CFR, it is men like Allan Welsh Dulles, one of the greatest exponents of community planning, intelligence and US intelligence that would strengthen the structure of the CIA, central US intelligence; journalist Walter Lippmann founding director of the weekly The New Republic and acute psychological action strategist; Otto bankers H. Kahn, and Paul Moritz Warburg, the latter born in Germany and emigrated to the United States where in 1913 designed and promoted legislation that would lead to the creation of the Federal Reserve Bank, the US private central bank that until our day exercises control over the entire financial structure of the nation.

At the end of World War II as part of the "new world order" of the postwar period, the Bank of the Federal Reserve would be complemented by the International Monetary Fund and the World Bank, also members of the CFR creations.

These three institutions together control the globalized financial system. It should be noted here that the only true globalization is now seen in the world is the financial system that has escaped any national control, because the economic and political systems today are temporarily centered on the national level.

Among the founders of the CFR, we find for example the geographer and president of the American Geographical Society, Isaiah Bowman, who would be responsible for the Anglo-American team redibujaría the map of Europe after the First World War and – Treaty of Versailles by – many disorders would bring in subsequent decades. CFR were two economists, Owen D. Young and Charles Dawes, who during the twenties would design and propel plans "refinancing" of the war debt imposed on Germany by the same Treaty. CFR members who were senior executives of the Bank and the Federal Reserve would generate distortions and monetary astringency that helped unleash the financial crisis of 1929.

Were CFR members who would press on public opinion – through the powerful media under their control as radio networks NBC and CBS and newspapers Washington Post and New York Times, to break the American neutrality in the new war unleashed in Europe from 1939.

THE HIDDEN FACE OF GLOBAL GEOPOLITICS

WORLD WAR II AND THE CFR

During this struggle in which the United States recently participate formally by the end of 1941, senior members within the CFR made up the **War & Peace Studies Project** which was integrated flatly the US State Department designing its policies towards Japan and Germany, and then he prepared another "new world order" after the anticipated Allied victory.

Thus, the CFR designed and promoted the creation from 1945 of the United Nations as a forum for global policy administration and some of its key economic agencies such as the IMF and the World Bank, through its members Alger Hiss John J. McCloy, W. Averell Harriman, Harry Dexter White, James Lovett, Dean Acheson, George Kennan, Charles Bohlen and others, as well as through conferences **Dumbarton Oaks** (to create the UN), **Bretton Woods** (to create the IMF, world Bank and GATT / WTO), Tehran and Yalta (conferences where the division of the world agreed in domain areas between the US and the USSR).

That war ended, President Harry S. Truman would establish the famous "Truman Doctrine" of national security which takes as its starting point the doctrine of containment – containment of Soviet expansionism – proposed by a member of the CFR at that time ambassador in Moscow: George Kennan, in a famous article appeared in the pages of Foreign Affairs and signed "X" as well as the directive NSC68 National Security Council drafted by Paul Nitze, the CFR. The same was the case of the so-called "Marshall Plan" designed by a CFR

194

task force and implemented by W. Averell Harriman and others.

Need is to investigate the way throughout this century CFR – alone or in coordination with other partner organizations – has exercised decisive influence over the widest range of ideological currents, political events, wars, acts of psychological warfare, economic crises and financial, encumbrances and defenestrations of high–profile personalities and other shocking facts – many clearly unmentionable – that have marked the course of humanity throughout the tumultuous century that just ended.

It is that it seems that we are all too busy and fascinated as passive spectators of the vertiginous events and facts that daily occur worldwide as a way to ensure that no one – or at least a few – comes to mind set attention elsewhere, to identify not so much the effects and shocking results of many decisions and covert actions, but rather the real and concrete origins of those same decisions and actions. For the success of this gigantic phenomenon of collective psychological action – as it it is –, the mass media play a vital and essential role. For they are the instruments whose goal is to promote the cancellation of the ability of independent and creative thinking among peoples.

The CFR effectively undertook a policy coup on US foreign policy with World War II. When war broke out, the Council began a "strictly confidential" project called the War and Peace Studies at the top CFR members collaborated with the State

Department in determining US policy, and the project was fully funded by the Rockefeller Foundation. The post–World War was already being designed by members of the Council, would enter the government to enact these designs.

The policy of "containment" toward the Soviet Union that would define US foreign policy for half a century was envisaged in a 1947 edition of Foreign Affairs, the journal of the Council on Foreign Relations. So were the ideological foundations for the Marshall Plan and NATO envisaged at the Council on Foreign Relations, with members of the Council recruited to enact, implement and lead these institutions. The Board also played a role in the creation and promotion of the United Nations, which were built later on land bought from John D. Rockefeller, Jr. According to writer and former Russian spy, **Daniel Estulin**, in his book "The Secrets of the Bilderberg Club":

"The CFR is part of an international group called Round Table or Round Table. Different branches in the world such as the Royal Institute of International Affairs in the UK and the Institute of International Affairs in Canada, Australia, South Africa, India and the Netherlands and the Institute of Pacific Relations of China, Russia and Japan. The CFR has its headquarters in the city of New York, in the Harold Pratt House building, a four –story mansion on the corner of Park Avenue and 68th Street, which was donated by the widow of Mr. Pratt, heir to the fortune Rockefeller Standard Oil. The CFR has much influence in the government, very few average Americans who know their existence, actually less than one in ten thousand, and many are even less aware of their real purpose".

THE CFR TODAY

Follow up activities CFR serves to get an idea about the discussions and strategies that are occurring within the US ruling class, at a time when US imperialism goes through a phase of global hegemonic crisis. In the broad area which means US foreign policy, CFR conduct, activities and proposed agendas on security, economic policy, energy policy and EU financial policy in the world. Therefore, monitoring is essential to know some important visions and projects of imperialism.

Its objectives are to identify and assess broad sets of political, economic, financial, social, cultural and military factors that encompass every conceivable facet of public and private life of the United States, its allies and the rest of the world.

The Council on Foreign Relations forms the core backbone network of this transnationalized capitalism and "borderless". Their networks are expressed through a multiplicity of organizations promoting the current global model, among which mainly include:

The Hudson Institute, The RAND Corporation, The Brookings Institution, the Trilateral Commission, The World Economic Forum, Aspen Institute, American Enterprise Institute, Deutsche Gesellschaft für Federal Foreign Politik,

Bilderberg Group, Cato Institute, Tavestock Institute and the Carnegie Endowment for International Peace, among others.

As previously he explained all these think tanks or "tanks thoughts" bring together the best technocrats, scientists and scholars in their respective fields, graduates of US universities, Europe and around the world. His tactical and strategic role is to identify threats and opportunities of the global environment, assess the strengths and weaknesses of the interests grouped within the CFR, and make broad strategic, tactical and operational plans in all areas where it operates the structure of transnational capitalism.

The CFR brings together the top managers of financial institutions, industrial giants and media, researchers and academics, military officers highest ranking, as politicians, public officials and deans of universities, colleges and research centers.

Different operating levels Zionism transnational capitalist from technocrats, executives and large "Charman" Washington Consensus (maximum expression of the real capitalist power) based in New York are contained and expressed in the Council on Foreign Relations.

They are members of the CFR a majority of presidents, managers and shareholders of Fortune 500 companies that together manage almost 80% of the US economy, employing over 25 million people, and have a market value equivalent two and a half times the GDP of the United States.

In the CFR all the media power of the Zionist Jewish lobby (focuses on the right and on the left): CNN, CBS, NBC, The New York Times, The Daily Telegraph, Le Figaro, The Economist, The Wall Street Journal, Le Monde, the Washington Post, Time, Newsweek, US News & World Report, Business Week, RTVE, etc., all in the hands of business networks that make up the CFR.

In operational terms the CFR forms a powerful center of geopolitical and strategic analysis and planning of the Zionist imperial capitalism in its transnationalized and global stages.

The enormous power of the United States, the scope of the CFR analysis covers the entire planet. In truth, the CFR forms a powerful center and geopolitical analysis and strategic planning. His research and evaluations are conducted by different researchers and working groups formed within the bosom of the CFR, dedicated to identifying threats and opportunities of the global environment, assess the strengths and weaknesses of the interests grouped within the CFR, and perform comprehensive strategic plans, tactical and operational in all areas to which he referred.

Although these intense, deep and efectivísimas tasks are performed within the scope of the CFR, the key to understanding their actions lies in the fact that the CFR never operates itself, but its individual members are those who do.

And it always from formal areas of action and power, which are multi and transnational corporations, international banks, international multilateral institutions, governments, universities, the military and the media. Those members of the CFR never invoke or even refer to their membership within the institution, much less invoked.

They are members of the CFR top managers of big banks like Chase Manhattan Rockefeller family that just merged with the bank JP Morgan, Bank of America and the current number, Citigroup, whose capitalization now exceeds 250,000 million; executives and opinion leaders of the world's eight multimedia monopolies; rectors and deans of the great universities and colleges like Harvard, MIT Massachusetts Institute of Technology, Columbia, Johns Hopkins, Princeton, Yale, Stanford, and Chicago; and – key factor in this real planetary wheel power – 150 key positions in the US government including the most significant positions in the armed forces.

Most of staff of the White House are occupied by CFR members. All these data come from a 1987 report published by the CFR, publicly available on its website itself.

The president of the CFR is the magnate **David Rockefeller** (active member of the Bilderberg Club). And speaking of the White House, the presidents of governments taking turns, but the power of the CFR, and its objectives are intact. George Wallace, Democratic presidential candidate four times in the decade of 1960–1970, made famous the slogan that no one gram of difference between the Democrat and Republican parties. Therefore, the CFR has behaved like a genuine employment agency for Democratic and Republican administrations.

MEMBERS OF THE CFR

Some powerful members of the CFR is David Rockefeller, Henry Kissinger, Bill Clinton, Zbigniew Brzezinski, George HW Bush, former Secretary of State Madeleine Albright, international speculator George Soros, Supreme Court judge Stephen Breyer, Laurence A. Tisch (president of the Lowes / CBS), the secretary of state Gral. L. Colin Powell, Jack Welsh (chairman of General Electric Company), W. Thomas Johnson (president of CNN and now director of AOL / Time-Warner) Katherine Graham (recently deceased president of the group Washington Post / Newsweek / International Herald Tribune); Richard Cheney (vice president of EE. UU., Former defense secretary George Bush (father), and former president of the Halliburton oil), Samuel "Sandy" Berger (adviser to President Clinton on national security), John M. Deutch (former director of the CIA by President Clinton), Alan Greenspan (governor of the Bank of the Federal Reserve), Stanley Fischer (head of the International Monetary Fund and current director of Citigroup ex-director), Anne Krueger (current deputy director of the IMF), James D. Wolfensohn (World Bank President) Paul Volcker (chairman of CS First Boston Bank and former governor of the Federal Reserve), John Reed (director and former chairman of Citigroup); Jeffrey Sachs economists, Lester Thurow, Martin Feldman and Richard N Cooper; former Treasury Secretary, former president of Goldman Sachs and current co-Chairman of Citigroup, Robert E. Rubin, former secretary of state by

President Reagan and "mediator" in the Falklands conflict, Gral. Alexander Haig, the "mediator" in the conflict in the Balkans, Richard Holbrooke, IBM chairman Louis V. Gerstner, the Democratic senator from Maine, George J. Mitchell, the deputy Republican, Newt Gingrich, and advisor to the president Bush's national security, Condoleezza Rice, Bush trade representative Robert Zoellick, Elliot Abrams, William Perry, Mark Falcoff, Paul Wolfowitz, Richard N. Perle and Richard Armitage, among many others.

The aforementioned characters make up the "two sides" of the Jewish lobby that controls operational and strategic structures of transnational capitalism that hegemonizes Zionist natural resources and economic-productive along and across the planet systems.

For those who want to investigate their real existence, you can visit the headquarters of the CFR in the residential Park Avenue corner 68th Street in New York City, where you can obtain a copy of the Annual Report which contains official descriptions of their activities and payroll of its more than 3600 members.

CFR within a set of strategic plans aimed at globalization of economy and finance, or which parts of the world will have peace and prosperity and which will sink into bloody conflicts, and decides to carry out the designing.

- **US Role CFR**
-

Since the US is a superpower in the world today, it is reasonable to assume that the world power structure – because it is administered by the world government, it does temporarily from its own territory and political and economic structure of the United States.

This does not mean that the American people necessarily part of this scheme (on the contrary, is a victim of all these plans), but rather that comprise its elites and ruling class; the so-called Establishment. It is, then, authorities operating within the United States (as do within the UK, France, Germany, Japan, Spain, Argentina, Brazil and Korea), but not necessarily belong to the United States (as their counterparts in other nations not represent those people, they not necessarily obey their interests).

To understand how it really works United States, we should remember that their policies – especially its foreign policy – are managed from Washington DC (themselves refer to their government as "The Administration") which is the seat of formal power. However, the real US government prevails from New York, the seat of royal power.

This is understandable since the real powers requires a solid and unbroken continuity and consistency to carry out complex strategies in space and time covering the entire planet and are projected through whole decades. These centers of power quickly realized many decades ago that there is nothing more inefficient and ineffective for continuity and consistency in the design and implementation of political, economic and social strategies, financial conditions, which democratic system with its high profile public and newspapers parts requires leaders to give permanent explanations to give to each step.

The better is to operate discreetly, from what is formally a mere gentlemen's club like the CFR, of which powerful and influential men are members, directors or presidents for decades without having to be accountable to absolutely no one outside his peers within the organization itself. Thus, 3.600 powerful individuals can exert a huge influence on countless billions of humans on the planet.

It is the central hub of a veritable network of powerful men and women, since the CFR is complemented by other US and international specialized similar organizations in the study of international geopolitical issues and promote the current global model: The Hudson Institute, The RAND Corporation, the Brookings Institution, the Trilateral Commission, the World Economic Forum, Aspen Institute, American Enterprise Institute, Deutsche Gesellschaft für Politik Federal Foreign Bilderberg Group, Cato Institute, Tavestock Institute and the Carnegie Endowment for International Peace, among others.

All these think tanks bring together the best men in their fields provided they are clearly aligned with the basic premises of the policy objectives of the globalizers: creating a private world government, systematic erosion of the structures of all states sovereign -nation (though not all in the same way or at the same time, it is understood), sociocultural standardization, the imposition of a speculative-usurious globalized financial system, alignment of world public opinion through a powerful psychological action on a global level, and management of a global war system that maintains the cohesion of the masses through permanent stoking against an "enemy", whether real or imaginary.

But then the question arises: What is globalization?

Globalization is a euphemism that conceals a deeper reality that mentors own system defined for almost a century ago as a "new world order" as defined by the then President George Bush in 1991. The main feature of the phenomenon of globalization is it sustains that although his power over economic and especially financial, in planning its global interests, forms a genuine political process.

Carl Schmitt (German political scientist) states that the natural realm of politics distinguish between friends and enemies, with the definition given enemy classical: not so much a inimicus, the personal enemy of each of us but rather in the sense of hostis, which is the enemy of the community, group, institution, or nation. Thus, it becomes hostis whole group, nation, ideology, religion, business, government, army or other organization or forces that actively or passively oppose the goals and interests of the globalization process.

Accordingly, the main hostis planners have identified globalization since many decades is the concept of nationhood and sovereign nation-state as its executive instrument. In short, to defend and promote their planetary interests which provides for a re-engineered model of the world, the promoters of globalization have no choice but to fight the roots of nationalism around the world and all the sovereign nation-state; each according to their characteristics, history, relative strength and permeability to align the globalization model.

In the words of Richard Gardner, one of the thinkers of the CFR: the " house of world order will have to be it built from the bottom up", urging an end run around national sovereignty, eroding it piece by piece, which will be achieved much more than with the old method of frontal assault.

The planetary model advocated by the CFR could be described as the creation of a sort of "factory" planetary creator of goods and services with its counterpart of a planetary "supermarket" consumption of these goods and services. In this model, there is no place for the sovereign nation-state, because it is a model based essentially on economic and financial concepts; It is a project developed and aligned with a set of very powerful private interests. This is eloquently reflected in the latest Annual Report corresponding CFR to 1999, in which the vice president of the CFR, **Maurice Greenberg** announces that in today's world no longer comes to designing only geopolitical but the axis of power today forms a true "geo - economics" which is simply laundering this reality that is the privatization of power. According to Greenberg, "In foreign policy it is time to change our central organizing principle of geopolitics to geo – economics;. Of traditional concerns the balance of power to economic and security concepts in my opinion, the greatest threat to security US come from a global economic collapse".

The Trilateral Commission

"In short, people will be unable to reason or think for herself. They will be able just babbling the news that was given the night before" Zbigniew Brzezinski

What is the Trilateral Commission?

Among the think tanks more powerful, who run the world politics after cameras, plus the Bilderberg, it highlights the Trilateral Commission (TC), which is an organism not published and integrates with executives of the largest US corporations, (US) Japan and the European Union (EU). Its aim is to reach agreements among industrialized countries in which the world economic system is unitarily planned and plays a major role in its relations with the East and answers the demands of the Third World function. Its action is aimed at strengthening its dominance as principal or dominant group in the current international capitalist system. Its political impact is reflected in the purpose of revitalizing the ideological conception of the West and the capitalist economic system. The unification of their economic, financial and technological potential allow them greater bargaining power as a bloc paying more attention to the danger of economic North-South conflict as outlined codes depending on the trilateral axis which is the economic strength of the capitalist world.

USA and its allies would take decisions that were necessary in international political relations as partisan. The CT would consequently an economic and political alliance in which decisions are consulted and acted under close cooperation. It means that the industrialized capitalist countries seem to want to structure a hegemonic power center where loyalty between them reaches higher degrees which can keep up with the developing nations of America, Africa and Asia.

The CT was born in 1973 with the aim of saving the crisis of capitalism against the threat of communist East and the ravages of the Third World. Within this context it is proposed to adjust the economic order without leaving existing structures. It is cited as one of its main ideologists **Zbigniew Brzezinski** who summed up his ideas as saying that **"the nation-state as a fundamental unit in the organized life of man ceased to be the main creative force"**.

International banks and multinational corporations plan and act in terms that far ahead on the political concepts of the nation state. "This view of **Brzezinski** shows the most active face of modern capitalism against which the Third World countries are preparing a strategy not eternalize as recipients of an unjust international economic order that asphyxiation. the approaches that seek to convey to regions of America, Africa and Asia would lead to perpetuate as mere appendages of the great powers. in different movements and global forums is being developed a true Third approach is demanding a new international economic order and particularly impulses of the "group of non - aligned" on the one hand and on the other through the "group of 77". However, it is good to stress that the designs of the Commission are to ensure the centralization of capital in the hands of a small part of the world and its flipside is the economic backwardness of the continents of America, Africa and Asia. The economic and political hegemony constitutes an obstacle to the development of Third World countries and jeopardizes world peace.

BRIEF HISTORY

After the Second World War US he entered a period of prosperity and economic hegemony becoming overwhelming world leader. The then unified economic assistance to Japan and the Marshall Plan in Western Europe woke European Economic Community industrial capacity of its partners. The military alliance of NATO in Europe consolidated liberal democracies and the communist ghost away. The need to neutralize in Asia to Russian and Chinese communist power led to the US presence in Japan created a powerful security system and had a marked influence of liberal–democratic court, which along with the aforementioned economic assistance, he soon transform Japan into a powerful and rich ally in the global arena. In a short time were defined three geographic poles: North America (United States and Canada), Japan and Western Europe integrated by industrial powers linked by strong common interests, supported their distinctly liberal democratic fundamental aspects related political values and generating opposition to the values of socialist Stalin's Russia. In 1957 the economic integration of Western Europe with the creation of the Common Market or European Economic Community (formalized EEC) and in Japan from 1960 to 1961 emerges at the global level as an industrial power. Industrial countries are intertwined in economic ties of interdependence while internal states of their economic strategies increasingly take into account the interests and convenience of their industry peers generating the formation of a global economic bloc. Rebuilt Europe and Japan in the postwar period already consolidated and in full development since the early 1960s, they ended up weakening the regions dependent on US hegemonic position within the trilateral system and its global primacy and opposing resistance finance by increasing dollar holdings. The US product meant 60% of Western descends in the seventies to 46%. The strong development of Japan, Germany and France, other factors such as the proliferation of industrializing nations in the South joined. With these sources capable of providing capital goods, technology and financing multiply. More and more multinational companies operating in the United States and the world. Increasingly, the corporate effort tends to focus on multinational corporations items. The large company resulting from the merger is one of several smaller corporation, represents a magnification of financial capital and therefore initiatives and ventures. The concentration stimulates the organizing capacity that can reach unexpected levels of efficiency. To be able to achieve exceptional quantities and qualities of supply, demand an approach thatcan facilitate marketing and dominate markets and set their guidelines is achieved. The inter – linkages between transnational of all kinds, the enormous exchange and community interests in order to insertion of subsidiaries in other countries, ultimately, the success of transnational corporations and the transfer of US leadership the three regions in question gives rise to Trilateralism. The situation is aggravated in the early seventies with the tensions referred to the international monetary system of 1973–1974 oil crisis, inflation and unemployment in industrial countries. As a result of the pressure of these factors the strategy and policy of trilateral system went into crisis. CT then emerged as formal institutionalization of society and potential partners to step out not only a circumstantial crisis but to launch a long – range program. The fact to note is that the community of interests of the three foci is gradually relegating him "unilateralism" to throat competition and the proud desire for national domain as classical operational strategies, and raising the desirability of mutual understanding between the parties, for increasingly frequent and charitable actions. Moreover, in regard to foreign investments of transnational 75% they are filed within the trilateral market. However, growth in the giant multinational phenomenon in the world, the Trilateralism indicates a current weakening of large corporations in the world market. The reasons would be, among others, the proliferation of moderate multinationals, the inefficiency of "gigantism", increased manufacturing and technological greater number, the appearance of emerging industrialized nations in the world southern adding new companies to the global concert, strengthening nationalisms and dissemination of new means of financing, among others.

DAVID ROCKEFELLER: MAN MOST POWERFUL OF CT

Despite having 101 years that conspiracy was directed and led by **David Rockefeller,** the greatest living representative of the most powerful family saga of the twentieth century, and founder and leader of the Trilateral Commission since 1973. This is, without a doubt, of the most powerful multinational ideologues in the world. However, more than one and two have come to regard the group as the true government of the globalized world. And to some extent not lack reason, because the Rockefeller himself made clear its main objective to create the group: **"Replace the sovereignty of peoples for world elite technical and financial".**

It all started during a two – day meeting –23 and 24 July 1972 in Pocantico Hills, a mansion owned by the Rockefeller family is forty kilometers north of New York. At that time, the magnate was convinced that new times began, so it was necessary to adapt them to maintain the power of the multinationals. The then US President, Richard Nixon, was an awkward character to Rockefeller, especially after the decision to impose the New Economic Policy in 1971. That standard hands and feet tied to companies, while the government greater power reserved for example, to impose caps on the prices of things. **"It is time to break the siege that are subject multinational companies to mobilize the global economy"**, Rockefeller, who, in a way, the need to initiate a process of economic liberalization arose said.

Thirty years later, the same David Rockefeller the need to strengthen the government discreet paying out of pocket was raised. He sent his emissaries looking for people with specific ideas that he believed essential for the world would face the end of the twentieth century. That was when he learned of **Zbigniew Brzezinski,** a Polish intellectual born in 1928 who moved to the United States with 25 years. They told –after know the content of some of his lectures in a think-tank, the Brookings Institution – that was the ideal man, since much of their approach fit the Rockefeller intended for discreet society.

THE HIDDEN POWER IN US?

Brzezinski believed that it was time to cut power space democracies and governments for the benefit of companies. In addition, it advocated the fall of the Soviet bloc and anticipated that the new political reality should be adapted in the future; changes in societies would provoke technology. Once Rockefeller decided that Brzezinski would be the ideologue of the Trilateral Commission, established lines of work of the group during the two – day meeting in that mansion of **Pocantico Hills** in 1972. The mansion, also known by the name of Kykuit or just as **"the Rockefeller country"** occupies fourteen square kilometers in the middle of which is a huge neoclassical building of forty rooms, although there are other buildings around, family archives, student facilities and even a nuclear shelter. There they have lived several members of the clan, who enjoyed notables invited to the lavish dinners were served in the lounges.

Every president since Johnson tested the culinary delights of the service, but there were also **Nelson Mandela, Kofi Annan, King Hussein of Jordan, Felipe González,** etc. A year later, David Rockefeller held meetings with president's twenty different countries around the world to introduce the idea. The aim was to facilitate the economic and political ties between the three blocks around which should establish itself a global financial market: North America, Europe and Japan. Of course, there was a secret agenda. The approach was that those three blocks form a shaft, but always under US control Similarly, support for underdeveloped countries was based on turning them into puppets of the most advanced, ie, in "governable democracies".

In fact, one of the first meetings of the Trilateral Brzezinski, and appointed director of the group in the United States, predicted that the coming conflict would no longer be among the Communist countries and the Western world, but between developed countries and those without they are. This was stated in the global meeting of the **Trilateral Commission in 1975 in Tokyo**. And the Polish thinker had noted that one of the missions of discrete society was blackmailing handle the Third World.

What the Trilateral Commission prepared, with twenty-five years ahead of schedule was the advent of globalization. However, their approaches were used to draw globalization opposite how we all interpret at first sense. They did not seek a borderless world, but a world in which all countries could become a natural market for the most powerful companies. After the 1972 meeting at the Rockefeller mansion and before the group public opinion was submitted in July 1973, the billionaire and the "wise" met on numerous occasions –another time in silence for Pocantico Hills– look for a candidate who could become US president They made several reports and interviewed numerous candidates until they found the little – known **Jimmy Carter,** who by then had expressed his desire to be a candidate for the Democratic Party but actually just had braces. Everything changed after the decision of trilateral conspiracy and suddenly began to fall on the candidacy of Carter a rain of millions to finance his campaign. He had launched the secret agenda of the conspirators. He won the election and shortly after the **"Cartergate"**broke though in a controlled manner without estridencias–, when the media discovered that twenty – six members of his team belonged to the Trilateral.

During the Carter administration, Vice President **Walter Mondale**, Secretary of State **Cyrus Vance**, Secretary of Defense **Harold Brown** and Treasury Secretary **Michael Blumenthal** were members of the multinational ideas created in the mansion millionaire. That is, five of the six most important government positions were in the hands of the powerful think-tank. The missing on the list is the post of secretary of Homeland Security.The sixth and most important, not infrequently, the real engine of international politics. During the time of Carter that position went to **Zbigniew Brzezinski. Can anyone doubt the influence of this group in political power?**

ORGANIZATION AND CHARACTERISTICS OF TRILATERAL COMMISSION

This organization brings together some 500 private within which there are businessmen, politicians, bankers, thinkers, economists, businessmen, trade unionists, executives of the mass media, among others. Those in the exercise of their public duties can not be members of the Commission during their management. Meetings are held annually in different parts of the world that last two to three days in which a previously prepared agenda and reports are drafted discussed. The CT has three presidents, one in Western Europe is French Georges Bertoin, David Rockefeller in the United States and Isamu Yamashita in Japan. The age of the three presidents is 70, 80 and 84 years respectively for what would be their next predecessors Charles B. Heck (North America), Paul Revay (Europe) and Tadashi Yamamoto (Japan). Every president has a staff in your area, located in New York, Paris and Tokyo. The contributions for financing theoretically come from each of the three parties in the following proportions: United States 50%, Europe 33% and Japan 17%. This percentage is indicative of the relative power of transnational sum of each of the three geopolitical areas corporations.

Bruno Cardeñosa in his book "The Invisible Government" (Mirror Ink, 2007), says:

On Friday May 17, 2007 took place in Brussels quote most powerful men and women gathered in the history of mankind. And it is not an exaggeration. In total, including businessmen, politicians and ideologues there were 350 guests, which highlighted several former European and American presidents, former CIA directors and members of the think tank best placed in the areas of power. Yes, despite the illustrious list that "escaped" from their countries to occupy the entire hotel had reserved for this purpose, in the media hardly knew anything, but in the work plan issues raised worldwide interest. And the secret–and the extreme security measures to protect the attending members is one of the hallmarks of the annual meetings of the Trilateral Commission.

Among other issues, one of the directors of the proposed meeting attendees take steps to mitigate the effects of **climate change,** without incurring penalize the profits of large companies. It was one of the few issues that deserved a briefing note, although very few media decided to give the green light to the note distributed by the Associated Press. Who made those proposals was John Deutch, who was CIA director from 1995 to 1996, besides being a chemical respected occupying the post of provost of the Massachusetts

Institute of Technology (MIT) and is part of the team of directors of the arms company Raytheon and bank Citigroup.

The proposal by former CIA director was to tackling climate change based on the idea that the damage was already done, so it was necessary to adapt to the new scenario. Therefore, he raised pollute the atmosphere with aerosols and placed in balloons and mirrors retain temperatures without modification, in order to balance the heating elements greenhouse stratosphere. In addition, he advocated nuclear explosions cause the upper layers of the atmosphere, in order to generate a series of springs that stabilize the situation. He also established the need to force the states to implement a new fuel tax a quarter of euro per liter of gasoline. Of course, the amount of the contribution of users should go to the coffers of the oil industry –the contaminante– to invest in the necessary measures to cope with warming. Such a proposal, no doubt, will become a reality within a few years.

CONTROL OF THE MEDIA

One of the priorities of the CT is the control of the mass media: newspapers, magazines, radio, television, cinema and all media that allows the control and direction of world thinking within the trilateral ideals. In U.S.A. which is the country with the most docilely guided by the mass media population, CT has control of the following most important media in the country: New York Times, CBS (Columbia Broadcasting System), Los Angeles Times, Time Magazine,

THE HIDDEN FACE OF GLOBAL GEOPOLITICS

Magazine Foreign Affairs and other national and international importance.

Despite this, US the press aware of being the fourth power and its undoubted influence at the national level, making it difficult independence has the goal of takeover by the Trilateralism.

TRADE POLICY OF THE EUROPEAN UNION

The trade policy of the European Union (EU) involves two institutional levels: the level of Union and national level. The legal bases in what refers to the common commercial policy are in Article 113 of the Maastricht Treaty. All major decisions are taken by the Council of Ministers representing Member States following the system of "one man one vote". The Council is supported by the CT which is responsible for providing proposals on policies to befollowed by the Council. Ministers of the Council members are interested in trade policies that reflect the interests of their own countries and in turn provide potential political and economic conflicts with countries that are not members of the EU, such as Japan or the US.

The power of multinational companies is reflected in the CT as the private club owners the world. CT currently belong to the people of US policy who bet on the war in Iraq, among which include Richard B. Cheney, Paul Wolfowitz, David Rockefeller, Madeleine K. Albright, Henry A. Kissinger, Robert S. Mc Namara, Zbigniew Brzezinski, among others.

The links in the Spanish press with the CT scandalize more than a naive reader. Ignorance about that club owners multinationals responsible for the current situation in the world, defined by some as "the government of the world in the shade" is amazing. Newspapers in Spain as El País, ABC, El Mundo, La Razon and others have had and have influence over members belonging to the CT which include Jesus de Polanco and his adviser Jesus Aguirre ("Duke" alba), Luis Maria Anson (La Razón, ABC and EFE) and the World by the Agnelli family of Fiat – controlled, among others. The current list of Spanish members of the CT is as follows:

-Ana Patricia Botin, Director of Banesto and Minister of Banco Santander Central Hispano;

-Jaime Carvajal Urquijo, Director of Dresdner Kleinwort Capital and Ford Spain;

-Alfonso Cortina, director and senior officer of Repsol-YPF;

-Pedro Miguel Etxenike, Professor of Physics at the University of the Basque Country and ex-Minister of Education (San Sebastian);

-Oscar Fanjul, Director of Hidroelectrica del Cantabrico and Honorary Chairman of Repsol;

-Nemesio Fernández Cuesta, Group Vice President E-Press Spanish;

-Antonio Garrigues Walter, Director of Garrigues & Andersen and Deputy Chairman of the Trilateral Commission in Europe;

-Mignon-Miguel Herrero, lawyer and international consultant, member of the Royal Spanish Academy of moral and political science and former member of the Spanish Parliament;

-Trinidad Jimenez, Secretary of the international section of the Spanish Socialist Workers Party (PSOE);

-Abel Matutes, Director of companies Matutes-Ibiza, former member of the European Commission in Brussels and former foreign minister;

-Antxon Sarasqueta, CEO of Media Capital, member of the board of the foundation of foreign policy and member of the board of the business group of Madrid;

Pedro Schwartz, CEO of IDELCO and professor of economics at the Autonomous University of Madrid;

- Mario Vargas Llosa, Writer and member of the Royal Spanish Academy;

-Emilio Ibarra, President of Banco de Bilbao Vizcaya;

-Pedro Solbes, Member of the European Commission-monetary affairs;

-Pedro Ballve, Director of Field cold food.

EUROPEAN TROIKA

"A committee built on rotten foundations". Yanis Varoufakis
Former Minister of Finance of Greece

DEFINITION

The concept of political triumvirate was invented by the Romans, as evidenced by the alliance of Crassus, Pompey and Julius Caesar in 60 BC, and the term Troika, comes from Russian and refers to a characteristic sleigh pulled by three horses, the the style of Roman intrigues.

The word spread in the Russian Revolution to designate trios of communist leaders. Thus it took the same meaning as in the Roman Republic (the triple political alliance), and the same fate: failure. Within the framework of the European crisis, the Troika comprises three institutions: **the European**

Commission (EC), the European Central Bank (ECB) and International Monetary Fund (IMF).

Essentially, the Troika "monitors" to countries with serious economic problems receiving financial loans from the EU and IMF. Despite having a lower interest rate compared to the capital market, these loans do not help the economies of the affected countries recover.

On behalf of the Troika are committing the most serious attacks against European peoples against its people, their dignity, against its economic recovery, for the sake of a supposed "fiscal discipline" and an "austerity" at any cost, that actually They constitute a strategy of impoverishment by dispossession of the working classes of the European countries. The Troika threatens us, watching us, controls us, and it also makes ghoulish following its dictates, its spurious interests, regardless of the dire consequences that their impositions bring the European population. Under the false flag of the famous "rescues" that are actually plans for creditors of private banks can charge, a series of suicide measures for the economy of states are imposed, leading to the population of the affected countries a mass impoverishment, to ensure the enrichment of the banks and big business.

The Troika is the Kingdom of Capital in Europe. Represents a set of anti – democratic organizations, of which there are only about the conclusions or ME (MOUs, as euphemistically call them) they publish on countries rescued those who "attend". But there is a total opacity around decisions that are shaping the future of European citizens, especially Greeks, Irish, Portuguese, Italian, Cypriot and Spanish. Between 30 and 40 experts from the three institutions are sent to the country to be examined to check that they are carrying out the measures imposed. Four times a year these "technical" (the colloquially called "Men in Black") examines States focusing on areas such as fiscal policy, the framework macro-economic, structural reforms and banking reforms, and ensures that they are meeting specified requirements. There is only a traveling team, but the European Commission and the IMF staff held in Athens, Dublin and Lisbon, in order to "ensure a continuous dialogue with the authorities" in the words of its leaders. In the Spanish example, men have controlled Troika especially the rescued financial institutions have met the objectives that imposed them.

Their work is based on a "very thorough" analysis of the data available on the country. These data are obtained after meeting with a number of partners from the Government, the Administration, stakeholders such as employers, workers, and academics. This technical work, mission chiefs, usually three, since each institution appoints one, discuss with political leaders program orientation and key measures to be taken, which are published in the Memorandum of Understanding. On the basis of this memorandum and the findings of the mission, the Euro group decides on each disbursement of financial assistance they deem necessary for each country. Experts who are part of these teams are employees of the institutions of the

Troika, and are selected according to their experience and knowledge of the subject to be treated in the country indicated, since they do not always send the same people to different countries rescued. Therefore, the team is not the same in each country and the number of people participating in a review mission can vary, and the profile of the team that meets the specific needs of the review mission.

The Troika is a criminal organization. It is the direct representative of that in Europe the ultra neoliberal policies of the IMF, responsible for the collapse of hundreds of countries around the world, and the stifling public debt policy are implemented. There is no real democratic control of their behavior, which makes it even more serious than the Troika has such a decisive role in the fate of countries that have borrowed money the EU or the IMF. Its counterproductive and political suicide being responsible for the high unemployment in affected countries as a result of their bigoted measures for ultra neoliberal convergence. The Troika is responsible (perhaps not the only or the last, because they are also responsible governments themselves that implement and applaud their actions) the growth of public debt, the impositions on the objectives of reducing the public deficit, and all privatization of public enterprises and services that are occurring in the European context. Troika measures are completely ruthless, as systematically attack wages and social welfare of the working population, imposing its unjust measures.

The Troika is a serious threat to democracy in the European Union, each of its Member States. It's like the "hand that rocks the cradle", the cradle of the markets, which are those who represent the real power in Europe.And as we have seen and tested in some countries (Greece or Italy, for example), if governments try to challenge the Troika and its policies, the pressure increases to a point where they have to resign to make way for the new governments expert, or technocratic governments. For citizenship, for the working class, the Troika is the cruelest political nightmare. Under this impeccable technical image, a group of bureaucrat's anonymous three powerful and macabre institutions that are not accountable to anyone, who rule the roost in the policies that determine the life of the people, and impose economic programs that pay hide the working majority.

While there are reasons for the economic difficulties at the national level in those countries – such as corruption and tax extremely low – which should not be underestimated, the Troika only focuses on national causes; however, the systemic issues at European and world level are more important. In addition, preferred by the Troika targets they are wages, working hours and social spending, preserving, again, only the interests of the wealthy.

The Troika first performed in Greece in 2010. It turned out that the economic and financial situation in Greece was not as prosperous as thought and as a final resolution, the country requested financial assistance from international institutions in May 2010. The EC, ECB and IMF undertook a mission to Athens and a few days later, a financial package was agreed with the first MoU. This started a downward spiral of wage and pension cuts, tax increases, layoffs and privatizations: the Troika had taken action on the matter.

After what happened in Greece, three other European countries were under scrutiny by the Troika: Ireland in December 2010 (formally abandoning the program of the Troika in December), Portugal in May 2011 and Cyprus in April 2013. Spain has a MoU which only includes conditions for the banking sector, but also forced to austerity by other measures. Other countries, such as Italy, are not officially under the yoke of the Troika, ie, they do not have an MOU, but are seriously under pressure to push through reforms and austerity measures. Fundamentally, the Troika ensures that ordinary people are paying for the systemic problems of the economy and mistakes made by financial institutions, which are the real causes of the crisis. At the same time, in recent years, European lawmakers have been steadily decreasing regulations and controls these financial institutions and large companies.

Therefore, it is important to see the Troika and its neoliberal policies not as an isolated issue but as an instrument in times of systemic crisis fits into a general trend of reform and neoliberal measures across Europe. These measures and reforms, defined by the term "economic governance", increasingly neoliberal impose more control, which favors large companies and financial markets and threatens democratic values and social rights achieved with great effort.

In summary, five keys are set to understand one of the organizations whose mere mention are cuts and austerity.

1. Although always associated with the European Union, the Troika is not a strictly Community body. This body is made up of **the European Commission**, the **European Central Bank** and the **International Monetary Fund**.

2. The fundamental objective of the Troika is to study the economic situation of countries to point out what measures and economic reforms should take if they want to consolidate their accounts and grow (However, the reality is much more raw, its true mission is loot the social justice of the people).

3. L to Troika points the way to the rescued countries. If those indications meet (usually cuts), they charge the rescue. If the country does not obey the Troika, it remains unfunded.

4. The imposition of economic measures the Troika has undermined sovereignty rescued as Greece States from Brussels dictating economic policy. For example, **the Government of Alexis Tsipras** insisted one of his speeches on the need to restore economic dignity.

5. The Troika is the body responsible for negotiating with government funding and in turn determines the conditions of repayment.

Figure 10. Christine Lagarde (IMF President, Mario Draghi (President of the European Central Bank) and Jean-Claude Juncker (President of the European Commission).

WHO IS BEHIND THE TROIKA?

Since 2007 they control the financial policies of the European countries most affected by the crisis. A set of experts is appointed to examine these states, study their budgetary policies, the macroeconomic framework, structural reforms and banking reforms, and ensure, to the dome, if they are meeting the specified requirements or not.

Note that this organization is undemocratic and that its actions are not entirely transparent. Internal differences arose almost from the first day, which is normal when there is a thinking head and director, but three. At its heart the confrontation between the IMF advocates economic growth, and the ECB believes in austerity as a cure to the economic crisis is cooked. This debate is being fed with the harsh criticism they are receiving the austerity measures imposed on Greece since 2010, which have plunged the country into a deep depression.

The IMF is an international institution composed of 188 governments. But within the IMF some governments have more weight than others. The distribution of power within the IMF is completely unbalanced; USA It has 16% of the vote. Be aware that decisions have to be voted by 85% to get ahead, which US You can veto any decision that does not like. Spain has no percentage is with a group of countries that control among the entire group only 3% of the vote.

The IMF has a fund, contributed by member states (including Spain), which used to lend to states in need. Needless to say that each loan has to be repaid with interest and that each loan allows the IMF to influence government the defaulting state. Therefore we can conclude that the IMF is public, international, but public. Although it does not behave as such, since much of its activity focuses on giving loans to companies and these are not controlled to lend them money.

The European Commission is an executive and legislative body of the European Union. It consists of 28 members and a chairman, all appointed by the European Parliament. We could say that is the governing council of the Union, therefore public and democratic. As democratic as the council of ministers, which no one actually vote but is elected among elected deputies.

The last institution that forms the troika is the ECB; the ECB is a public body that replaces today in many of its functions to the central banks of various countries. Your funds are nourished mostly of contributions from member states of the Euro, to a lesser extent thrives on the creation of money and contributions from private banks (in theory have to provide the ECB 2% of deposits their customers).

It is inexplicable for example, that the ECB does not inject money in any case directly to the states where he gets the money and if you do too often multinational companies. The ECB has taken out a billion dollar purchase plan debt but makes purchases in the secondary market. What does this mean? The state takes the debt (it borrows at a very high interest rate) is buying a bank and the ECB buys the debt to the bank (at a rate much lower interest). Round business for the banking system. **Does that make sense? Why the ECB will not buy the debt at a moderate rate or other favorable payment terms, directly to the country that cleared?**

The IMF and the ECB act as a usurer with states, when they lend money, take political control of the defaulting country and force him to make legislative changes, all aimed at thinning the states. Privatization of all state enterprises, tax increases, limiting the rights of workers, etc. It seems they do not want these loans to be repaid, in order to seize and states seem to do their best to please the expectations of usurers. The European Commission, the last leg of the troika, supports the other two in all its measures, behaving like an enemy state it represents.

It is assumed that the legitimacy of these institutions is given by the vote of the people, because they have been created and are supported by the representatives we elect in the elections. But clearly it is not, it seems that democracy is confined only to national parliaments, some parliaments that are continually pressured by these institutions to act against themselves and workers.

Austerity measures have multiplied Troika debt Spain for three, they have increased the salaries of zero point seventy workers have severed all social spending. Shirt austerity.

What is meant is that black men are people who have only one loyalty, money, benefit those who buy them. In reality we live in a dictatorship disguised as democracy, the dictatorship of capital. The crisis, that they use to win more at our expense and put ourselves in the place they think belongs to us, helps us to see what some behind the disguise.

Today modern states make large investment funds, vulture funds, and the mega – speculators who amass their fortunes in futures markets and in general, those sharks with a speculative attack on the bags can sink a currency, as it happened at the time with **George Soros** and his attack on the British pound. These loan sharks are those who tell the states and supranational institutions (IMF), because they also lend them what policies must do to return the money, or what is the same, what part of the social pie / "public" they will eat them being privatized for the benefit of creditors.

The main problem of capitalist societies is not their puppets but their handlers, the capital. This should be done without denying that criticisms of the boards of directors of capital are the institutional apparatuses. But that is secondary.

"Democracy" as the criticism of his absence is not that we should exorcise evil, nor the spear that will destroy capitalism. It is no longer a matter of how not choose or representations, the weighted weight of each country, according debatable criteria, lack of equal opportunities in politics or lower order as many questions stake. It is that democracy is a story for dummies, a lie sleeping masses, the means of making them accomplices to the consequences of policies against them ("do not complain, has democratically decided"). The voter totally ignores what to do with their votes (and in this I do not appreciate any between right and "left" difference) and also know all about the voting, when voting, and the impact of their vote.

RAUL OJEDA

THE EUROPEAN PARLIAMENT THE TROIKA SAT ON THE BENCH DEFENDANT

The European parliament has investigated the Troika and its working methods. MEPs held discussions and field visits; the conclusions are reflected in two reports approved by the plenary on 13 March 2014.

The Committee on Economic and Monetary Affairs of the European Parliament conducted an assessment of the Troika, whose speakers were the Austrian MEP Othmar Karas and French Socialist Liem Hoang Ngoc. At the same time, the parliamentary committee on Employment and Social Affairs held a second report led by Spanish socialist MEP Alejandro Cercas. The two reports focus on, respectively, the working methods and social impact.

The report adopted by the commission of Economy recognizes the difficulties faced Troika and the results achieved in the midst of a critical situation. But it also underlines the internal problems of this device that brings together three different institutions, whose responsibilities, decision-making structures and transparency are not equivalent.

Maladaptive measures

The report also criticizes the Troika managed to not adjust the measures imposed on the particular circumstances of each country. It proposes best solutions for the future. According to the report of the Committee on Employment focused on Greece, Ireland, Portugal and Cyprus, the four countries need a recovery plan for employment and social protection. According Fences, adjustment programs should not serve to weaken the collective agreements signed by the partners, or to cut or freeze minimum wages or pension systems -poniéndolos in some cases below the threshold of poverty, or to hinder access to health care, medicines or affordable housing. The field research included a delegation from the European Parliament will travel to Portugal on 6 and 7 January, to Cyprus on 10, Ireland 16 and 17, and Greece on 29 and 30 January. And personalities who participated in the decision of the Troika as Olli Rehn, Vice-President of the European Commission and former president of the European Central Bank (ECB), Jean-Claude Trichet came to the Parliament to exchange views with the MEPs.

The European Union looted the peoples of Southern Europe

Parliament's rejection of Cyprus to tax bank deposits "is part of the glut that has the people of southern Europe before this forced looting of bank accounts", said Francisco González Tejera analyst at RT.

" This looting of the bank accounts of the population, in this case of Cyprus, has finally destroyed the credibility he had left the Troika and the EU", today explained the expert Tejera to analyze the situation created after the Cypriot rejection European rescue.

On 16 March 2015 the ministers of the European Union, the IMF and the ECB announced the decision to establish a tax on bank deposits of Cypriots, which generated unrest in the markets threatening to turn the country into a 'financial hell' and repeat the scenario of the crisis of 2008. According to Tejera, that decision is to "steal the 6,75% of the savings of pensioners, the housewives, the most disadvantaged", but the people Cyprus "has not allowed this abuse of the working class southern Europe is committed".

"They want to behead the people, looting, swindling the people of the south, whom they consider inferior, and generate insecurity, generate fear" is the policy, already widespread Troika, EU and Angela Merkel, explained Tejera, to " behead the people, looting, scamming villages in the south, whom they consider inferior, and generate insecurity, generate fear".

Francisco González Tejera, all you have done in Cyprus is "keep social rights and labor rights of the people". "It is the line to follow, implemented by the Troika and Angela Merkel to continue trampling the peoples of southern Europe, we are already saying 'enough' to this dictatorship are creating to take away the rights and the historical achievements made during many year", he added.

Could there be reprisals?

In response to the question whether the actions of Cyprus today could trigger retaliation, Tejera said the message is clear: "Enough of looting and no need to make other policy and end this dictatorship to which they are subjected the peoples of southern Europe".

"Retaliation will not exist if we planted as it did Iceland"

Given this scenario, Tejera believes that "retaliation will not exist if we planted as it did Iceland". The solution to reverse this situation of deep crisis and "permanent abuse" is, leave the euro – says Tejera, leave the European Union and build a Europe of peoples and solidarity" since "not only subject us impoverishment but stress is permanent", adding that "we need to plant us to avoid retaliating and continue trampling on our rights".

RAUL OJEDA

NEW AMERICAN CENTURY

"The process of transforming the US the dominant force of tomorrow will be long, if not involved some catastrophic and catalytic event like a new Pearl Harbor" New American Century Project

DOES THE PAX AMERICANA?

The **Monroe doctrine** "America for Americans" remains – in essence – the main engine of foreign policy of the United States in its **relationship of domination** of Latin America, which is so deeply rooted in the consciousness of American citizens who believe the political and military interference by the government in other nations of the world, is for the good of humanity, the development of peoples for democracy and freedom.

THE HIDDEN FACE OF GLOBAL GEOPOLITICS

The Monroe Doctrine was expressed by the President of the United States, **James Monroe**, in the seventh annual message to Congress on December 2, 1823. The following is the relevant part of it: (...) "a proposal bythe Government of the Russian Empire made through the minister of Emperor here resides, has been handed a total and instructions to the Minister of the United States in St. Petersburg to resolve by amicable negotiations the respective rights and interests of the two nations on the northwest coast of this continent. A similar proposal has been made by His Imperial Majesty the Government of Great Britain, which has also been accepted. The Government of the United States wished for this friendly procedure show the high esteem that invariably has the friendship of the Emperor and his request to cultivate the best understanding with the Government. In discussions arising from this interest and in the agreements which must end, it has been judged that that opportunity is the chance to assert, as a principle in which the rights and interests of the United States are involved, that the American continents, for being a free and independent they have assumed and maintain, henceforth not be considered as an object of future colonization by any European power (...) it was stated at the beginning of the last session that were making great efforts in Spain and Portugal to improve the condition of the people in those countries, and apparently I was doing it with extraordinary moderation. It must be emphasized that the results have been very different from what was then anticipated. Of the events occurring in that part of the globe, with which we have a close relationship and which comes our origin, we have always been anxious and interested spectators around.Citizens of the United States share the most friendly feelings for the freedom and happiness of our friends on this side of the Atlantic. In the wars of the European powers, the problems that concern them, we have never taken part, nor has our policy. Only when our rights are invaded or are seriously threatened, it is when or we resent injuries or make preparation for our defense. With the movements in this hemisphere we are necessarily more immediately connected, and for reasons that are obvious to all enlightened and impartial observers. The political system of the allied powers in that regard is essentially different from those of America. This difference comes from those in their respective Governments; and the defense of our own, which we reached after the loss of much blood and wealth, which was designed by the wisdom of its most illustrious citizens, and under which we have enjoyed a happiness without equal, this whole nation is devoted. We must, therefore, for the frank and friendly relations between the United States and those powers to declare that we will consider any attempt on their part to extend their system to any portion of this hemisphere as dangerous to our peace and security. With the colonies or dependencies of any European power we have not obtrusive, and we will. But with the governments who have declared and maintained their independence, and whose independence we have, on great consideration and on just principles, acknowledged, we will not consider any intervention for the purpose of oppressing them, or controlling in any way their destinations by any power European otherwise than as a hostile predisposition towards the United States. In the war between those new Governments and Spain we declared our neutrality at the time of recognition, and she have adhered and continue to do so, provided that no change occurs by which, in the opinion of the competent authorities of the Government, should become a change of attitude by the United States, which is essential for safety. The latest developments in Spain and Portugal show that Europe is still convulsed. This important fact can not be argued strongest proof that the allied powers should have thought more carefully at any satisfactory principle for them, have intervened by force in the internal affairs of Spain. To what extent such intervention should be carried out by the same principles, it is a matter in which all independent powers whose governments differ from those are interested, even the most remote, and surely there is no more interested in why the United States. **Our policy towards Europe, which was adopted at the beginning of the wars that have so long plagued the place of the globe, it is however the same, which is not to intervene in the internal affairs of any of those powers; considering the de facto government as legitimate; to maintain friendly relations with them, and to preserve those relations by a frank and firm policy, knowing in all cases of the just claims of every power, without submitting to any offenses. But on these continents circumstances are eminently and evidently different. It is impossible that the allied powers could not extend their political system to any portion of these continents without endangering our peace and quiet; nor can anyone believe that our southern brethren, if the leave, would adopt spontaneously. It is equally impossible, therefore, that we could see an intervention of any kind with indifference. If we look at the strength and resources of Spain compared with** those of the new governments, and the distance separating them, it is obvious that Spain will never submit. It is then the policy of the United States to leave the parties to resolve the situation on their own, hoping that the other powers follow the same behavior"

The **Monroe doctrine** involves two evident premises:

1. The principle of self–defense.

2. The principle of self–determination.

James Monroe led arrogantly that the former Spanish colonies assumed as his own doctrine, considering himself or his government, the protector and legitimate interlocutor of the independent republics in Latin America and the Caribbean. But instead of giving real protection to the mestizos and indigenous people of Latin America the US government encouraged – with the example of the European pioneers in North America – exploitation and extermination. Even I knew protect the indigenous population of their own country, which was a victim of the policy of expansion of the US government. Thus, indigenous peoples, such as the Sioux, Cheyenes, Cherokees, Apaches, Irokeses and many others, were expelled from their territories, discriminated, massacred and killed and those who survived the genocide were held in Indian reservations. **Who defended these peoples of mass destruction? What European nation dared to prevent genocide?** If you were European settlers who deceitfully, theft and violence exploited and vilified large ethnic majorities, often with the support of the governments concerned.

Theodore Roosevelt and Big Stick policy

With its new imperialist vision in the early twentieth century, the United States reaffirmed the Monroe Doctrine and President **Theodore Roosevelt** (President 26th US) issued Corollary 1904 (Roosevelt Corollary) for the interpretation of the Monroe Doctrine. That is the policy of the **Big Stick or Big Stick**. The expression is the US president, taken from a West African proverb, "Speak softly and carry a big stick, and come away" (speak softly and carry a big stick, you will go far).

In the corollary states that if a country in Latin America and the Caribbean placed under US influence threatened or endangered the rights or property of citizens or companies, **the US Government I was forced to intervene in the internal affairs of the country to reorder deranged, restoring rights and property of its citizens and its companies**. Under the Big Stick policy the use of force is legitimized as a means to defend the interests –in the broadest sense of the US, which has resulted in numerous political and military interventions across the continent.

The Big Stick also refers to US interventions caused by the "disability" of local governments to solve internal affairs from the point of view of the US government, and protecting the interests of citizens and organizations.

In this sense, Roosevelt postulated that internal disorders of the Latin American republics were a problem for the operation of US commercial companies established in those countries, and that therefore the United States should be attributed the power to restore order, first pressuring local warlords showed the benefits of enjoying the political and economic support of Washington (talk smoothly), and finally resorting to armed intervention (the Big Stick), should not obtain favorable results to their military interests.

US interventions in Latin America

The different US governments throughout the nineteenth and twentieth centuries have amply demonstrated that the aspiration to world power – Theory – and dedication to achieve it – practice – are two sides of the imperial currency. The United States achieved their imperial purpose after World War II became a powerful nation that the Roman Empire July Galius Caesar and the Emperor Augustus, who comprised a territory, inhabited by over 50 million women, men, elderly and children, which extended from the current Iraq to the British Isles. **Never before in world was history there a more powerful than the United States Empire.**

On March 12, 1947 President **Harry Truman** announced the US postwar foreign policy before the two chambers of the United States Congress: At this stage of world history nearly every nation must choose between alternative ways of life. Very often, the decision is usually not free. In several countries recently they have been implemented by force totalitarian regimes against popular will. The US government has raised frequent protests against coercion and intimidation carried out in Poland, Romania and Bulgaria, in violation of the Yalta agreement. I must also say that in other countries there have been similar events. One such way of life is based on the will of the majority and is distinguished by the existence of free institutions, representative government, fair elections, guarantees of individual liberty, freedom of speech and religion and the right to live without political oppression.

The other is based on the will of a minority forcibly imposed by the majority. Rest in terror and oppression, a controlled press and radio, in fraudulent elections and the suppression of individual freedoms.

The **Doctrine-Truman** was directed in the first instance to counter the "danger of the world communist revolution" and was the touchstone of the Cold War. To some extent, the Truman doctrine can be seen as the adaptation of the Monroe doctrine to the new global political situation. The world after World War II became bipolar. For Truman represented the Soviet Union without all the "kingdom of evil", which implied that the United States was by conclusion, the earthly paradise.

In this international context, the Truman administration developed from 1947 a new strategic concept for National Security. The law of 26 July 1947, known as the **National Security Act**, has a historical importance postwar since it represents the legal basis of military power of the United States in the world. This law ruled the creation of the Ministry of Defense, Air Force, National Security Council and the Central Intelligence.

The doctrine that gained popularity and importance for his openly imperial character is known as the "Bush Doctrine", executed following the false flag of September 11, 2001 against the Twin Towers in New York. The concept of National Security Strategy dedicated to the transformation of national security institutions in North America to meet the challenges and opportunities of the XXI Century, published by the same President George W. Bush on September 17, 2002, reads as follows:

"The presence of American forces overseas is one of the most profound symbols of the US commitment to our allies and friends. Through our willingness to use force in our own defense and in defense of others, the United States demonstrates its resolve to maintain a balance of power that favors freedom. To deal with the uncertainty and meet the many security challenges we face, the United States will need bases and stations within and beyond Western Europe and Northeast Asia, as well as arrangements for temporary access to the deployment of US forces a great distance"

The US military interference in the internal affairs of other nations has always followed the same manual:

1. "Protection" to US citizens.

2. The defense of US interests in the respective country.

3. Conservation of supposed democracy.

4. Capture – dead or alive – Terrorist fashion.

US imperialism has found something that many philosophers have emphasized: "The peace of an empire always means, regardless of the degree of goodness" and the sense of justice,the emperor, the military subjugation of peoples and the intrinsic desire to expand and occupation of other territories. The different doctrines are always based on politico–military, commercial and cultural ideological interests of the powerful nation. Without wars empires have never existed or will exist.

War is a lucrative business for large industrial and financial capital, with a high profit margin, especially if we consider the three dimensions of the phenomenon called war: Preparation, Execution and Prevention. Weapons and war means destruction, and peace, construction and rearmament. According to the Institute of Peace Research in Stockholm (SIPRI, acronym in English) of 100 companies linked to the production and trade of weapons, 46 are American companies with a turnover in 2000 of more than 96 billion American dollars.

Samples of multiple interventions US

Historically, these interventions do not start from the Monroe doctrine, but preceded it, and the doctrine came to consecrate a policy that was already part of reality, as Examples include:

- 1798-1800, undeclared naval war with France: this territorial dispute included actions such as those carried out in the Dominican Republic, in the city of Puerto Plata, where they captured a French ship.
- 1814-1825, the Caribbean. Repeated fighting between pirates and American ships on land and sea in the vicinity of Cuba, Puerto Rico, Santo Domingo and Yucatan were fought.

These were not the only prior to 1823, the year of the declaration of the Monroe doctrine, there were enough other, all the same announcer sign of doctrine.

- 1831, Argentina. On December 28, waving French flag, the corvette USS Lexington destroyed Port Soledad, Falkland Islands. A party landed and destroyed the settlement, taking prisoners to most of its inhabitants.
- 1835-1836, Mexico. During the War of Independence of Texas, ranchers and slavers take large tracts of Mexico, north of the Rio Grande. US General Gaines occupies Nocagdoches, Texas, with the imaginary pretext that there is danger of an "indigenous uprising".
- 1845, Mexico. Annexation of Texas and California, belonging to Mexico. Manifest Destiny is satisfied: the white man must invade territories "backward" peoples, usurping their wealth enslaving its inhabitants.

- 1846–1848, Mexico. United States formally declared war on Mexico with the aim of conquering more land; military occupy, by order of President Polk, the territory between the Rio Grande and Nueces rivers to provoke Mexico.Le snatching half of its territory. In a bitter struggle they enter Mexico City.

- 1855. The American adventurer William Walker, operating in the interests of bankers Morgan and Garrison invades Nicaragua and proclaims himself president. During his two years of government also invade neighboring countries of El Salvador and Honduras, also proclaimed head of state in both countries. Walker restored slavery in the territories under its occupation.

- 1890. United States form the Pan American Union to accelerate its plans to convert to Latin America in its "backyard".

- 1898, War Spain–USA. The United States declared war on Spain at the time that the Cuban independence had practically defeated the colonial military force.

American troops occupied the island of Cuba, known patriots, and Spain was forced to cede to the United States territories of Puerto Rico, Guam, the Philippines and Hawaii. In Puerto Rico, from 1898 to 1947, the US imposed the (colonial governor always American), and he appointed administration officials, usually Americans. On July 25, 2012 marked the 60th anniversary of the founding of the Commonwealth, a formula that allowed the election of Puerto Rican governor, acknowledged flag and anthem, but that did not alter its colonial condition.

– 1903, Colombia. US promote segregation of Panama, then part of Colombia, and acquire rights to open the Panama Canal. Years later, former President Theodore Roosevelt –the actual segregating of Panama would say, "I took the Canal Zone while Congress was debating". "In Colombia it was later paid the ridiculous sum of $ 25 million in compensation".

– 1912, Nicaragua. 2,700 US Marines invade Nicaragua "to protect US interests during an attempted revolution", ushering in an occupation that would remain almost continuously until 1933.

– 1914, Mexico. During the Mexican Revolution, the US Navy bombards the port city of Veracruz, an attack apparently motivated by the arrest of US soldiers in Tampico. The Mexican government apologizes, but President Woodrow Wilson ordered the Navy attack on Veracruz. One hundred Mexican soldiers, several cadets from the Naval Academy and civil groups resist heroically. The occupants remain for several months. 1914–1917 Campaign undeclared hostilities against the Mexican Revolution. General Pershing invaded northern Mexico, pursuing the revolutionary Pancho Villa.

– 1926, Nicaragua. Augusto Cesar Sandino aims to create a popular army to fight the foreign occupiers. 1926–1933, an increase of revolutionary activity causes the landing of 5,000 Marines "to protect US interests". National Guard of the Somoza family is formed. Marines conducted major operations against the revolutionary Sandino. The United States then made the first aerial bombardment in Latin America. Attacked the village of El Ocotal. 300 Nicaraguans killed by bombs and machine guns Yankees. (1928). After his withdrawal, the

National Guard traps and finally fusila Sandino (1934). The military dictatorship ruled for 45 years.

- 1947, the United States begins to gradually impose the Inter-American Treaty of Reciprocal Assistance (Rio Treaty).

- 1948 Foundation of the Organization of American States.

- 1954, Guatemala. The CIA orchestrated the overthrow of the democratically elected government of Jacobo Arbenz in Guatemala. Organizes an army of right-wing exiles, who, with the help of aerial bombardments, attacks the city of Guatemala. The bombing comprises internal coup military forces trained by the United States, with the support of the church. They followed almost 40 years of violence and repression that culminated in the policy of "scorched earth" 80s More than 150,000 people were killed. Arbenz had nationalized US company lands of the United Fruit Company.

- 1960, Cuba. President Eisenhower authorized the realization of large-scale covert action to overthrow the government of Fidel Castro.

- 1961, Cuba. Bay of Pigs Invasion. A brigade of trained and directed by the US, with air and logistical support, mercenaries landed on the island. The invaders are defeated in less than 72 hours at Playa Giron. Since then, the forces of the CIA have landed many times in Cuba for sabotage, biological warfare, murder, contact their agents and other hostile acts and armed.

- 1965, Dominican Republic. US send 42,000 troops to the country marines to repress a movement trying to restore to power the previously ousted and democratically elected progressive president Juan Bosch; around 3,000 people.

– 1973, Chile. The military Augusto Pinochet took power in a coup supported by the CIA against elected socialist president Salvador Allende.

– 1989, Panama. It was the tenth third US invasion to Panama. US authorities, led by George HW Bush justified the estimated deaths of more than seven thousand Panamanians intend to capture General Manuel Antonio Noriega for alleged links to drug trafficking.

– 1994, Haiti. More than 24,000 US troops with supporting warships, helicopters and modern means of warfare invade Haiti under the pretext of ensuring the transfer of power from the dome coup, led by General Raoul Cedras, the elected President Jean Bertrand Aristide.

THE POWER OF MACHINERY BELICA OF AMERICAN

After the Second World War and throughout the period of the "Cold War" expansionist activity and US occupation, he was limited by the presence of Soviet power. But after the fall of the Soviet Union, the **Pax Americana**entered conditions positioned anywhere on the planet. According to an annual report published by the Stockholm International Peace Research Institute (SIPRI), institute that bears the statistics of military budgets of 159 countries for the year 2004 in the world one thousand and forty billion dollars (US $ were spent 1.040.000.000.000) in military budgets, of that amount, the United States is accounted for forty-seven percent (47%) as the country spent, according to SIPRI, four hundred fifty five billion dollars (US $ 455 billion).

THE HIDDEN FACE OF GLOBAL GEOPOLITICS

The United States presented a rapid growth between 2002 and 2004 due to the implementation of military plans referred to in its draft 1997: "Project for the New American Century" (PNAC) (Project for a New American Century). This project was revised and implemented since September 2000 under the name of "Rebuilding America's Defenses: Strategy, Forces and Resources for a New Century". (Reconstruction of the American Defenders: Obligations and Resources for the New Century). In this project, the requirements for the consolidation of the empire in the world for the next hundred years are described. According to this document, theUS should:

1. To strengthen its military position in their bases in southern Europe, Southeast Asia and the Middle East.

2. Modernize its armed forces by increasing the military capability of the Air Force, Navy and Army.

3. Develop and install a missile defense global platform that includes domain of outer space.

4. Check the common cyberspace on the planet.

5. Raise the annual budget for defense spending to a minimum of 3.8% of Gross National Product (this target was met in 2004, as this year's defense budget was equivalent to 3.9% of the Gross National Product).

After the disintegration of the Soviet Union is no nation in the world with enough military power to endanger the territorial sovereignty of the United States and yet, despite the end of the Cold War, undefeated empire continues to deploy new military bases (in 9 of the 15 former Soviet republics have already installed base) and sea power more than thirteen task forces are still scattered in all oceans on the planet. As its flagship aircraft carriers Kitty Hawk, Constellation, Enterprise, John F. Kennedy, the Nimitz, the Dwight D. Eisenhower, the Carl Vinson, Theodore Roosevelt, Abraham Lincoln, George Washington, John C. Stennis, Harry S. Truman and Ronald Reagan, kept sailing the seas of the world in the style of the cold war. An army of more than 500,000 people made up of soldiers, technicians, spies, educators, administrators and contractors, is deployed in more than 702 bases in 130 countries around the globe (not including the most recent in Kosovo, Afghanistan, in Iraq, in Kuwait, Kyrgyzstan, Qatar, Uzbekistan, Paraguay and Honduras). They do not guarantee the collection of taxes as formerly did the Roman centurions, but if they respond by subtracting the benefit provided by a complex neo-imperial covert action, economic self – righteousness, of preventive wars process, and invasions that provide them access to the riches of the world in the name of peace, freedom and the fight against terrorism.

General **Martin Robertson**, commander of a military base in the region of Camp Lemonier in Djibouti, France, said that the only way to put into action the "preventive war" was proving "global presence" and that, in his view, means gaining hegemony over any place where you have no control. The idea, he says, is to create a "global aballaría able to ride the stakes of any border and neutralize the" bad guys "as soon as we manage to identify them".

In order to increase its military presence abroad, the Pentagon (military brain of the empire) is repositioning new bases, six of them in Iraq and one in Kuwait which, incidentally, covers an area equivalent to one quarter of the territory of that country (who ended up invading Kuwait?) But what Colin Powell categorized as **"new family of databases"** begin to unfold in European countries like Romania, Poland and Bulgaria in Asian countries like Pakistan (where already there were four), India, Australia, Singapore, Malaysia, the Philippines and, incredibly, even in Vietnam, and in African countries such as Morocco, Tunisia, Algeria, Senegal, Ghana, Mali and Sierra Leone. The Pentagon proposal is to build a chain around al- basis General Powell Persian Gulf to join the already existing in Bahrain, Qatar, Oman and the United Arab Emirates. All this growth of military power of the United States goes beyond the hackneyed goal of confronting terrorism, the real reason for building this ring new bases around Ecuador is to expand the empire and strengthen military occupation planned as strategy domination of the planet and this plan (Project for a New American Century) was made long before the terrorist attacks of 11-S.

MACABRE PROJECT: THE NEW AMERICAN CENTURY

From 1997 he was baptized with the name "Project **for a New American Century**", but in fact the bases were created for the last great superpower struck with an overwhelming proposal domination aiming to put the world under the absolute control economic aura of Pax Americana. Within this project is the documentation proving this new imperial tendency. That proposal is identified with the name of **"Rebuilding America's Defenses: Strategy, Forces and Resources for a New Century"**, was developed in September 2000 (long before the terrorist attack on the twin towers which was in September 2001) and, as already stated, the requirements are described to empower the United States as the dominant empire for the next hundred years. George Bush when Bush assumed the presidency in 2001, are the authors of the "Project for the New Century" who also assume the leadership of the Pentagon, the Ministry of Defense and the White House, so when the towers were They pulled down the doors opened for this team warmongers put into practice his dream of a planetary empire. US Vice President for the period 2001–2004 and 2004–2008 **Dick Cheney** (Jewish former president of Halliburton, manufacturer of weapons and one that managed to have the largest contracts of the "reconstruction of Iraq "), together with the Minister of Defense **Donald Rumsfeld** and President of the Defense Policy Board **Richard Perle**, are founding members of the "think tank Washingtonian" creator of the project in 1997. Who was the Deputy Minister of Defense Paul Wolfowitz (the 30- 03- 05 was elected President of the World Bank) during the first Bush term, it was the ideological father of the group that developed the project and responsible for its management was a Pentagon official named Bruce Jackson who later went on to lead one of the largest companies gunsmithing: the Lockeheed Martin.

Figure 11. Members of the Project for the New American Century or English PNAC (Project for the New American Century), an ideological and political group based in Washington DC.

Advisers Project for the New American Century are the same that formed the so – called **Friends of Democracy** which sponsored the bloody confrontation in Nicaragua and El Salvador. Are the same actors during the Cold War organized the **"Committee on the Present Danger"**, stating that a nuclear war with the Soviet Union would be wise for the United States. And they are also the ones who created the **"Committee for the Liberation of Iraq"**, under the coordination of Condoleeza Rice (National Security Advisor and from January 2005 was Secretary of State in the Bush administration) formulated the plan to prepare psychologically the American people about the need for a war against Iraq. Condoleezza Rice said: "and I report" Rebuilding America's Defenses "is a plan with due ideological and financial support developed during the administrations of those who, for decades, have led the destinies of the empire".

This project has now been taken up strongly by those who, from a fundamentalist perspective intended to wage an endless crusade to establish what they define as "the new place of America in the World", a euphemism to cover up what appears to be the great battle for the planet's resources and step (according to fundamentalist Zionists who run the project) by the so - called promised land. The plan was designed to answer a simple question: **How can we justify the project for a new act of war managed to reposition US as the only super power?**

The destruction of the twin towers of the World Trade Center in New York was the trigger that allowed the US government argues four good reasons to justify the initiation of a new war:

1- The search for weapons of mass destruction "unstable countries".

2- The collaboration of governments identified as belonging to the "axis of evil" with terrorist groups like Al Qaeda.

3- The pursuit and capture of terrorists operating in countries brigands.

4- The demolition of dictatorships for the establishment of democratic governments.

The invasion of US troops Afghanistan and Iraq served to elucidate these reasons, but after almost two years of investigations and battle after these invasions facts have shown, irrefutably, the falsity of these arguments.

· No weapons of mass destruction were found
· There was no link between the Iraqi government and Al Qaeda.
· Al Qaeda terrorists have not been captured in Iraqi territory.
· A dictatorial government was overthrown, but someone who violates human rights, who closes the media and who is equally bloodthirsty, the president appointed by the empire Iyad Allawi, a former CIA agent, has been fingertight in a fit of rapture Of cholera, personally was responsible for executing 8 detainees for acts of resistance to the invaders.The renewed military action of George W. Bush as a direct executor of the policies of the US empire, obeyed four purposes:

The prime purpose was to avoid chaos was coming to the impossibility of maintaining the myth of sustained growth of the economy of the United States, **Alan Greenspan**, is the president of the most powerful central bank in the world: the Bank of the Federal Reserve U.S. This character, now become the "great guru" of monetary policies in the country that drives the world's economy said the September 17, 2004 on CNN: "is unstoppable need to start increasing rate benchmark interest federal funds".

Analysis of **"The Trap of false growth"** and result in the virtual collapse of the empire, was based on the fact that the economy of the United States, still has not come out of the great recession in which he was for the moment the arrival to power of President George Bush and, rather, what has happened is that, from that moment, has implemented an abnormal growth based on an expansionary credit policy and financing of its growing fiscal deficit by placing public debt bonds (Treasuries).

According to that, it is known that in recent years, the imposition of a very low rate of interest has allowed credit expansion and increased demand and, of course, as a result, the abnormal growth of the economy The United States.

But the problem is that this option of growth through the expansion of demand, has now become untenable, and has become the debt of the average consumer in a lethal trap, trying to remove it, generate unpredictable consequences for the economy of the empire and the pocket committed US taxpayers.

During the administration of George Bush, the purchasing power of domestic and imported goods it increased considerably thanks to the so expeditious and inexpensive way to access credit. Clearly, using low cost raw material abundant in many Third World countries, the availability of cheap labor and low costs means not having to respond to severe fiscal or environmental protection laws, they have made these countries very attractive places for the location of manufacturing plants of US corporations.

This means that much of the US imported goods are produced by US companies whose products no longer carry the label "**made in USA**" and this logically has helped increase the huge trade deficit that has that nation.By July 2004 the amount of this deficit amounted to 385 billion dollars.

The problem arises when it is observed that since 2001, maintaining the excessive consumption of the US market and momentum that this consumption provided its economic growth (two – thirds of the US economy depends on consumption) he was sustained on the decision of the Federal Reserve Bank, to keep the benchmark interest rate to 1%.

The existence of such a small benchmark interest turn has remained very low interest mortgage loans, purchase of vehicles, consumer credit and credit cards and this has made the credit in the preferred mechanism of the consumer the acquisition of any goods or services. This, of course, has led to an expansion of demand that has made possible to maintain sustained growth in the domestic US economy and Asian and Latin American countries mentioned.

But the study of the behavior of the interest rate during the Bush administration, allowed to infer that the failure of that growth was due to the supposed economic recovery announced since 2001, was rather a recovery funded by the US consumer (increasingly indebted day).

In addition to the expansion of demand by facilitating access to credit, the Bush administration, in its attempt to prove that would pull the country out of recession, implemented another stimulus to growth: increased public spending through the budget.

What followed after 2001 was accelerated growth of the annual budget. This budget, for many years has been in deficit, but over the last three years this deficit (corresponding to the difference between the amount of the annual budget and the availability of tax revenue needed to cover sum) arrived at the sum of 395 billion dollars.

Over the past 30 years, the mechanism of coverage budget deficit of the United States has been addressed through the Treasury Bonds placement. During this period the massive investment dollars (mainly oriented to the acquisition of these bonds) emissions, recycling of petrodollars nations of **OPEC** (Saudi Arabia, Kuwait and Venezuela lesser extent) have been commissioned to solve the problem.

Similarly, the central banks of China, Japan and other countries maintain their dollar reserves by buying Treasuries. The total of these loans amounted to $ 1.3 trillion. If this amount is added the acquisition of Bonds made by OPEC countries, especially Saudi Arabia 860 billion (US $ 860 billion) plus own debt to domestic investors, the US public debt would present the world's largest with an amount currently exceeds 3.7 trillion dollars.

Then came 2008 and with it the great crash of the US economy (As William Engdahl said that the "bubble of false recovery Bush" explode sometime after 2005), and the most affected were the millions of homeowners who struggled to pay off their mortgages (especially those who signed mortgages under the scheme of variable interest). Bines estate market collapsed under the falling prices and the inability to place new housing units. The bank entered in difficulty for the recovery of loans and mortgage system went into recession.

NEW AMERICAN CENTURY AND OPEC

Large buyers of Treasury of the United States, China and Japan, bonds are highly dependent on the US consumer market but, in turn, are also great iron plaintiffs oil and other important raw materials.

If the raw materials and inputs in general, materials double their price, (this would happen if a barrel of oil exceeds $ 50) investment capacity of these countries in Treasuries could be substantially reduced. This fall could only be stopped by an increase in the interest rate that would make investment more attractive in these roles, (the increase in bond interest drag upward the interests of consumer credit and this would lead to a further reduction in demand with the serious consequences already mentioned for the economy).

On the other hand, if OPEC countries decide to trade their operations selling oil in euro replace the dollar as did Iran, Iraq and North Korea (and why all three have been placed on the list of "axis evil") the acquisition of Treasuries would suffer a loss of nearly 600 billion petrodollars a year.

If the oil price continues to rise and the dollar continues to weaken against the euro (and it seems that it will happen), China and Japan in addition to being unable to continue investing their reserves in Treasury Bonds, try to get rid of those papers on the stock Exchange and would create a price drop to drag the current values (already overvalued) the rest of the papers and publicly traded goods.

If all this is added the "stock market bubble" (prices higher shares representing assets), a climate of upheaval and financial deterioration similar to what occurred in 1930 could be created.

The inability to place treasury bonds would be very difficult for the United States to cover its current budget deficit. This situation would cause a contraction of the economy caused by the sharp drop in demand. Many companies would cease its operations or would be forced to declare bankruptcy. Unemployment would rise to unsustainable levels creating a vicious circle of unemployment.

A depression with these characteristics would impact dangerously close to the entire financial and productive system in Europe and Asia. The global economy would be severely affected, (perhaps this explains the indefatigable Bush is receiving support from the UN, his failed attempt to stabilize the disaster that has caused in Iraq).

The government of George Bush with his advisers Pentagon launched a crucial and dangerous alternative: the use of war to achieve direct control of oil production on a global scale and in this way to lower prices, to meet their growing needs energy and continue to cover her swollen budget deficit by recycling petrodollars to its economy.

Therefore, the drop in oil prices was a long – term plan of the Elite Crime (ET): "Oil prices are a highly effective weapon of economic warfare (...) It is used by the transnational elite (the network of elites based largely on the G-7 that impose and manage the NOM of neoliberal globalization) to subordinate Russia and to integrate into this new order to any country still resist, as Venezuela or Iran", says Greek analyst **Takis Fotopoulos**, in an article published in the Russian newspaper 'Pravda' and on the website of the Canadian research center globalization 'Global research'.

This fall is "induced" and "is part of a long – term plan", which also includes economic sanctions and blocking new projects to facilitate distribution, adds Fotopoulos. For the US, however, low energy prices could help stimulate growth to 3.5% next year, instead of 3.1% forecast in October year, analyst estimates. Whereupon, according to the expert, it is not surprising that Saudi Arabia, one of the leaders of the Organization of Petroleum Exporting Countries (OPEC) and traditional ally of Washington, has opposed in the Vienna summit to quota reduction production to regulate the market.

In the era of globalization, the transnational elite uses to fight any nation that resists the abolition of its sovereignty, says Fotopoulos. Also it stresses that the aim is to get a severe economic downturn in all these countries, including Russia, and cause "velvet revolutions" accompanied possibly also by changes of regimes.

THE HIDDEN FACE OF GLOBAL GEOPOLITICS

American Centuria and oil of Venezuela

In 1999, the Iranian government decided to trade its oil operations in euros. In 2000 the Iraqi government did the same. In 2001, the Bush administration said Iran and Iraq as belonging to the "axis of evil" and a year later, 2002, the United States Army was invading Iraq.

Venezuela has a democratically elected government, which has no weapons of mass destruction and its territory hides terrorists, however, according to the statement by Michael Ruppert in "The Unseen Conflict" alone was enough that his ambassador to Russia Francisco Mieres (2000) let float the idea of the possibility of a shift to the euro so that "coincidentally" a year after a coup backed by the United States occurred.

The rescue of national sovereignty implemented by the government of Hugo Chavez, as the proposal called Bolivarian Alliance for the Peoples of Our America (ALBA), caused great concern among the doers of the foreign policy of the White House because it obviously is beyond the scope of the geostrategic interests of the empire. ALBA seen as an alternative to the one identified as Free Trade Area for the Americas (proposed FTAA), promoted by the US, proposed a new way of establishing trade transactions could not use the dollar as a medium of exchange.

The possibility that the United States could sponsor a new coup or even intervene militarily in Venezuela is something that should be seriously analyzed and which should be established contingency plans.

Another country identified by Bush as belonging to the "axis of evil" is North Korea who decided since December 2002 to replace the dollar with the euro in their business operations.

But what would be the impact on the economy of the United States; would the decision of OPEC countries to trade their oil sales in euros?

When US consumers purchase imported goods are sending dollars to producing countries such goods and when these countries buy oil from OPEC nations they will pay the same dollars. OPEC countries in turn put these dollars back into the US economy by investing in shares of stock, bonds, mutual funds or any other asset that allows them benefits. This recycling of dollars by OPEC countries, as has already been said, makes an annual amount ranging between 600 and 800 billion "petrodollars".

Moreover, in order to avoid attacks or speculative manipulation of their currencies, central banks of countries hold reserves in dollars equivalent to the amount of money in circulation in their respective markets amounts, so that the greater the pressure to devalue, the greater the tendency to increase the dollars in reserve. This circumstance, of course, helps to give greater strength to the dollar as a reserve currency. This hegemony of the dollar largely is due precisely to the fact that as all transactions in the oil market are made in dollars, then the dollar is, by far, the single currency through which you can buy oil.

According to the statement by Dr. Ali Rodriguez Araque Former President of Petroleos de Venezuela, SA (PDVSA) and former Secretary General of the Organization of Petroleum Exporting Countries (OPEC). Of the 85 million barrels produced in the world 30 million are placed by OPEC in the international market. If the average cost was maintained at $ 48 per barrel. If these 30 million were traded on OPEC euros, how the US economy is hurt? Let's get the account: 30 million barrels for $ 48 would be 1440 million dollars a day multiplied by 365 days a year would, 525,600 million dollars a year (525.6 billion reasons to invade any country) All this without taking into account that the United States would need to purchase euros to cancel the value of 10 million barrels per day currently buys from the OPEC countries.

It is for these reasons that the Pentagon, according to an article by **William Clark** published in the Sydney Morning Herald on May 30, 2003 has planned a period of five to seven years of war and is the same reason why, in the recent book by Wesley Clark, the author states that whatever the geostrategy of "war on terror" followed by the US with the problem of "Global Peak Oil" she always include other very distant from the Middle East scenarios, such as Africa (Sudan?) and the Andean region in South America (Will Venezuela join?).

The fourth purpose relates to the way in which the Bush administration can justify the expansionist behavior of the

United States taking advantage of the expectations on the foreign policy of this country, they have the 20 million Christian Zionists who believe and promote the realization of the "Seventh Dispensation".

This waiver seventh which is also known as the Millennium Dispensa says an apocalyptic vision of the future of humanity. This vision is established in a biblical prophecy that, according to the beliefs of respected scholars and teachers of Dallas Theological Seminary, Moody Bible Institute, influential Jews as Baruch Ben-Yosef Temple Mount Yeshiva and of politicians like George Bush and Tony Blair, it is in its phase of imminent execution.

Dispensationalism is perhaps the most influential theological concept in the United States. The dispensationalist thought of Christian Zionists called, had its beginning as a religious movement in England in the eighteenth century under the leadership of John Nelson Darby, however, were the evangelists Cyrus Scofield and DL Moody who at one time were responsible for disseminating this sectarian religious doctrine among American evangelicals. Within the ranks of dispensationalism are also former presidents like Jimmy Carter, the late Ronald Reagan and President George W. Bush.

It is important to remember that Venezuela, **the country with the largest reserves of unconventional oil on the planet**: Wednesday January 19, 2011, the Minister of Energy and President of Petroleos de Venezuela SA (PDVSA) Rafael Ramírez announced that at the end of 2010 Venezuela had a level **of**

217,000 million barrels of oil, and to this date and at a volume of reserves was achieved **297,000 million barrels of oil** of which**220,000 million** are from the Orinoco Belt. Of them in 2010 86.400 million barrels were certified, bringing in a 40.64% its proven oil reserves, which would place Venezuela as the country with the largest oil reserves in the world even above Saudi Arabia – although 75% of them correspond to extra – heavy crude in the Orinoco oil Belt.

Companies that make these certifications for PDVSA are oil companies have been areas for possible exploitation in the Orinoco or companies that specialize in these matters. One of the companies contracted by PDVSA, Ryder Scott certified proven the Carabobo area, which contains several blocks of 500 square kilometers each reservation. According to PDVSA said in 2007:

"The international company Ryder Scott certified tell 129.14 billion barrels of Original Oil In Place (POES) in the Carabobo area of the Orinoco Oil Belt, of which 45 000 548 million was discovered in the Carabobo Block 1, 30 000 660 million in Block Carabobo 2 28 000 650 million in the Carabobo 3 Block and 24 000 291 million in Block Carabobo 4. it is expected that a recovery factor of 20%, estimated at 25 billion 92 million bookings are developed barrels in the Carabobo area ".

In addition to the traditionally exploited deposits of light crude oil conventional western Venezuela, Venezuela has large deposits of heavy crude oil and extra formerly classified as bitumen – the so – called Orinoco Belt, a similar size and extension to deposit sand Athabasca tar in Canada.

The extra – heavy oil from the Orinoco Belt, even though less viscous than Athabasca–which means it can be extracted by more conventional – media, is yet buried to greater depth – what meaning it can not be extracted by surface mining as with the Canadian. Estimates of recoverable reserves in the Orinoco Belt between 100,000 and 270,000 million barrels. In 2009, the USGS updated this figure to 513,000 million barrels (8.16×10^{10} cubic meters).

GREED AND UNREALIZED HAZARDS OF WAR MONEYMAKER

Long before George Bush Jr. **started the hunt against Saddam Hussein** in Iraq in 2003, Washington had developed the mechanism of the distribution of this important spoil of war that promised access to the second largest reserves of world oil and colossal reconstruction country. If not for that document of 99 pages prepared by the USAID (US Agency for International Development) was leaked to The Wall Street Journal and then to The Guardian, it is possible that many companies in Spain and the UK they would have been without its share of the treasure. USAID had sent a secret invitation to five large US companies to submit bids for the reconstruction of buildings, bridges, hospitals, roads, airports, ports, water treatment plants, etc. The initial floor that offered the government to these companies was $ 900 million, with the promise that **the work would be made** (...) although theywere made. One of the representatives of these government

273

enterprises favorite (or perhaps the other way around) summed it up with these words: "the truth is that there is a huge irony here asking for contracts to rebuild bridges still not bombard ". The costs of that war were covered by public funds (public debt of the United States increased from 6 to 16 billion dollars in 10 years), while the benefits of the reconstruction of Iraq and the exploitation of oil remained in private hands.

Dismay in London

Filtration of this news caused consternation in the government of Tony Blair, in March 2003. The British troops shared on equal risks with US troops in Iraq, so did Tony Blair that it was not fair that US only stay with the spoils of war. The London Times warned of this scandal and 3 June 2003 asking what right "only US companies would be the beneficiaries of this war". The Bush administration was taken for granted possession of oil and would boost the arms industry and therefore had signed a commitment to companies whose main role was building. **By the juicy contracts for construction companies that left the large surpluses liquefy the oil.**

The five companies were contacted by the USAID **Halliburton Company (through Kellogg Brown & Root), Bechtel Corp, Parson Engineering, Lewis Berger Group and Fluor Corporation.** These five companies were deeply entrenched in the government and its contributions to the political world totaling more than $ 55 million, 68% for the Republican Party. Kellogg Brown & Root and parent company Halliburton Company had been directed since 1990 by Dick

Cheney who, besides his salary, received an annual check for a million dollars and when he resigned in 2000 to enter the Bush administration, received a prize 20 million as retirement.

For the United States, control of Iraq meant **control of the second largest oil reserves worldwide** where 70 oil fields, only fifteen were exploited. In turn, the British British Petroleum and Shell had long beensuggesting to the Iraqi government that he must accept foreign oil and divide the proceeds from the exploitation of oil. This forced a change in the law giving the National Oil Company of Iraq monitoring oil fields, saying that oil was a state resource that should be exploited by the state. The modification consisted of putting a word and leaves the supervision to "existing fields" that were less than a third of Iraq's oil. Thus, 70% of the "non – existent" fields were opened to oil transnationals.

Large construction

The US construction giant had begun to divide the spoils left by the wars of the Middle East since the end of the Cold War in 1990. Lewis Berger Group and Halliburton accumulated great experience rebuilding cities in Kuwait, Turkey, Georgia, Afghanistan, Jordan and Uzbekistan. On March 24, 2003, and after giving smaller contracts to open, USAID awarded closed a contract to Halliburton for 4.800 million dollars to reopen and operate the only deepwater port in Iraq is the Umm al Qasr.

The Bush administration assured Congress that the war would be quick and with few casualties, and would pay for itself. Deputy Defense Secretary **Paul Wolfowitz** said that oil revenues over the next two to three years (2004–2007) would bring to Iraq from 2 to 3 billion dollars, which would be enough to rebuild the country and establish democracy.

However, the March 20, 2003 the Chicago Tribune said the government was lying, and that Republicans would shame of fiscal irresponsibility when shooting public debt. The newspaper noted that **the Iraq war could exceed 100 billion dollars**, a sum greater than the annual budget of Energy, Commerce, Housing and Urban Development, Interior and combined Justice, and that in a decade the total cost could exceed 600 billion. 2008, when they met five years of the start of the invasion of Iraq, Joseph Stiglitz estimated the cost at $ 3 trillion, five times more than estimated by the Tribune.

According to the Watson Institute for International Studies at Brown University, the Iraq war has cost $ 1.8 trillion. It increases to $ 2.2 trillion when we add future costs of care to veterans, and $ 3.9 trillion when the interest on the national debt is incorporated until 2053 (from the 90 wars financed with bank credit).

Even the New York Times, certainly wiser than in those years, now says ten years after its inception, the Iraq war still haunts the US in the nearly 4,500 soldiers who died there, more than 30,000 Americans wounded have come home, the more than 2 billion dollars spent on combat operations, reconstruction, the deficit and lessons learned about the limits of leadership and power. The main objective of the Iraq war was to end the state industry and allow access to transnational oil companies. Ten years after the invasion entire oil industry is privatized and totally dominated by foreign companies. Today no one denies that this war was about oil and that the only ones who won were Exxon, Chevron, Shell and BP.

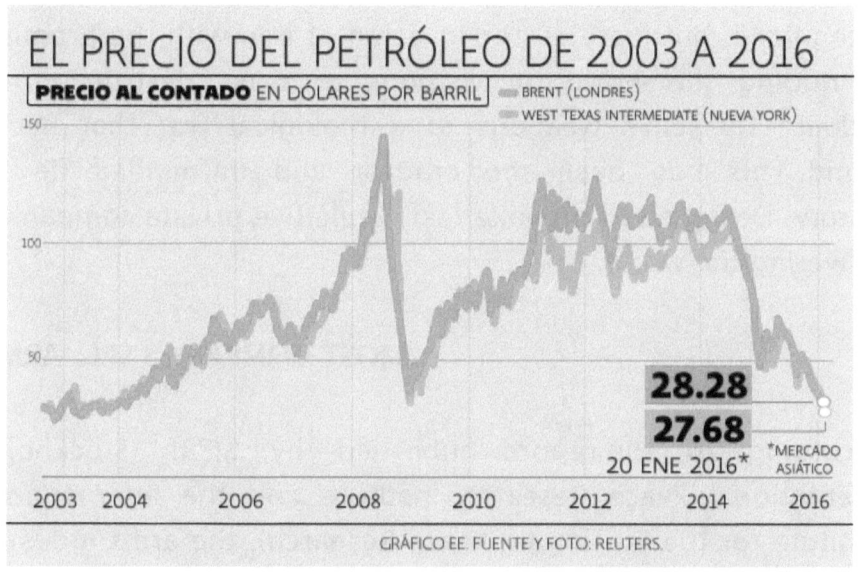

Figure 12. Variation in oil prices from 2003 to 2016.

Iraqi oil was once state-owned, facilitated water and electricity to the population. Since that wealth was privatized in a few hands, Iraqis must pay water and electricity at high prices. In addition, as oil companies import their workers, unemployment in Iraq is over 50%.

Contrary to what the Bush administration said Iraq does not need transnational oil companies to tap the wealth. Before the US invasion, Iraq produced 2.5 million barrels of oil a day. Since the invasion, this average has dropped 2.2 million barrels and even 1.7 million barrels. Iraq's oil is cheaper to produce and their cost in 2003 was less than 60 cents a barrel. Years when oil averaged $ 25 a barrel, thus offering a spectacular return on investment.

The Bush administration said it was for oil, as it is now recognized, but justified the invasion of Iraq with the promise of ridding the world of weapons of mass destruction of Saddam Hussein's weapons to a biological war that never found. This has been the crudest and unfounded lie in history. Designed to provoke fear, while five private companies delivering the world.

MOST COMPANIES SELL ARMS

According to the report published by SIPRI (Stockholm International Peace Research Institute and the International Institute for the Stockholm Peace Research), the arms industry is one of the economic sectors that have grown in recent times. 465,770 million dollars is what they have perceived sales amount in 2011 the hundred largest companies of weapons and military equipment, an increase of 14% over the previous year.

Thus, the SIPRI yearbook reflects the deep and sustained vigor of the defense industry, able to successfully cope with the financial economic crisis of 2008. Although usually not publicly report the performance of these companies, their products and armed services absorb much of public budgets, and receive numerous benefits unlike other industrial sectors.

According to the publication, the hundred most rentables sector companys account for half a billion dollars annually in relation to public spending. It should be noted that most factories are privately owned weapons. According to the list published by SIPRI, almost half of the hundred most profitable companies in the sector are of US origin. Here are the top ten companies sold more weapons in 2011 (sales and net income in US dollars million, the figures in parentheses refer to the data of 2010):

1 (1) – Lockheed Martin (USA). Aircraft, missiles, electronics, aerospace. Sales: 36,270 $ ($ 35,730). Net earnings: $ 2,655. Employees: 123,000.

2 (3) – Boeing (USA). Aircraft, electronics, missiles, airspace. Sales: 31,830 $ ($ 31,360). Net earnings: $ 4,018. Employees: 171,700.

3 (2) – BAE Systems (UK). Aircraft, artillery, electronics, missiles, military vehicles, ships. Sales: 29,150 $ ($ 32,880). Net earnings: $ 2,349. Employees: 93,500.

4 (5) – General Dynamics (USA). Artillery, electronics, military vehicles, ships. Sales: 23,760 $ ($ 23,940). Net earnings: $ 2,526. Employees: 95,100.

5 (6) – Raytheon (USA). Missiles, electronics. Sales: 22,470 $ ($ 22,980). Net earnings: $ 1,896. Employees: 71,000.
6 (4) – Northrop Grumman (USA). Aircraft, electronics, missiles, warships, airspace. Sales: 21,390 $ ($ 28,150). Net earnings: $ 2,118. Employees: 72,500.

7 (7) – EADS (European Union). Aircraft, electronics, missiles, airspace. Sales: 16,390 $ ($ 16,360). Net earnings: $ 1,442. Employees: 133,120.

8 (8) – Finmeccanica (Italy). Aircraft, artillery, electronics, vehicles, artillery, missiles. Sales: 14,560 $ ($ 14,410). Net earnings: $ 3,206. Employees: 70,470.

9 (9) – L–3 Communications (USA). Electronics. Sales: 12,520 $ ($ 13,070). Net earnings: $ 956. Employees: 61,000.

10 (10) – United Technologies (USA). Aircraft, electronics, motors. Sales: 11,640 $ ($ 11,410). Net earnings: $ 5,347. Employees: 199,900.

WHY DOES THE US HAVE ABOUT 800 MILITARY BASES AROUND THE WORLD?

US has about 800 military bases throughout the world, the maintenance costs about 100,000 million dollars a year to taxpayers in the country. The amount of these bases could be much higher if you take into account the still open facilities in Iraq and Afghanistan.

Most US bases were built after World War II. The Korean War and the Cold War contributed to the acceleration of the expansion of the military infrastructure of the North American country to other states, says American University professor, David Vine, in his new book 'Nation bases'. How to US military bases abroad harm US and the world ('Base Nation. How US Military Bases Abroad Harm America and the World').

In an attempt to contain Soviet communism, US forces they expanded across the globe, particularly in regions considered by Washington 'vulnerable' to the influence of the USSR. The portal But even after the end of the Cold War, much of the military infrastructure built at that time still operational until today publishes 'Vox'. Currently most US troops you are stationed in allied countries: Japan, Germany and South Korea. This April US He expanded its military presence also in Latin America. The US airbase at Soto Cano in Honduras, also known as 'Palmerola', 86 kilometers from Tegucigalpa, has a new special unit. According to a recent report from the US Department of Defense and the information of your Personal Data Center Defense, the **US has military bases in at least 74 countries** (mostly in Europe, Africa and Latin America) and troops around virtually everyone.

Among the analyzed data it highlights that there are currently more than 40,000 US troops and 179 military bases in Germany; more than 50,000 troops and 109 military bases in Japan; more than 28,000 troops in 85 bases in South Korea and tens of thousands of troops with hundreds of bases throughout Europe. The portal Quartz, which has requested a clarification of the data to the Department of Defense for its inconsistency (no answer), has developed a research led by David Vine, associate professor of anthropology at the American University (Professor USA), in the which **reveals US global military presence** Data from the Department of Defense, the press and Google Maps.

Figure 13. US military presence around world.

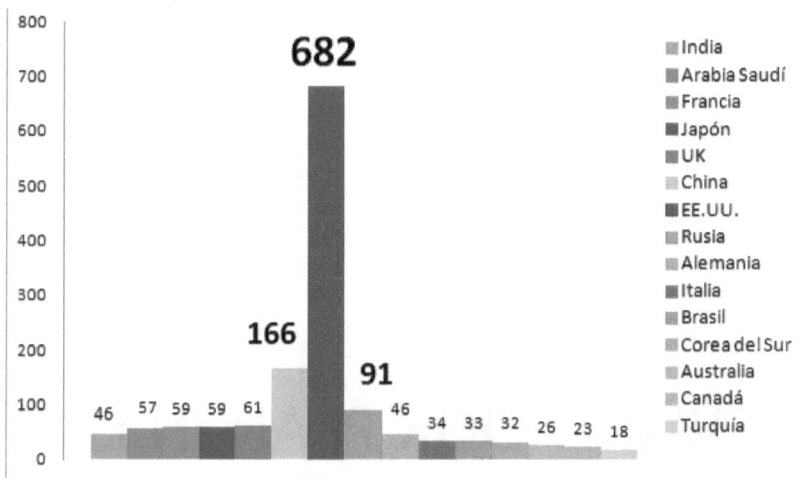

Figure 14. Top 15 countries with military spending expressed in billions of dollars annually. Source: SIPRI

NEW CONDOR PLAN IN LATIN AMERICA

"There is a new Condor Plan: a military dictatorship no longer needed, submissive judges are needed, a corrupt judge, who even dares to publish private conversations, which is absolutely illegal is needed". Rafael Correa

LATIN AMERICA, THE BACKYARD OF THE UNITED STATES OF AMERICA?

A blind man was sitting on the sidewalk. On his knees he had a cap. On one side, it chalked a sign saying "**Help me, please, I'm blind** ". Marketing specialist approached him, wrote something on the poster and, without a word, he left. Hours later, the cap was full of money. The advertising expert returned. He recognized by the blind for his steps. She asked him what he had written on the poster. "**The same message, but with other words**", said the publicist. Now the sign said: "**We are in the spring and I can not see it** ".

Please do not forget the parable described above; however, the political relations of the United States with Latin America have historically been marked by the asymmetries of political, economic and military power.Without doubt, the independence of the United States in 1776 – the first on the continent – and the beginnings of the American industrial revolution in 1877 are factors of political and social and economic development that played a decisive role in the dynamics of unequal dialectical development of the respective companies. However, these developmental theories – however interesting they may be – explain only partial aspects of asymmetric bilateral relations, not, the arrogant behavior of US political and military, diplomatic and commercial level with Latin America.

It is an indisputable fact that the relations of the states of Central and South America with the US government always developed in a vertical plane, especially during the nineteenth and twentieth century. This hierarchical relationship, whose character and content is imperialist, was made possible by the infamous metaphor of "backyard". The Monroe doctrine americanus demarcated the limes.

At the White House Monroe, Single, racist and xenophobic, Latin America was simply "the backyard", the Wider Caribbean the "Pool" and Panama the "armory workshop".

The special interest of the United States for Panama, dating from the time of the war with Spain in 1898, when the

US government began to take the first steps as a candidate to become empire nation. The topography of the Isthmus of Panama had all the advantages of strategic land-based military operations must meet. The construction of the canal in the early twentieth century not only shortened the trade route intercontinental shipping but also conditioned the installation of military bases for the "eventual" strategic defense of the Panama Canal and understood maritime area between the Great Basin Caribbean and North Pacific.

In the world, the American pre – eminence as an "agent of good" diluted like sugar in coffee, and became a state that finances terrorism. In a joint commission meeting in Washington by the Center for Strategic & amp; International Studies (CSIS), **Richard Armitage**, Assistant Secretary of State for the Middle East during the first term of **George W. Bush, and Joseph Nye**, a Harvard professor, concluded: "Since the Sept. 11, 2001, the United States has exported terror, fear and fury".

At that time, **Joseph Nye** established the difference between persuasion exercised by the United States to convince other countries to support them in their plans, called soft power, and coercion with which they can force them to go after them, called hard power. After the unfortunate outcome of the war, there was a change of attitude in the Bush administration with the request for funds to strengthen civilian power in Iraq, formulated by the Pentagon chief, Richard Gates.

Aware of this, Nye and Armitage proposed a third way, called smart power. What does it consist of? – The ability to combine soft power and hard power, so as to draw a compelling and successful strategy to improve the degraded image of the United States.

In a way, the committee chaired by Armitage and Nye wanted to be like the publicist who encountered the blind. He tried to encourage a change in strategy. Or, at least, to urge it on the eve of the departure of the neocons in the White House after the 2008 elections afternoon, Father Bush turned to matters that should be a priority, as an Israeli–Palestinian peace.

Yes the United States to implement smart power, **how they should behave the other countries**? In the book "The Power " **Dick Morris**, famous for having advised **Bill Clinton** in 1996 reelection and his Argentine partner, **Luis Rosales**, international relations expert, said that "Latin America can not escape from the proximity of the United States "and that" its success or failure will inevitably be associated with its policy of linkage to the US market".

Unlike the nineties, when there was another speech that was not the exaltation of free trade, Morris and bring as novelty Rosales conversion in the region since the rise of Hugo Chavez and other leftist leaders orientation.

The same said the head of the Brookings Institution, Strobe Talbott, deputy secretary of the State Department in the

Clinton administration, before the inauguration of Cristina Kirchner: "The biggest challenge for Latin America is the nexus between politics and the economy". That has been immersed a message: Latin America is the most desired area by the claws of the American empire, if any government opposes US foreign policy obviously you have problems. Reasons? – There are too many.

In view of the above in the text above quoted: one of the most momentous official documents is the strategic program **"US Southern Command Strategy 2018 Partnership for the Americas"**, which claims that "the countries of Latin America and the Caribbean are strategically important national security and economic future of the United States".

"Latin American and Caribbean nations are strategically important to the national security and economic future of the United States. The long-term interests of the US are best served by a hemisphere of stable, secure, and democratic nations. A prosperous future for all rests on a foundation of shared values; efficient governments; free societies; and open, market–based economies'.

"The major long-term interests of the United States are better served in a hemisphere of stable, secure and democratic countries. The prosperous future for all rests on a foundation of shared values, efficient government, free societies and open market economies". That is, the strategic plan of the Southern Command specified as part of its strategy not only that the continent is of strategic importance but is essential to control what kinds of societies, governments, democracy and economies need in the rest of the continent for their own defense.

Similar documents, sometimes with a huge bias according to political orientation of governments, can be found in both files southcom and the fourth fleet. Such as in which he mentions being "attentive to the potential geopolitical turbulence that could impact citizens and US military personnel in the region, particularly in Cuba, Haiti, Bolivia and Venezuela". Except Haiti, three countries that during 2012 there were no major conflicts, and where the Southern Command wielded as arguments to stop the ear the change of government of Fidel Castro to Raul Castro and implementation of economic reform, wage protests in Bolivia and Hugo Chavez Commander disease (for the year came the document still alive) in Venezuela. Three ALBA countries, economic bloc referred to again in the same document as a block influenced by Iran.

Also they disclosed there and in other documents not only detailed military exchanges with countries in the region, but a great concern from the challenge of them buy weapons and the growing influence of China, Russia and Iran, especially Iran (sic) over the region who dedicate a special section unlike China and Russia they are treated together.

In those documents, to rule out interference in internal affairs case of a new adventure, it is added that Latin America has been the first US expansionist doctrine developed (Monroe

Doctrine in 1823) self – proclaimed defender of the continent, also they have dedicated to the region's first major military agreements (the Rio Treaty in 1947, two years before the formation of NATO) and the dedication of more civilian personnel and military Southern Command) to the countries of the continent, which realizes a clear and sustained strategy on the continent of almost 200 years.

While in the past decade and a half US He has lost its absolute and unquestionable dominance in the fields of economics and global politics, leading to a multipolar world full of disputes of various kinds that put in check, recognized by the Department of State, the Pentagon and intellectuals far – right like former Carter adviser, **Zbigniew Brzezinzki**; nevertheless, still remains its military dominance, controlling half the military budget at the global level. Against this background the strategy for Latin America and the Caribbean rages. It is of paramount importance to US not lose control of your own backyard, dividing the countries in the region, plaguing the area of military presence and encouraging and supporting alliances and coups in countries with governments that do not meet the requirements of US security. From our side is, at least, it is clear about those objectives to act accordingly.

Against this, as if it were blind, publicist wrote "the same message, but with other words". So far from God, so close to the United States, the ideological blindness is sometimes worse than biological, paraphrasing Mexican President Porfirio Diaz (1830–1915).

How Panama became a military camp in the United States?

To explain the military presence of the United States in Panama and direct government interference in the internal affairs of that country must be taken into account three important historical periods in the evolution of the Republic of Panama.

The first is framed in the early nineteenth century, when Thomas Jefferson – 3rd President of the United States, was thrilled with the idea of Alexander von Humboldt to build a canal in the Isthmus of Panama.

"The Isthmus of Panama, is a landform located in Panama, between the oceans Pacific and Atlantic, linking South America and Central America. It has a length of about 700 kilometers; its width varies between 50 and 200 kilometers, and is rugged by the Cordillera de Talamanca. North is the Gulf of Mosquitos and south the Chiriqui and Panama. The Panama Canal crosses the Isthmus, allowing ship traffic between the two oceans that unites".

In 1831, the outbreak of civil war neogranadina, Panama separated for more than a year of New Granada, with the intention of forming a Colombian Confederation, maintaining its autonomy. In 1855 the State of Panama is created, federated to New Granada (now Colombia). The first explicit reference to the rights of US military intervention in Panama appears in the treaty **Mallarino–Bidlak**, 1846 signed between Washington and Bogota. The document gave the United States permission to build a railroad transistmeño, whose Atlantic terminal would be the island of Manzanillo on Lemon Bay. With the railroad, United States intended, on the one hand, a faster way to connect its east with the west coast; and, second, to counteract the British presence in the area, especially in Nicaragua.

The second period begins in 1903, when Panama became Republic, egged on and supported by the government of **Theodore Roosevelt**. This phase lasted 33 years and ended in 1936, when the United States gave up the right to interference in the internal affairs of Panama, established in Article 136 of the Constitution of Panama of 1904, which gave the government of the United States the right to intervene in any part of the republic in order to restore peace and public order. The United States tacitly became the protector and guards the independence of Panama.

Even existed in this period, two Panamas: The Spanish-American and the Canal Zone. The first, a protectorate with all of the law, and the other a political-military and commercial enclave with its own code of law, approved by the United States Congress on June 19, 1934.

The last period begins in 1939 with the ratification by the US Congress **tried Schubert Hull-Alfaro** (or also known as Arias-Roosevelt Treaty). Politically the treaty guaranteed the sovereignty of the Republic of Panama, by eliminating the clause authorizing the US to intervene in Panamanian affairs. It was also agreed that the defense of the canal by the Americans would be replaced by cooperation and shared responsibility in the operation and protection of the Canal.

Economically the United States pledged to cooperate to eliminate smuggling; It is also authorized Panamanian products free access to the canal area, giving them the opportunity to sell directly to merchants ships were in the channel region.

In other considerations, the US government pledged to enforce the laws of customs and immigration and the Republic of Panama, and also to facilitate Customs offices at the terminals Panama channel ports. Another significant achievement for Panama was the increase in the annual lease payment Canal from $ 250,000 to 430,000. The United States renounced the maintenance and operation of the Canal, but still provides some level of security
 This phase ended December 31, 1999, when the Panama Canal was under the trusteeship of the Panamanian government. **The start of a new era in Panama?**

To ensure the strategic defense of the canal during the Second World War, the United States launched a military cordon composed of military bases and naval and ground forces. The danger of sabotage canal and maritime ambushes by the fleet of Hitlerite submarines in the Caribbean Sea served as political–military argument to legitimize the existence of headquarters Defense Command Caribbean US military in the Isthmus of Panama.

After World War II ended, the United States strengthened its military presence in Panama, establishing permanent headquarters **Command South Defence**, which controls and directs the strategic defensive operations in Central America, the Caribbean and South America. The headquarters of the Southern Command of the US Army was recently moved to Miami in 1997, ie, I cincuentaiocho years later the outbreak of the Second World War.Officially – – US military bases were closed two years later.

However, the Isthmus of Panama remains listed by the US Department of Defense as strategic military base operations in the framework of the "National Security".

But, there are no military bases in Panama?

If accurate information **Movement for Peace, Sovereignty and Solidarity between Peoples** (MOPASOL) in Panama are operated 12 military naval air base. Moreover, former Panamanian Minister of Security, **Jose Raul Mulino** confirmed publicly in October 2012 the construction of four new US military bases on Panamanian soil, which would mean that in the territory between Panama and Colombia would be running about twenty – five military bases modern.

Under the premise of the so- called war against drug trafficking, the united States justify and maintain its military presence in Central America, the Isthmus of Panama and Colombia. The Colombia Plan is an economic–military project between the governments of Colombia and the United States, conceived in 1998 and officially launched in 1999 by former Colombian President **Andres Pastrana**, and whose priorities apparently eradicating socio-economic causes poverty, civil violence and the escalation of the war against drug trafficking. Undoubtedly, drug use is a serious, serious social problem that affects not only Americans (main consumers of narcotics in the world).

The Plan Colombia began in 1999 with a budget of approximately $ 7,500 billion, whose completion was planned for 2005.

Depending on the facts, currently the Colombia Plan is only a vile excuse of political-military strategy of the US National Security The war on "narco-terrorism" justifies facing Congress and the American society, the military presence of the United States in the region.

However, such socio-economic programs such as the Programme for Prosperity and peace in Colombia, conceived and government of the United States funded, are doomed to failure, since these pseudo plans are not aimed at eradicating truly factors poverty and socio-economic inequality in countries where the insurgency is strong and organized. Both the **Colombia Plan**, such as the **Bell Trade Act** in the Philippines in 1946 or the Alliance for Progress in 1961, are programs that are part of a political-military-economic strategic overall counterinsurgency plan for full control of the region.

The establishment and consolidation of its advanced military and political–military and ideological training of the "terrorists" are part of the strategic defense plan. It is no coincidence then, as stated above, that Panama was for many years the headquarters of the Military School for the Americas, also known as the School of dictators and Murderers School. There's darkest criminals and terrorists Latin American military formed.

Terror School of the Americas

The School of the Americas was established in Panama in 1946 and until 1984, where at present and since 2000 operates the Panama Canal Melia hotel. He was born with the initial designation of **Latin American Training Center, Ground Division** (Training Center for Latin America. Division of Earth). Its main mission was to foster or serve as an instrument to prepare Latin American nations to cooperate with the United States and thus maintain a political balance countering the growing influence of Marxist ideology or political movements of left-leaning organizations. All this in the new international context of the Cold War between the Allied Powers and the Soviet Union.

In 1950 it was renamed: **United States Army Caribbean School** and moved to Fort Gulick, also in Panama; that same year the Spanish language was adopted as the official language of academia. In July 1963 the center was reorganized under the official name **United States Army School of the**

Americas (USARSA), or more popularly known as **School of the Americas**.

More than 60,000 military and police personnel up to 23 countries in Latin America graduated there, some of them especially relevant for their crimes against humanity as : **general Leopoldo Fortunato Galtieri or Manuel Antonio Noriega,** and then transferred to Fort Benning, Georgia 1984. There were trained and trained in the "art" of torture, psychological warfare and the guerrilla struggle. Definitely, Fuerte Amador love for the social–economic justice and freedom of action and thought, conspicuous by his absence. The president of Panama, **Jorge Illueca**, described the School of the Americas as "the **largest gringa base for destabilization in Latin America**", and major international newspapers she was nicknamed "The School of Murderers".

The story of death surrounding graduates of the School of the Americas is very long: hundreds of thousands of Latin Americans have been tortured, raped, murdered, disappeared, massacred and forced to take refuge in other countries by soldiers and officers trained in that school. Bloodthirsty graduates **USARSA** pursue educators, union organizers, religious workers, student leaders, and the poor and peasants fighting for the rights of victims.

US imperialism historically strategically prepared to fight the "Soviet communist subversion" in their backyard. Cuba, which has become the "Caribbean brothel" of the American Mafia, became the night of December 31, 1959 to the morning of January 1960, with the triumph of the Cuban revolution, the enemy number one US society. The Cuban revolution since then, the thorn in the side of the government of the United States.

As mentioned earlier in July 1963, the government of the United States decided to rename the "newly **School of the Caribbean** "; probably because it was assumed that the "communist threat" was not limited only to the region of the Great Caribbean Basin, but extended to the entire American continent. The name "Military School of the Americas" wore better with the character and content of continental and anticommunist military training center. In 1984, after the agreements which regulated the transfer of the Panama Canal to the Panamanian government were signed, the "School of the Americas" was moved to Fort Benning in Georgia / USA. Since then the "School of the Americas" (SOA) ceased to exist and instead appeared the Institute for Security Cooperation in the Americas (WHISC, its acronym in English).

There are two periods in the political and military history of the US government in Latin America that essentially influenced and conditioned the promotion and development of the "School of the Americas". The first period begins with the outbreak of the First World War in 1914 and ends in 1960 with the defeat of Dictator **Fulgencio Batista** in Cuba. The second period extends from 1961, symbolically represented by the mercenary invasion at theBay of Pigs to the present.

The special interest of the United States in Latin America, dating from the early nineteenth century, but with the opening of the Panama Canal in August 1914, the area of Central America and the Greater Caribbean became a military strategic area of government of the United United. It was precisely **John F. Kennedy**, US President who promoted and encouraged decisively and resolutely counterinsurgency doctrine since 1961.

Kennedy, who was convinced that the war against "international communism" not only had to fight with military means, but also through a strategic political, economic and ideological plan would be the basis of the alleged "peaceful revolution" in Latin America.

The Alliance for Progress was funded by the **United States Agency for International Development**, but soon was exposed, the agency served only to strengthen unity among the Latin American oligarchy, the military oligarchy and the Catholic Church. The Alliance for Progress was actually the unity of the ruling class in terms of promoting the retreat of the poorest countries in the Americas.

After the Cuban revolution, came the first guerrillas in Venezuela and Colombia, as a response to poverty and extreme social inequality in most living of the poor. In El Salvador the mid-twentieth century 67% of fertile land was in the hands of a 4% of the population, while 96% of all landowners owned 33% of arable land. In Colombia the situation was similar: As of 5% of the population belonged to 80% of the arable land, while 66% of the population owned 5% of the land. At this inequality level land kleptocracy of officials, submission of nationals to the guidelines of the government of the United States and to cap governments, the brutality with which the repressive forces and paramilitary punished peasants were added and laborers (thousands of forced disappearances).

Plans military training of the "School of the Americas" were adapted to the counterinsurgency strategy of the Kennedy administration. The military learned in SOA torture, disappearance and death are the ideal tools to ensure "freedom and peace" among the peoples of Latin America, or in the best way: everyone involved is forced to continue the policy US outer.

From 1961 to 1990, about 36,000 Latin American officers and NCOs visited the "School of the Americas terror". Most of them were Colombians (5827), El Salvador (5642), Peru (3465), Panama (3003), Bolivia (2669), Venezuela (2462), Chile (1968), Ecuador (1869), Honduras (1550) and Dominicans (1700).

From 1981-1990 the situation in Latin America radically changed and the focus moved to El Salvador and Colombia, two countries with similar political and social structures. Both countries not only have in common one of the best coffees in the world, a high poverty rate and extreme violence, but also in their territories operated the largest and best-armed guerrilla armies in the history of the political-military struggle in Latin America. No wonder then, that Colombia and El Salvador occupy the first two places in the number of graduates of the "School of the Americas". Among the outstanding students of the "School of Dictators", stand out:

1. **General Manuel Noriega**, Panama: former CIA agent. In 1992 he was tried in the United States and sentenced to 40 years imprisonment on charges of being linked to the Medellin cartel and Pablo Emilio Escobar Gaviria.The penalty was later lowered to 30 years and then 20 for "good behavior". In early 2008 he remained in jail in Miami awaiting your situation is defined. France requested his extradition, ratified in January 2008 by a US judge.Noriega was convicted in 2010 by a French court to seven years in prison for laundering drug money. A French judge granted parole in September 2011 requested by his lawyers, considering that Noriega served more than half his French sentence: year and a half has been detained in France and two years and a half he was detained in the United States awaiting approval of his extradition to Paris. Noriega remained in the Paris prison of La Santé until his extradition to Panama on December 11, 2011.

2. **General Efrain Rios Montt**, Guatemala: the May 10, 2013 was sentenced to 80 years for genocide and crimes against humanity, but this sentence was overturned on May 20, 2013 by the **Constitutional Court of Guatemala** (CC) because Jazmin Barrios judge president of the Court of First higher Risk a, did not comply with the rulings of that court, being a senior legal authority for that reason committed disobedience and contempt.

3. **General Hugo Banzer**, Bolivia: Bolivian dictator between 1971 and 1978, it is estimated that during its first rightist government about a hundred political prisoners were missing, having been subsequently found in the basement of the Ministry of Interior (Current Ministry of Government of Bolivia) cells torture and bones human. Banzer since 1988 occupies a place of honor in the Hall of Fame of the School of the Americas.

4. **Colonel Roberto D'Aubuisson,** El Salvador: founder of the far – right party **ARENA** and death squads in the 80's former ambassador Robert White said in 1986 the United States Congress that D'Aubuisson participated in planning and execution of the assassination of Monsignor Oscar Arnulfo Romero. However, D'Aubuisson was never formally accused to justice. He died in bed as the dictator Pinochet, without paying to society for the crimes committed.

5. **Colonel Natividad de Jesus Caceres Cabrera**, El Salvador: second in command of the Atlacatl Battalion, responsible for having made the slaughter of El Mozote. Caceres Cabrera, along with Lieutenant–Colonel Domingo Monterrosa and Major Jose Armando Azmitia Melara (both deceased) directly responsible for this slaughter.

6. **Manuel Contreras**, Chile: director of the Chilean secret police (DINA) during the dictatorship of General Pinochet. Contreras was sentenced to 289 years in prison for kidnapping, disappearance and murder.

Summarizing

During the Cold War, the "School of the Americas" played a leading role in military training under the strategic concept of counterinsurgency war of low intensity and the dirty war, also in the anti-communist indoctrination of thousands of Latin American officers and NCOs.

With the fall of the Soviet Union in 1991 disappeared the "communist enemy". Instead came the international drug trade, also called Muslim terrorism and drug trafficking. With the birth of the "new enemy" of Western society – although drug trafficking has always existed–the government of the United States pulled off the military–political argument to continue to maintain its military bases and training centers throughout the planet. It is possible that the common American citizen is misinformed, but the politicians who govern this powerful and great nation – Democrats or Republicans, doves or hawks – are people with highly educated and knowledgeable, who surely know that while persist causes of poverty and social inequality in Latin America, the danger of social revolutions remain latent. While the danger of Marxist revolution hides in its "backyard", the military presence of the United States will remain an unavoidable reality.

THE HIDDEN FACE OF GLOBAL GEOPOLITICS

CONDOR PLAN

In recent years, the transnational elite headed by the US government have developed new forms of intervention in Latin America and around the world (New Plan Condor). These procedures are carried out within the framework of capitalist globalization and under the rhetoric of **"promoting democracy"**.

"Plan Condor was an operation that involved the coordination of actions between rights - wing dictatorships recorded in several countries in South America (Chile, Argentina, Brazil, Paraguay, Uruguay, Bolivia, Peru and Ecuador) between the 70 and 80 in which he was involved unrestrictedly US".

The New Plan Condor seeks coordination of right–wing leaders in Latin America to isolate the regional context the nations with progressive governments.

Political revanchism right to destroy and discredit the social progress made by socialist governments sought. This is evidenced by the arrival in December 2015 the neoliberal government of Mauricio Macri in Argentina, whose first steps were massive layoffs, censorship of the media, privatization and attacks against countries that do not share their policies, such as Venezuela.

According to **William I. Robinson** (Professor of Sociology at the University of California, USA) in his book "Promoting

Polyarchy" (Promoting Poliarqula), published in 1996, the agenda of the Transnational Elite has two dimensions: promotion poliarquía and promotion of neoliberal capitalist globalization.

But who are the victims of promoting capitalist poliarquía? There are three categories of white countries:

1. Countries selected to effect a "transition" of dictatorships or authoritarian regimes polyarchic elitist regimes. This is not to "destabilize" these countries, but to organize a transition under the hegemony of neo-liberal civilian elite. For example, in South Africa in the early nineties, in Chile under Augusto Pinochet, in the Philippines under Ferdinand Marcos in Panama with the US invasion of 1989, in Haiti under Duvalier, etc. At first, the new strategy for promoting polyarchy was formulated for this category of countries. Once running the new strategy, they expanded the focus to include as white, two other categories of countries.

2. Countries US and the transnational elite (ET) attempt to destabilize and overthrow. These categories are listed in recent years, Nicaragua under the Sandinistas, Haiti under **Jean-Bertrand Aristide**, Cuba since 1959, Venezuela in 1998, and Bolivia since 2006. And outside Latin America, one can cite Iran today, and the Hamas government in the Palestinian territories. In these countries, programs promoting polyarchy are part of the projects of aggression, destabilization, terrorism and counter – revolutionary campaigns very broad.

3. Countries where nationalist, revolutionary, or simply progressive forces that challenge the new neoliberal order, popular forces are on the rise and represent a potential threat to the dominance of local elites and transnational agenda. In these countries, the promotion programs polyarchy are designed to strengthen local neoliberal elites, to mediate and de-radicalise popular struggles, and to avoid coming to power through elections or other means. In this category, currently included El Salvador, Colombia, and Mexico, for example, and also included Bolivia before Evo Morales and Venezuela between 1989 Caracazo and the election of Hugo Chavez in 1998.

A question arises: What is the modus operandi of the new policy intervention? Let's see:

Programs promoting polyarchy operate on several levels. On the first level is the overall design, and operate at this level the highest levels of the American state apparatus: **the White House, the State Department, the Pentagon, the CIA and other agencies.** At this level, decide on assembling promotion programs polyarchy as a component of the overall policy towards the country or region concerned.

At the second level, assigned million, spread across several channels (including USAID, the National Endowment for Democracy, known by its acronym, NED, CIA, the State Department), a series of American and international organizations closely linked with the state and with the foreign policy of Washington. Numerous agencies receiving funds for the "promotion of democracy". Among the long list include the International Republican Institute (IRI) and the National Democratic Institute for International Affairs (NDIIA), official foreign policy arms of the Republican and Democrat parties respectively; the Institute for Free Labor and the International Labor Solidarity, among many that could be cited. All these organizations and actors constitute a complex network of American political intervention.

At the third level, this interventionist network provides "grants" to a series of similar groups in the country intervened. These large grants include: funding, management, political patronage, and so on. Every American interventionist agency specializes in a particular sector of society in the country intervened. For example, IRI and NDIIA typically work with political parties in the country involved, the Institute for Free Labor with the unions, and so on. The goal is the penetration and control of civil society in the involved country, as US strategists have become good Gramscians – know that to beat their opponents and to make domination, they need win hegemony in civil society.

Therefore, interventional network seeks to penetrate and capture the civil society in the country intervened instrumentalises a number of local groups, including: the political parties and coalitions; unions and guilds; business chambers; the media; civic and neighborhood associations; student groups, youth, women; etc. The goal is to strengthen related organizations or create parallel organizations competing with organizations of the popular sectors and try to outshine the radical groups, reinforce the hegemony of local elites, and inculcate the transnational agenda. All these groups are presented as "independent" and "non-partisan" but actually function as instruments of US policy and the transnational elite.

A powerful indicator that a country is subject to an interventionist operation is when a real invasion by an army of American and international non-governmental organizations, "technical", "consultants", experts", etc. occurs. Made programs "strengthening of political parties and civil society", civic education" workshops "leadership training" and "training of the media" and so on.

For example, the "Mongoose" in Venezuela operation: One of its main tasks was to recruit agents in the field to their destabilization plans and to perform a variety of provocations, trying to put in check the constitutionality in the brotherly country. And the CIA determined that some of the young Venezuelans could be the center of its work recruitment. Thus, he began his efforts to move closer to them through different avenues. Forms of recruitment of its agents have been made, without distinction, in various ways, but basically this work has done the CIA from the US embassy in Caracas, through its operating officers, concentrated in the Office of Culture and the Press.

In other cases, the recruitment work has been done through the use of covers of the Agency as USAID, NED, Provide, the Center for Dissemination of Economic Knowledge for Freedom (CEDICE), European NGOs (among which German Konrad Adenauer Foundation, Friedrich Naumann Stiftung and the Spanish Foundation for Analysis and Social Studies – FAES), student bodies linked to European and Latin American rights and as well as by groups of "exiles" based in Florida.

The media integrated network interventional give wide cubertura to network activities, exaggerate their drag to give an image of strength and so on. This is a crucial component: it is the media disinformation, or more precisely, the use of means to carry out psychological warfare, the ideological war. In this new era of globalization, the media plays a major role in political and social processes in the battle for hegemony. Interventional media network use what is known as black propaganda; character assassination (demonization of opponents); called "blowback" (when implanted information invented a means of communication determined and then the information is collected and disseminated widely by other local and international media); the use of what **Joseph Goebbels** (Minister for Public Enlightenment and Propaganda of Nazi Germany between 1933–1945) called the "big lie" and so on.

The overall objective of the network is to eroding the social basis of counter-hegemonic project, the popular project, to implement the project of the transnational elite to popular sectors, the discontented, the middle class; go exploiting and harvesting the frustrations and grievances, legitimate grievances of the population. Cynical tactics used, as provocations; create "incidents"; violent clashes; economic attrition (sabotage, hoarding, provoking shortages); tender "balls"; stoke an atmosphere of insecurity, uncertainty, and anxiety. Coincidence? – Everything has been pre – planned.

Above all, the network interventionist advantage of the economic difficulties faced by popular projects. They seek to aggravate these difficulties and make it impossible for material improvement of the masses, as the popular transformation projects have as their reason for solving the material problems of the people, and this rationale has to be subverted. Also they take full advantage of the errors of grassroots leaders, popular and revolutionary leaders, opportunism and corruption within the popular field and within the state and the revolutionary parties. Even they seek to promote this opportunism and corruption, pursue cultivate "endogenous" allied to the popular and revolutionary projects.

In the strategic lexicon, this is called political and psychological warfare.

We must be clear: once the popular and revolutionary forces lost hegemony in civil society, the government and transnational elite have practically won. For example, in Nicaragua, the Sandinista revolution could not be defeated militarily. The Sandinistas defeated the armed counterrevolution. However, the Sandinistas lost the hegemony within society between 1987 and 1990; years when the United States went on to implement the strategy of promoting polyarchy.

As for electoral processes, they endow the interventionist network with the opportunity to deploy all its instruments and resources to put into action the whole range of tactics and maneuvers. But they are not omnipotent.When the election results will come out the butt and win popular candidates, as in the cases of Haiti or Venezuela, Bolivia and Palestine, then cry "fraud" with great fanfare, quickly assembled machinery of disinformation, and pass the phase destabilization.

Finally on this point: it is important to emphasize that the new forms of American political intervention does not replace but combine with the full range of domestic and international interventional instruments, including military aggression, covert operations, economic blackmail, sabotage; the actions of paramilitary and terrorist units; putschists attacks, etc., as witness our fellow Cubans, Venezuelans and Bolivians.

>> **Nicolas Maduro: Venezuela is experiencing the most serious threat in recent years by US interference.**

The interventionist and interventionist US strategy in Latin America in the 1970s and 1980s, it was based on military coups to overthrow governments and regimes and dictatorships forming pro-American; An example of these actions were the overthrows of governments of Salvador Allende in Chile (1973); Isabel Peron in Argentina (1973); the coup of Juan Maria Bordaberry in Uruguay (1973).

Intervention elements of internal order

The series of lawsuits against major leadership progressives, the growing threat of paramilitary groups, the criminalization of movements advanced and blows to the economy of the countries of popular consciousness, are part of the reconfiguration of Operation Condor in Latin America, according analyst and journalist, **Miguel Jaimes**.

Among the elements involved Condor internal order of the countries Plan, Jaimes quoted in an exclusive interview with the Telesur website:

–The Constant attack on the economy and the productive apparatus of the South American countries and progressive: The maneuvers for lower oil prices, food shortages in Venezuela, as well as sabotage in the price of the parallel dollar and other related indicators economic, part of Operation Condor. These aim to create despair among the population and also affect the funding of social programs.

–Death Leaders and lower average basis of socialist and popular parties: referred to as examples of persecution of popular leaderships murder of indigenous leader Berta Caceres (Honduras) and the young deputy Robert Serra (Venezuela). These actions aim mainly play down the leaderships solid influential parties and demoralize its members.

–Use Of media to criminalize political leaders and sink campaigns: In addition to seeking to be processed and banished from the political arena, it is believed that the media seek to influence the atemorizándola population, manipulating and legitimizing powers. One example is that a former president like Alvaro Uribe (Colombia) "constantly appears in the media with his views on military intervention in a sovereign nation, calling the military to do so, who is he to do? And Why what the media have given so much deployment that?".

–Violence And drug trafficking: An evil that grows throughout the continent and even appropriates the poorest populations in order to create free for drug trafficking between South and North ports. It is a form of terrorism even in Venezuela has been developed with the interference of criminal gangs from Colombia and, according to the analyst, not only to generate fear and establish a market, but also gain power.

–Criminalización Of leftist movements, corruption and attacks on the environment: It seeks to support the media blame solely on corruption movements and leftist parties, although many of them are those who have initiated the struggle for the clarification of these cases. It seeks to establish an association between crime and leftist leaders. He also said that the attacks on the environment for resource exploitation are partly made by the executor and capitalist arm of the US

–NGOs And manipulation of youth: organizations like Sumate, led by former deputy Maria Corina Machado right and directly linked to the 2002 coup, are responsible for generating movement on the streets with young used to promote violent actions. According to leaked documents, USAID and the NED invested more than 100 million dollars between 2002 and 2012 in sponsoring opposition groups and create at least 300 new NGOs in Venezuela.

PARLIAMENTARY BLOW

The new Condor Plan is based on soft and parliamentary coups, as presidents have publicly denounced as Venezuela, Nicolas Maduro and Rafael Correa Delgado of Ecuador.

The parliamentarian is that the basis for implementation within the same legal system of the country: motion of censure, investigations of judicial nature (impeachment), declaration of "inability to govern" to force a resignation, among others.

The private media and the political and economic elites play an important role in the implementation of these new shares, to manipulate information and laws to destabilize the country.

>> **Guillaume Long** : **progressive countries live a constant threat to its democracy**

The parliamentary coup strategy reduces the political cost of stakeholders and to change the direction of a country and its foreign policy without "bloodshed", appealing and excusing the "rule of law" and "democracy".

The parliamentary coup has become political operation more profitable foreign intervention to alter the correlation of forces, eliminating important political leaders and radically changing international power schemes and regional blocks of influence.

The most recent example of parliamentary coup is **Brazil**, whose president Dilma Rousseff was away from the office for 180 days to face impeachment for allegedly making up the fiscal accounts in 2014 and delay payments to the Central Bank, although the right not presented evidence of these crimes.

On August 31, 2016, eight months and 17 days after onset, the process of "impeachment" against **Dilma Rousseff** came to an end. Around 13:30 local time (1630 GMT), **61 senators voted to remove the president from office permanently**. 20 rejected the measure and there were no abstentions. And so Michel Temer Brazil assumes command until the end of 2018 amid strong protests by their cuts and privatization policies.

Honduras 2009

The coup against President Manuel Zelaya with the participation of the armed forces, however the Honduran Parliament participated in the overthrow of the president, the head of Congress, Roberto Micheletti, he initiated an investigation against Zelaya for alleged "violations of the rule of law".

Honduran parliamentarians appealed to express political uprising record where Zelaya was allegedly "violating" the rule of law. Parliament was based on the Special Law Regulating the Referendum and Plebiscite to carry the dismissal of the legally elected president. When completing the parliamentary and military coup, Manuel Zelaya was removed from the country.

>> **The Network of Intellectuals, Artists and Social Movements in Defense of Humanity (REDH) rejects institutional coup attempt in Brazil**

Subsequently it established a transitional government in Honduras supported by a military junta until the expiration of the constitutional term of the deposed president, to make way for new elections. Without the participation of former President Zelaya.

Paraguay 2012

Since coming to power of Fernando Lugo in 2008, the Paraguayan oligarchy tried to torpedo social initiatives included in the government program that led him to the presidency. In Paraguay was used as a central resource to bring the dismissal of Lugo the "Slaughter of Curuguaty".

The purpose of the charge was none other than justify the coordinated actions siege and media pressure by the "international community" tied to US interests. Before the impeachment in parliament Colorado Party had tried to dismiss about 23 times.

Venezuela, the attack continued

Since 2002 the first strong attacks against the Bolivarian Revolution are recorded. Only in 2002 a coup against President Hugo Chavez, this left 19 dead and an oil strike destabilized politically, socially and economically the country.

Venezuela filed a complaint with the Organization of American States (OAS) with documents showing US involvement in the coup of 2002. Among other tests, the national Government officials said US State DepartmentThey made an intense political lobbying to justify the coup in Caracas.

In addition, by denouncing Venezuela highlighted the meeting between US Ambassador Charles Chapiro the putschist Pedro Carmona, on days close to the deposition of President Chavez.

In 2014 another 43 Venezuelans died as a result of opposition violence. The images of the "guarimbas" gave around the world as part of a media war that suggested the violation of human rights by the Venezuelan government.

Photos of the "Arab Spring", also promoted by the West, were widespread and attributed to alleged attacks by Venezuelan police officers against the people.

After that, a campaign of "solidarity" of the international right to Venezuela, although it has been the same opposition that promotes impunity with **the momentum of the amnesty law.** The statute would free Leopoldo Lopez, a former opposition mayor who made irresponsible calls to violence, in addition to the 43 deaths he left hundreds injured.

The circumstantial triumph of the Venezuelan opposition in parliamentary elections on December 6, 2015 paved the way to accentuate the attacks against the Government of Nicholas Maduro.

From the Parliament, the right has tried to sabotage the social and economic agenda of the government with a veil of legality, by driving laws such as Amnesty and the Law of Property Housing Mission, which aims to privatize more than 1.2 million new homes built by the government plan for the Venezuelan people.

Other recent attacks from right to Venezuela as shortages, hoarding and economic warfare, are part of the Condor Plan to dominate the country the Bolivarian Revolution introduced and promoted the integration of the South.

Venezuelan shelves **register a flasher in terms of basic products.** They appear for a while, but they fail to be for another term. This occurs mainly with milk, sugar, corn flour and wheat and personal care products. But a curious phenomenon: for a while disappears milk, but are all products made with milk.

Alerted a few months ago the former President Cristina Fernandez at the meeting of Mercosur when he remembered that marks 40 years of the Condor Plan and warned. **"It was created to overthrow democratic governments may now be loosely constructed somewhere a new plan, it will be more subtle and sophisticated. In some cases they can be vultures and condors not, but are always birds of prey. We need to strengthen our democracies than ever"**. Perennial imperial eagle flies over Latin American territory, accompanied by vultures and condors are savored and not find the hours to strike out and enjoy the feast. There shake up or devour us like 40 years ago. United States comes with the fury of the waves of a troubled sea. He wants to destroy everything, like a hurricane.

A few weeks ago the US government through the DEA launched a media bomb against Venezuela, was announced as breaking news, talking about a drug shipment intercepted in Haiti bound for the United States, commanded a nephew and Nicolas Maduro godson. In seconds the news at the expense of the empire it spread throughout the world. And the next day was headline news in printed newspapers worldwide. Of course it was a false note, a strategic plan to put Maduro in the eyes of the world as a family and government working with drug trafficking. The Venezuelan government demonstrated the falsity of the accusation but none of the media note released deigned to ask for an apology for such defamation. Much less the US government and the DEA.

Why launch a media well and pump at this time? Because this is December 6 parliamentary elections in Venezuela. Part of it was right plan the assassination of Secretary of Democratic Action, Luis Manuel Diaz gave Lilian Tintori tone for worldwide denounced a "state terrorism" and accused the government of Nicolas Maduro of trying to end his life. Do not forget that this white shirt held in the private bunker when conservative Macri won the presidency of Argentina. Albeit with the minimum of 679,000 votes, ie; that those who voted were those political zealots who do not know what it means or what round. A few hours of being declared president lambasted the ruffian Venezuela because he wants her out of Mercosur.

And do not doubt for an instant that will support and money as president of the Argentine people, a coup against Maduro and Dilma. That like as 40 years ago did other traitors of the oligarchic dome of South America, it would also be a member of a joint planning an invasion of the Southern Cone and also implement but is himself as similar to Night and Fog decree Adolf Hitler. We would back daylight to Death Squads. Macri has the support of the Latin American oligarchy, the business sector and former presidents and right–wing presidents. Despabilemos or devour us.

Advancing the imperial eagle, vultures and next to the footmen traitors condors have to take a look at how have Mexico, Central America and the Caribbean who are American colonies, how have Peru, Paraguay and Colombia, full of military bases Americans in order to be as close as possible to the countries with progressive governments to ensure the success of a military invasion. You have to see how they have captured to Argentina in recent days. How a coup against Dilma is forged. Now go against Brazil, they do not want to Brazil in the BRICS. Because, who make up the BRICS? Brazil, Russia, India, China and South Africa. What do these names mean for the capitalist empire? Goodwill and unity.

The governments of Lula and Dilma are the only ones who have worked towards that part of the society living in poverty. The United States wants oil from Brazil and Venezuela. Dies himself as the desire for oil in Syria, for that reason the military invasion and bombing. As he stood with Iraq's oil, (that of Mexico, Peña Nieto handed it alone, dropping his pants) think that you can also do the same in South America. **The president of the Brazilian Congress approved impeach against Dilma. Who is this scoundrel?**

One of the most powerful right-wing politicians in Brazil. It bears the letter a criminal investigation for accepting a bribe of five million dollars as part of a system of corruption that tries to ruin Petrobras. Dilma's government did not allow these vultures and condors devour the state enterprise and in response this whippersnapper imposes a political corruption trial that seeks to give a coup to progressive government and thus end the progress of the region. Despabilemos or will devour us.

This detractor as Lilian Tintori, Leopoldo Lopez and Henrique Capriles in Venezuela, orchestrated countless marches white shirts calling for an end Dilma government. Like the managers of Clarin and La Nacion in Argentina who attacked the government of Cristina and organized marches Nisman white shirts with a cause.

"The United States is trying to regain control in Latin America with the support of right-wing forces", he warned the Argentine popular movement Patria Grande

Rousseff claims to have "strength, courage and courage" to face the 'impeachment' warnings were broadcast after the vote in the Chamber of Deputies of Brazil on the impeachment of President Dilma Rousseff. River Plate grouping denounces the imminence of a coup in the South American country and states that the will of millions of Brazilians who chose Dilma "is replaced by a group of lawmakers representing the concentrated economic power and in its most are suspected of corruption". According to the Argentine movement, USA tries to regain control of the American continent with the aim to "align the countries of Latin America and the Caribbean" to their strategy.The new Condor Plan activates another sinister Operation Condor in Latin America Patria Grande recalls that during the 70s and 80s, USA He enlisted the help of military forces within the same Latin American countries to install "docile to his political governments". Thus emerged the Condor Plan",from which coordinated the kidnapping, torture, murder and disappearance of thousands of compatriots with the aim of annihilating the popular mobilization and terrorize the population to install neoliberal policies". The new US strategy is the so-called "soft coup" through which "is intended to legitimize the dismissal of governments disadvantages through the joint between the private media sectors of the judiciary and Parliament", the popular movement. "Invariably, in all cases the change of government is done by right-wing political parties, which support democracy only when they succeed, but they just operate against fall outside the government", he added. "Wishes imperialism" In this situation, the Patria Grande Popular Movement expressed its solidarity with the people of Brazil, which at this time is "in the streets repudiating the coup". Patria Grande also expressed concern "about the course of events developing full affinity with the wishes of imperialism: the electoral triumph of Mauricio Macri in Argentina now followed the coup in Brazil". Cut social rights, limit the economic sovereignty to the transnationals, it is what is mentioned by the movement as trends of "new cycle of neoliberal adjustment on the continent". Unit processes "In these circumstances, we need to intensify and deepen the political debate and the process of unity among grassroots organizations in each country and across the continent.

Must coordinate the struggles and mobilizations in solidarity with the processes assaulted and in each country, prepare to assume drive a new cycle of resistance, with the aim of building the political alternative of peoples",concludes Patria Grande. The movement According its founding manifesto, Patria Grande is defined as a grassroots organization left, anti-capitalist, anti-imperialist, internationalist, feminist, inscribing on their banners and slogans the struggle for socialism for the

XXI century democratic character, our American and ecosocialista.

NEW CONDOR US PLAN LATIN AMERICA FLIES TO ELIMINATE THE LEFT

When the ALBA (was founded in December 2004 Bolivarian Alliance for America, then turned–ALBA–TCP) and 5 November 2005 in Mar del Plata, Argentina, was buried the FTAA (Free Trade Area of the Americas) air of economic and political integration seemed to become an unstoppable hurricane, the embrace of Chavez, Lula and Kirchner, was followed by the triumph of Evo Morales in Bolivia and its Plurinational Revolution, Rafael Correa and the Citizens Revolution in Ecuador, Daniel Ortega and the Frente Sandinista National Liberation Front in Nicaragua, Fernando Lugo in Paraguay with the Patriotic Alliance for Change, opened a new horizon for our continent.

The example of resistance of the solitary Cuba is permeated in the people of America, human dignity began to prevail over the vile money and social policies were the focus of progressive governments, a new era was traveling the roads of change in societies exploited and discriminated against for more than 500 years began building the second and definitive independence.

The empire did not remain expectant before this situation, although his main interests were in the Middle East and North Africa did not forget what always defined its "backyard" and was setting up a network of NGOs, foundations and economic structuring with media groups with an interventionist policy waiting for the right time to take the blow.

Driving times local oligarchies and coordinating them with the great transnationalized economic groups, with the support of judicial and parliamentary powers, the soft blows were launched.

Manuel Zelaya ousted in 2009 attempted assassination of Rafael Correa in 2010, dismissal of Fernando Lugo in 2012, permanent harassment Hugo Chavez and after his death his successor Nicolas Maduro and the loss of the parliamentary majority in the last elections of members the Bolivarian National Assembly amid a permanent external aggression and economic warfare, defeat in the plebiscite of Evo Morales by a press operation, electoral victory of the candidates of the US Embassy in Argentina in 2015 and the recent dismissal of Dilma Rousseff in Brazil They show that nothing is casual but causal, and directed from the centers of imperial power north of the Rio Bravo.

Progressive governments in the region are trapped between the legality of democracies built in times of independence of the colonies and reformed in the post-war liberal proposals and under the political tutelage of the US and the preaching of the hegemonic media in what can be called a true "Information Control Plan Condor", which initially conditioned the implementation of reforms and policy alternatives.

Only three countries in the region have made constitutional reforms that break with the reactionary legality of the status quo conservative, giving a change to the conception of the role of the State and the economic model in the functioning of society, contrary to the neoliberal logic, recognizing the plurality ethnic our people and looking for a model more participatory democracy: Venezuela (1999), Ecuador (2008) and Bolivia (2009), but none of them communication and information was established as a social good that can not be held capital companies or individual entrepreneurs.

It is tremendous as two of the key countries in continental and main supporters economy economic integration agreement more important in volume and mainland territory, MERCOSUR, have been dominated by business, media and judicial mafias, subservient to imperial north.

Start with a methodology similar coordinated media and judiciary, Cristina Fernandez and Dilma Rousseff suffered systematic attacks on the right, leading to the loss of the elections for the Front for Victory Cristina and Dilma dismissal.

The successors of both presidents, Mauricio Macri, in Argentina and Michel Temer in Brazil were reported in WikiLeaks as informers or collaborators of officials of the US embassies in their respective countries, detail not less that we must consider when we analyze what It is happening today.

North attacks on Mercosur have a clear objective shared today by Argentine and Brazilian destroys rulers. The entry of Venezuela to it, an interesting reversal of the regional agreement, if only a trade agreement is going to a social–political–economic inclusive treaty, a member state hinge made with other economic–political treaty produced social ALBA–TCP, led by Cuba and Venezuela, a full integration of the Bolivarian state to Mercosur, of the Bank of the South (developed occur to that business bourgeoisies both Brazil and Argentina opposed) conditions were given an integration process with South Central America and the Caribbean, creating a huge regional market, not tied to US policies.

The coup in Brazil, not only dismisses Dilma Rousseff, but, as in Argentina, produces a brutal decline in social policies, putting the state in a place of subsidy economic corporations, which gives them the address of the and seeks to redirect the BRICS (international economic agreements Brazil, Russia, India, China and South Africa) could in the short term to put the US trade dominance in check, and suffer a hard cimbronazo to withdraw Brazil whose policy be tied to the designs IMF and WB without any doubt.

The dismissal of Dilma and the assumption of Temer comes at a time where it is trying to strike a blow also within the Mercosur, not allowing Venezuela became president pro-tempore, while drench the coup attempts against Maduro, the

Paraguayan right next to Brazilian and Argentina generate the conditions for the disintegration of the regional agreement, albeit for different reasons, agree with the objective, besides being subservient to American foreign policy.

A Argentine businessmen linked to transnational and led by Macri, seduces joining the Trans Pacific Treaty and participation in an active and inclusive Mercosur consider it an obstacle in its objectives, must be removed, even if it means giving in political and economic sovereignty large corporations and central countries, USA to the head. Therefore we affirm the principle of the note that the colonial restoration in the Americas is planned and implemented from Washington, beneficial ownership of disasters ahead with the implementation of the policies of the Washington Consensus in our territories.

It should be recognized that these advances on the right are also produced by the inaction of progressive governments who thought they could develop social policies, generating an internal market that lifted millions of people out of poverty and poverty, recovering for the people the surplus production, mainly of commodities and extractive exploitation, while trading with large corporations of monopoly capital, control root without changing the economic and political matrix of the country.

They are not within capitalism genes to resolve hunger, unfair distribution of income, equity in the exercise of power and social justice, so no stable agreements with the owners of capital and empire as its factual Control, will only be temporary and tactical, and both Argentina and Brazil in this decade won neoliberalism, their governments failed to dismantle the structures of economic power, or taking substantive measures such as the nationalization of banks and foreign trade and reform land according to the new needs of agricultural production, nor a policy on the media and their owners were given and missed the opportunity, when they could, to modify the feudal constitutions we have and dismantle the judiciary, become a political party the imperial service.

The formation of political cadres and design policies of territorial occupation, fostering the development of social movements and indigenous peoples, dismantle and replace the old party structures in the territory, the permanently rely on popular mobilization was a necessity to face the reaction was coming and to ensure a destiny other than our America.

You could not negotiate with menial empire, we must learn for the future, there can be more Cobos (Vice President CFK) or Temer in popular governments, a change process must be deepened with every step to sustain and advance, but the enemy destroys you. It is now expected that all the guns aimed at the Venezuela Bolivariana, we must defend and rely on a mobilized people, millions in the street to recover the popular initiative on the continent and resist the colonial restoration with the unity of the people, the only way to build a better world.

USA INCREASES IN LATIN AMERICA WITH MILITARY PRESENCE IN HONDURAS AND SPECIAL UNIT PROJECT IN ARGENTINA

USA He expanded its military presence in Latin America. The US airbase at Soto Cano in Honduras, also known as 'Palmerola', 86 kilometers from Tegucigalpa, hosts this Wednesday a new special unit.

According to the portal defensa.com, the Palmerola, which usually accommodate between 500 and 600 US soldiers permanently receives an additional 250 marines now, at least four heavy helicopters and amphibious high speed catamaran, designed to transport troops and means between ports within a theater of operations.

The new unit, called 'Task Force Purpose Special Air-Land Marines-South' or 'SPMAGTF-South' (from 'Special Purpose Marine Air-Ground Task Force-South'), will be operational in the region between June and November. From April 1 the base and houses the unit, reports in turn, La Iguana TV (http://laiguana.tv/).

The new force is "crisis response". Its stated mission is collaboration in training with forces in the region, humanitarian assistance and anti-drug operations. The creation of the new force came a week after the visit of the head of the US Southern Command, John Kelly, to Honduras, where he participated in the Central American Security Conference Crime, attended by representatives and heads of the Armed Forces 14 countries, including Canada, Mexico, Colombia, Dominican Republic, Haiti and Costa Rica.

At the time, former Honduran President **Manuel Zelaya** declared its intention to convert Soto Cano into a civilian airport with funding from ALBA, a decision rejected by the US ambassador in Honduras. Zelaya was deposed in a coup in June 2009. The base is key to Washington's interests in the region, was leading the coup against Zelaya, it highlights the chain Telesur. The new Honduran government canceled the decision of the previous government and the Palmerola remained in place. The news of the creation in it of a new special unit coincides with the intensification of tensions between the US and Venezuela and the proposal made on March 30 by Secretary General of UNASUR, Ernesto Samper, to remove all US military bases in the Latin American territory.

How will Argentina with two US military bases?

According to **Carlos Aznarez** (Journalist and Argentine Writer) agreements that the current government of Mauricio Macri has already launched through the Ministry of Defense and consisting install, in principle, two bases of the NSA (Agency of National Security) Misiones and Tierra del Fuego, and also generate exchange missions with US troops for joint both in the territory and in other Latin American countries exercises. Thus, the current government efectiviza the notoriously traitorous foreign policy turn away from the CELAC, UNASUR and the BRICS. It also ignores the recommendations given by the owner of the UNASUR, Ernesto

Samper that it is time that the US bases "withdraw from the continent". At the same time, both Macri as his foreign minister Susana Malcorra, assail against Venezuela and the ALBA countries and reinstall carnal relations with the US, asking meekly join the Pacific Alliance, a coalition of countries that are not just issues economic but put in place by action or omission interventionist actions of great significance.

In this context, it appears that what at the time tried to effectuate the former Kirchner governor of Chaco, Jorge Capitanich, in the airport facilities in that province and was paralyzed product of popular mobilization and the good sense to some officials Local Chancellery, now takes shape to do it in two strategic areas geopolitical level and that profoundly affect national sovereignty. Missions say is talk of the Triple Frontier and the Guarani Aquifer, one of the most important sources of water in the world, and a territory that since Ronald Reagan on, always aroused desires in Washington. So much so that on one occasion, George Bush Jr., was about to place it as a "military target to bomb" with the mendacious excuse that there are "trained" Palestinian and Hezbollah militants.

Therefore, Macri and his combo of sepoys have given the green light to install a base radar installation and observation "to combat drug trafficking and international terrorism" (sic) is very bad news, not only for missionaries who have already begun to mobilize, but also to the troubled situation now living in South America. In fact, already they have been personado several "observers" US Southern Command and the NSA, who are touring the area and apparently inclined to be **Puerto Iguazu** (on the border with Brazil) place to install this gringo interventionist sanctuary. Even some means of Misiones ensure that this decision has created a stir among some Argentine military officers and that would not have been consulted. Other unconfirmed rumors, but frankly credible in the times indicate that for several years, that territory is visited by US military commanders with the intention of observing what is now about to become reality. Something like the invasion of Israeli soldiers is taking place in southern Argentina and southern Chile. Under the guise of "vacation" of the brutal invading rush against the Palestinian people, like their US counterparts, they take the opportunity to do "intelligence" to Tel Aviv on highly coveted swaths of national territory.

Faced with such a scenario, and knowledge of the impunity with which in recent months has moved the macrista government to lash out against national interests and the population itself, is that several popular organizations missions and are considering nationalizing the subject and (as happened with the base failed Chaco) generated in the first instance an information awareness campaign to the population to help in situ subsequent demonstrations. Also, by parliamentary means, missionary deputy Daniel Di Stéfano presented at the National Congress a draft resolution requesting the Executive Branch details on the installation of two military bases in the Argentine territory. In the case of Tierra del Fuego, the basis of "observation" and "scientific experimentation" would be installed in the vicinity of Ushuaia, and as it is easy to understand would be a true "Trojan horse" to influence a highly strategic territory at whose geopolitical and military consequences are unpredictable because a few miles is the NATO base in the Falklands, and Argentine Antarctic territory, a stronghold also coveted by the US for the importances of continental ice for water supply in the future.

Finally, it is worth remembering that the United States usually use several ways to carry out their military interventionism: in some cases used the excuse of "advice and humanitarian assistance", generating campaigns against dengue, zika or what you put by hand. In this context, first they landed nurses, doctors and paramedics, and then always military observers whose tasks have nothing to do with the primary objectives announced appear.It occur, among other countries, in Honduras, in Peru, in Paraguay and the Dominican Republic. In other cases, without much ado, "manage" with government allies or submissives installing observation bases, placing radars and other technological gadgets that do not provide more public information. Or open, as they have already done 36 times, military bases across line (there are 761 worldwide) with runways and takeoff of bomber aircraft and troop presence in uniform and weapons. Cases of Colombia, Panama, Peru, Chile (with its base of "peacekeepers" in Concon), Curacao, Guatemala and several small islands spread over the Caribbean. Now the Viceroyalty of Mauricio Macri wants to join the dangerous habit of ceding territory and ensure impunity for the actions of US civilian and military personnel in northern and southern Argentina. If you are not facing radically now, before it can realize, then there will be opportunity to bemoan what has not.

Figure 15. Map of the Guarani Aquifer, a huge natural reservoir (almost entirely underground) of fresh water.

THE HIDDEN FACE OF GLOBAL GEOPOLITICS

EEE.UU. president, Barack Obama, traveled to Argentina in late March 2016 to sign several cooperation agreements. Including the unrestricted trade liberalization, assistance in the Triple Border, coordination of military missions in Africa, giving asylum to Syrian refugees, the creation of Fusion Centers Intelligence cooperation of security forces in the Southern Command and the field nuclear, and the fight against drug trafficking and terrorism.

The Nobel Adolfo Perez Esquivel, Peace Prize winner said at the time of the signing of agreements that these actions are a Trojan horse for interventionism in Argentina as happened in Colombia.

"US never was an ally of Argentina, only had good relations when we gave our sovereignty and resources, that is the essence of TPP, the new FTAA", he said.

TERRORIST FINANCING

"Forgiving terrorists is God's, but send with it's my thing" Vladimir Putin

In an article published by the international analyst **Walter Goobar**, founder of the **Twenty Magazine** and **Weekly looks south** at: **https://mundo.sputniknews.com**, he explains that the writer and former Russian spy **Daniel Estulin** published a bestseller in which It reveals how the US government and its allies support jihadism to destabilize the Middle East and Africa.

While drench the Russians bombed the Islamic State in Syria, writer, analyst and former counterintelligence agent of the Federal Security Service of the Russian Federation (FSB, the agency that replaced the KGB after the collapse of the USSR) **Daniel Estulin**, who became known for revealing the existence of the Bilderberg Club, a club of millionaires who strategically choose the political, economic and social events in the world, he returns to the present with its latest and controversial book, **Out of control** (Editorial Planeta). A volume in pointing to the United States and its partners, UK, Saudi Arabia and Israel, as promoters and financiers of Islamist terrorism with the aim of destabilizing the Middle East and North Africa, from Syria, Iraq, Lebanon, Yemen, to Libya (but believe it, ask yourself how are these countries at present).

"The Anglo-American, in connivance with the rich Arab oil countries led by Saudi Arabia, have created an army of the Caliphate with the jihadists who have left the war in Syria, something that jihadists would never have achieved alone", he says Estulin in this interview along with colleague **Cynthia Garcia** at the National Radio microphones.

– Why Russia at this time has become a kind of "executive arm" of the fight against ISIS, when an Anglo-American creation?

– The Russians are the only ones who are really fighting against the Islamic State. Neither US nor Britain, nor Saudi Arabia have any intention of fighting against the Islamic State. They have used the supposed war againstISIS to undermine and destroy the regime of Bashar al Assad, Syria and destroy the nation-state to produce a regime change to put someone kinder to the Anglo-American interests. In that sense, the Russians are showing that this American and British rhetoric of fighting terror is a lie, a chimera, because –at the end of the corporal said the Russians are demonstrating how much can be done in a short time if there is a true desire to end Islamic terrorism.

Estulin, nominated for a Pulitzer Prize for his 2014 book **TranEvolution, The Coming Age Of Human Deconstruction**, said that the fight against terrorism is a chimera, a smokescreen. To explain his claim goes back to 2008. When **Bradley Birkenfeld**, an analyst and American banker who worked for the Swiss bank UBS, "found 19,000 secret accounts in that entity, which together accounted for 54,000 million dollars". Accounts which "shared the US government, Britain, Saudi Arabia and terrorists".

OPERATION OF RUSSIA AGAINST ' EL' IN SYRIA

With all this information, Birkenfeld "went to the United States Department of Justice to declare on this issue. The government allowed him to testify in closed session of the US Senate, which was present then Senator Barack Obama. When years later, as president, Obama says he does not understand where they get the money for terrorists, I know there are lot idiots but not all are".

After that, remember that the US government, rather than reward Birkenfeld, "put him in prison, and many others who worked for Booz Allen Hamilton Inc, which was Edward Snowden and was an expert in financing terrorism, whose history is linked with this", said Estulin. Among those imprisoned by US to know their links with Islamist terrorism also points to Scott Bennett and several agents of the NSA

(National Security Agency US). So Snowden fled the country because he knew he would suffer the same fate.

"Bennett and Birkenfeld agreed in jail and compared notes and completed the information that they needed to put together the puzzle. When Bradley was released from prison threatened the government with exposing this information, and to cover his mouth was paid 104 million dollars for allegedly discovered accounts in UBS Americans who did not pay taxes. Lie". About the UK, the former spy emphasizes that it is the "center of terrorism, as ten of their groups are based in London because the Crown and MI6 (secret services) permit" and adds that seven lieutenants of bin Laden operate from there, including quotes Abu Doha, Abu Abdullah and Abu Qataba, who works for the secret services according to the Times.

"When Brad Birkenfeld discovers these bank accounts, also discovers how terrorism is financed. Not that you give them a Visa card so they can get cash from an ATM. The money was channeled through a foundation called Optimus. the Foundation had as one of its greatest frontmen Abdullah Aziz, who was prestanombres Osama bin Laden and Al Qaeda, who -through the Optimus Fundation- funded in 2008 the presidential campaign of Sen. Barack Obama, through the counsel of UBS for the Americas, Robert Wolf", he says.

But what are the US objectives pursued are and the United Kingdom with the financing of these groups? Destabilize certain countries to obtain "control the world. It is a war for survival for natural resources". A plan already laid out in the '70s of the last century. "Then the Bernard Lewis analyst spoke Arch crisis. If the two maps included in the book you can see that terrorists are in the nerve centers of regime changes look. And it is not because they are good or bad. The Americans Russians, anyone who supports (...) support them in turn".

THINGS ABOUT ISIS AND AL-QAEDA THAT DO NOT WANT YOU TO KNOW

The Islamic State, ISIS or Daesh, was created by the CIA (USA), the MOSSAD (Israel) and MI6 (UK) to appropriate the strength of Syria. Professor **Michel Chossudovsky**, a Canadian economist and director of the **Center for Research on Globalization**, in Montreal, has collected 24 truths that Western governments do not want the people know about ISIS (or Islamic State) and Al-Qaeda (...) **How is it possible to continue the game in the United States aimed at creating a global police state?** Through the destruction of peoples, cultures and ancestral remains of ancient civilizations. Barbarism in maximum dimension.

The US government's war directed against the Islamic State is a great fallacy. The problem of "Islamic terrorists", carrying out a preventive war around the world to "protect American interests" is used to justify military agenda. The Islamic State of Iraq and Syria (ISIS) is a creation of the US intelligence. The "program against terrorism" of Washington in Iraq and Syria is to support unreservedly the terrorists.

The invasion of the terrorists of the Islamic State in Iraq from June 2014 was part of a carefully planned military operation intelligence and secretly supported by the US, NATO and Israel. The mandate of combating terrorism is a fiction. United States is the "number one state sponsor of terrorism". The Islamic State is protected by US and its allies eternal. If they had wanted to eliminate ISIS brigades, they could well have bombed military apparatus when they crossed the Syrian Desert to Iraq in June. El–Arab Syrian desert is an open territory. With jet fighter aircraft (F15, F22 Raptor, CF-18), would have been, from a military perspective a fast and convenient surgery.

Below are great truths about terrorism refuting media manipulation are presented. Interpreted by the media as a humanitarian enterprise, its large – scale military operation directed against Syria and Iraq it has resulted in countless civilian deaths. It could not have been accomplished without the unwavering support of Western media, who have defended Obama's initiative as an operation to combat terrorism. (Consulted Source: Michel Chossudovsky, the US war against terrorism, GlobalResearch, Montreal, 2005, Chapter 2).

1. The United States has supported **Al Qaeda** and its affiliated organizations for almost half a century since the heyday of the Soviet–Afghan war. For example, in April 2016, a recent report by the **British Institute of IHS Jane's Defense**, said that **the official website of Federal Business Opportunities** (FBO) has presented in recent months two requests seeking companies that take care of the transport of weapons of Constanta

(Romania) to the Jordanian port of Aqaba, the shipment included "**AK-47 rifles, PKM machine guns, heavy machine guns DShK, RPG-7 rocket launchers and anti – tank systems 9K111M Faktoria**" detailed IHS Jane's. A boat with about a thousand tons of weapons and ammunition left Constanza in December 2015 towards Agalar (Turkey) and then go to Aqaba. Another boat with more than two thousand tons of weapons left late last March and followed the same route to Aqaba. "We knew that the rebels in Syria are a lot of weapons during the high official fire. We also know that these rebels periodically deliver half of their weapons from Turkey and Jordan to Al-Qaeda in Syria (also known as Frente Al- Nusra)", the author of IHS Jane's. Moreover, neither Turkey nor Jordan uses such weapons Soviet design. This shows that these weapons are going to Syria, where denounced as a large number of sources, will be delivered to terrorist groups fighting for more than five years ago to overthrow the government of President Bashar al-Assad.

2. Training camps of the **Central Intelligence Agency** US (CIA) settled in Pakistan. In the ten year period from 1982 to 1992, some 35,000 jihadis from 43 Islamic countries were recruited by the CIA to fight in the Afghan jihad against the Soviet Union. Thousands of ads, paid for with CIA funds, were placed in newspapers and newsletters around the world offering incentives and motivation to join the Jihad.

3. On February 2, 1983, President **Ronald Reagan**, receives, in the Oval Office of the White House in Washington, under the portrait of George Washington, the leaders of the so – called

"Freedom Fighters" radical Islamic fundamentalist financed and armed by the CIA. The mujahideen (or mujahideen) in Islam are the fighters of Jihad (holy war). It was the origin of Al-Qaeda and the Afghan Taliban, which eventually would turn against USRonald Reagan at that meeting official said Taliban futures were present: "They have the same moral level as the founders of the United States parents".

Figure 16. Reagan met with the Afghan Mujahideen.

4. Something that does not know the people, the United States spread the teachings of Islamic Jihad in textbooks "made in America" developed at the University of Nebraska: United States spent millions of dollars to supply Afghan girls and school children text books full of violent images and militant Islamic teachings, which were part of covert attempts to encourage resistance to the Soviet occupation. An article published by **the Washington Post, March 23, 2002** reveals:

The manuals, which were filled speeches on jihad and showed drawings of guns, bullets, soldiers and mines, have served since then as the main curriculum of the Afghan school system. The White House defends the religious content saying that Islamic principles permeate Afghan culture and books are absolutely in line with US law and policy. However, legal experts wonder whether the books violate a constitutional ban of using taxpayer money to promote religion.

USAID officials said in interviews that left the Islamic materials intact because they feared Afghan educators reject books that lacked a strong dose of Muslim thought. The agency removed its logo and any mention books on the US government, USAID said spokeswoman Kathryn Stratos. "The support religious institutions are not a policy of USAID", said Stratos, "but we continue with the project because the main purpose is to educate children, which is predominantly a secular activity". Published in the dominant Afghan languages Dari and Pashtu, the textbooks were created in early 1980 through a grant from USAID to the University of Nebraska-Omaha and its Center for Afghan Studies. The agency spent $ 51 million in college education programs in Afghanistan from 1984 to 1994.

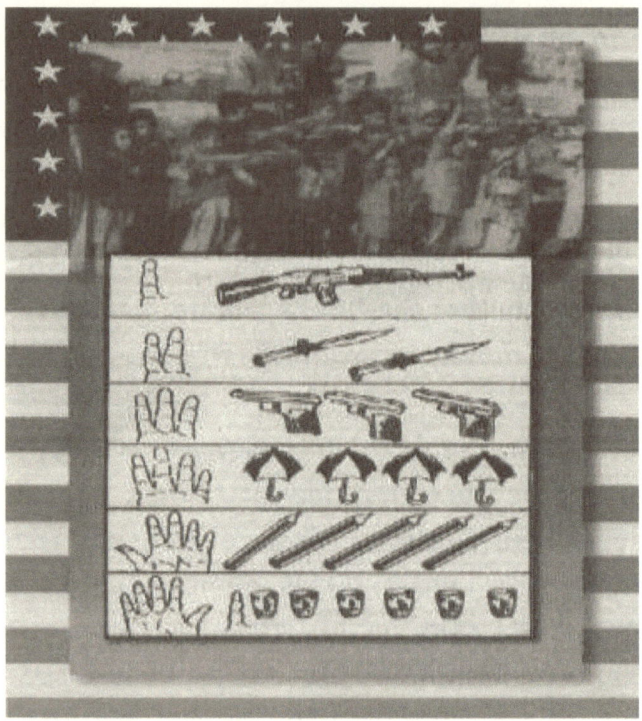

Figure 17. Texts supplied to the jihadists.

5. In 1979, the director of the secret service of Saudi Arabia, Prince Turki **Al Faycal**, recruited **Osama Bin Laden**, who was then 22 years, to manage the operations of the CIA in Afghanistan financially. Its mission: to raise funds, attract Islamic fundamentalists and arm them to fight the army of the Soviet Union, which had just invaded the country in support of pro – Soviet government of the People's Democratic Party of Afghanistan (PDPA). The CIA invested about 2,000 million dollars in operations whose aim was simply to achieve the failure of the Soviet Union during the Cold War and reduce its influence in Central Asia.

In August 1988, before the expected success of the anti-Soviet resistance, Bin Laden -Graduated in Business Administration at King Abdul Aziz University in Pakistan created a database with detailed information Mujahideen 35,000 volunteers from 40 different nations, who had fought in the Afghan war. That file was simply called "Al Qaeda" ("the base" in Arabic) and today named the most feared and persecuted of the world terrorist network.

Bin Laden, the collaborator in the shadow of the CIA, came to be considered by the same United States Department of State a "dangerous terrorist"",one of the most significant sponsors of Islamic extremist groups worldwide". Beside him, the Al Qaida was held by Ayman Al Zawahiri, a surgeon pursued as head of Islamic Jihad in Egypt, who had also fought in Afghanistan, and Mohamed Atef, killed by the United States in 2001.

Figure 18. Bin Laden when he was considered a hero.

According to Professor **Chossudovsky**, Al Qaeda was behind the attacks of September 11. In fact, the terrorist attack in 2001 provided a justification for waging war against Afghanistan, arguing that Afghanistan was a state sponsor of terrorism of Al Qaeda. The attacks of September 11, therefore, were instrumental in laying the foundations for the "Global War on Terrorism ".

6. The Islamic State or ISIS was originally an affiliate of Al-Qaeda, created by US intelligence with the support of the British MI6, the Israeli Mossad, the intelligence services entity of Pakistan and the General Intelligence Presidency of Saudi Arabia (GIP or Ri'āsat Al-Istikhbarat Al-'Amah (سة رذ ١ الـ عامة الا سـ تخ بارات). According to Israeli intelligence sources, published on the website **DEBKAfile**, this initiative has been to "a campaign to recruit thousands of Muslim volunteers in countries Middle East and the Muslim world to fight alongside the Syrian rebels. The Turkish army accommodates these volunteers, train them and ensure their entry into Syria".

There are members of Western Special Forces and Western intelligence agents within the ranks of ISIS. Members of the British Special Forces and MI6 have participated in training jihadist rebels in Syria.

7. Western military experts hired by the Pentagon have trained terrorists in the use of chemical weapons. "The United States and some European allies are using defense contractors to train the Syrians on securing stockpiles of chemical weapons in

Syria rebels, according to a senior US official and several high – level diplomats CNN ".

Figure 19. News about as US and allies train Syrian rebels handling of chemical weapons.

8. The brutal beheadings carried out by terrorists of ISIS, part of the training programs sponsored by the CIA in fields of Saudi Arabia and Qatar and aims to cause fear and shock.

Figure 20. Decapitations by ISIS.

9. Israel has supported ISIS brigades and Al Nusrah of the Golan Heights, in their fight against the government of Al–Assad and Hezbollah Shiite forces. Jihadist fighters have met regularly with officials from the Israeli Defense Forces (IDF) as well as with Prime Minister Netanyahu.

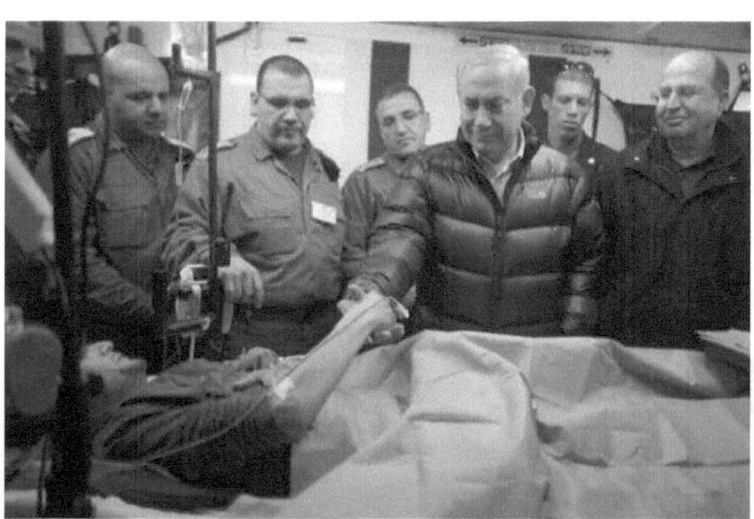

Figure 21. Netanyahu with a mercenary of the war in Syria, being cured in a hospital in Israel.

The high command of the IDF tacitly acknowledging: "elements of global jihad in Syria, members of ISIS and Al Nusrah, are supported by Israel".

10. ISIS soldiers within Syria, working under the orders of the Western military alliance. His tacit mandate is to wreak havoc and destruction in Syria and Iraq. A proof of this is found in this photo, in which US Senator John McCain meets with terrorist leaders jihadists in Syria.

Figure 22. US Senator John McCain meets with terrorist leaders jihadists in Syria.

11. ISIS militias, which are currently the alleged target of a bombing campaign by US and NATO under the mandate of the "fight against terrorism", still secretly supported by the West. Shiite forces fighting ISIS in Iraq and members of the Iraqi army itself have repeatedly denounced the military aid provided by the United States to ISIS terrorists, while at the same time fighting against them.

Figure 23. News on military aid provided by the United States terrorists ISIS.

12. The ISIS project to create a caliphate is part of an agenda of US foreign policy, which aims to divide Iraq and Syria in separate territories: A Sunni Islamist Caliphate, a Shi'ite Arab Republic and the Republic of Kurdistan.

13. "The Global War on Terrorism" (GWOT) is presented as a "clash of civilizations", a war between values and competing religions, when in fact it is open for a conquest war, guided by strategic objectives and economic.

14. United States sponsored terrorist brigades of Al Qaeda (secretly supported by Western intelligence) that have been deployed in Mali, Niger, Nigeria, Central African Republic, Somalia and Yemen. These various affiliates of Al Qaeda in the Middle East, sub – Saharan Africa and Asia are sponsored by the CIA as "intelligence assets". They are used by Washington to wreak havoc, create internal conflicts and destabilizing sovereign countries.

15. Boko Haram in Nigeria, Al Shabab in Somalia, the Islamic Fighting Group in Libya (LIFG) (with the support of NATO in 2011), Al Qaeda in the Islamic Maghreb (AQIM), Jemaah Islamiyah (JI) in Indonesia, among other groups affiliated with Al Qaeda are secretly supported by Western intelligence.

Figure 24. A terrorist group Boko Haram created to destabilize the African continent.

16. The United States also supports terrorist organizations affiliated with Al Qaeda in the Xinjiang Uighur Autonomous Region, China. The underlying objective is to trigger political instability in western China. Chinese jihadists are reported to have received "terrorist training" in the Islamic state "in order to carry out attacks in China". The declared aim of these jihadi organizations (objective that serves the interests of the US) is to establish an Islamic caliphate extending west of China.

Figure 25. Terrorism sponsored by US in China.

17. The terrorist threat is a homegrown production. It is promoted by Western governments and media in order to override civil liberties and the installation of a police state. They are used to create an atmosphere of fear and intimidation. In turn, arrests, trials and sentences of "Islamic terrorists" sustain the legitimacy of the state of Homeland Security United States and an iron law enforcement that is becoming increasingly militarized. The ultimate goal is to instill in the minds of millions of Americans that the enemy is

real and the US Administration will protect the lives of its citizens.

The ultimate goal is to instill in the minds of millions of Americans that the enemy is real and that the US Administration will protect the lives of its citizens. The same is true of countries like France, UK or Australia.

Figure 26. Militarization of European countries.

18. The "anti-terrorist" campaign against the Islamic State has contributed to the demonization of Muslims in the eyes of Western public opinion is increasingly associated with the jihadists.

19. Anyone who dares to question the validity of the "Global War on Terrorism" is labeled as a terrorist and subjected to anti-terrorist laws.

Finally, the ultimate objective of the "Global War on Terrorism" is to subdue the citizens, totally depoliticize social life in America, prevent people think and conceptualize, from analyzing facts and challenging the legitimacy of inquisitorial social order governing the United States and other countries. Consulted   Source: http://www.globalresearch.ca/twenty-six-things-about-the-islamic-state-isil-that-obama-does-not-want-you-to-know-about/5414735

RAUL OJEDA

FALSE FLAG

"We'll know our disinformation program is complete when everything the American citizen creates is false" William Casey

HISTORICAL FLAGS ATTACKS YOU SHOULD KNOW FALSE

False flag operations, designed by governments for charging their enemies, are one of the dirtiest tools of political struggle. The truth is that there are many false flag attacks documented throughout history, as well as numerous projects false flag operations that never materialized, but which was written record.

False flag operations designed by governments in order to appear carried out by their enemies, are one of the cruelest tools of political struggle.

The portal **Infowars** has published a list of forty-two false flag attacks that have been recognized by governments that perpetrated or prepared. It is interesting that a quarter of the false flag operations listed are in the United States, which has used more than once to provoke internal conflicts enemies or justify invasions countries. We present the countries most often listed. Learn about the most significant transactions in world history:

1– In the 20th century, Japan had special rights over an area of southern Manchuria, China. But China began to coalesce under the orders of Nationalist leader Chiang Kai-shek, which worried the Japanese. The Japanese leaders decided then to invade the country, but had to submit to China as the aggressor. His plan, which is now known as Mukden Incident, self-sabotage involved a Japanese railway. In 1931, Seishiro Itagaki Colonel organized the attack on a stretch of railroad tracks in Mukden and then blamed the incident to the Chinese. This was used as a pretext to invade Manchuria city.

Figure 27. Invasion of Manchuria.

This is known as the "Mukden Incident" or the "Manchurian Incident". The International Military Tribunal in Tokyo said: Several of the participants in the plan, including Hashimoto (an officer in the Japanese army senior), have admitted on several occasions their participation in the plot and have stated that the objective of the "incident" was give an excuse for the Kwantung Army (a group of Imperial Japanese Army) occupied Manchuria.

2- In 1939, Hitler needed a great pretext to act against Poland. So Operation Himmler, which aimed to present Poland as an aggressor in Germany originated. The plan took place the night of August 31 and is considered the first chapter of World War II. It consisted of Nazi military dress uniform of the Polish army and make them tormenting the German border cities. Having presented the reason to initiate war, Germany attacked Poland the next day and World War II had officially begun. During the Nuremberg Trials one Major SS Nazi admitted that under the orders of the head of the Gestapo, he and some other Nazi agents forged attacks against its own people and several facilities which blamed the Poles, to justify the invasion from Poland.

Figure 28. Justification for invading Poland.

3- On the night of February 27, 1933, an arsonist set fire to the German parliament building. The Dutchman Marinus van der Lubbe said it was responsible for starting the fire, saying it was a communist who wanted revenge of capitalism. Hermann Goering, interior minister of Prussia, immediately announced government plans to quell the communist uprising. Goering said he already had a list of communists to stop. His quick response and effort to blame the whole communist party event led to believe that Goering organized the fire as a false flag operation against the Communists.

Figure 29. Fire in the seat of the German Parliament in 1933.

4– Soviet leader Nikita Khrushchev admitted in writing that the Red Army of the Soviet Union bombed the Russian town of Mainila in 1939, by which accused Finland as a base to launch the "Winter War" against the country.President Boris Yeltsin agreed that Russia was the aggressor in the war.

Figure 30. Starting the "Winter War" against Finland.

5- The Russian Parliament, President Vladimir Putin and former President of the former Soviet Union, Mikhail Gorbachev, admitted that the Soviet leader Josef Stalin ordered his secret police executed 22 thousand military and civilian – ente Polish officers in 1940, for then blame the Nazis.

Figure 31. The slaughter of Katyn.

6- The British government admitted that –between 1946 and 1948– bombed five ships that transported Jews trying to escape the Holocaust and shelter in Palestine. They created a false group called the "Defenders of Arab Palestine" which falsely claimed to have been responsible for the attacks.

7- Israel admitted that in 1954 an Israeli terrorist cell operating in Egypt planted bombs in several buildings, including those where American diplomats were. They left "evidence" to see Arabs as responsible. One of the bombs exploded prematurely, allowing the Egyptians to identify those responsible. Several of the Israelis involved admitted the fact.

8- The Ajax Operation, 1953, was a plan of the British and US intelligence to overthrow the Iranian leader Mohammed Mossadegh, the democratically elected. Iranians working for the CIA posed as communist partisans of Mossadegh. They organized an attack on the home of a cleric to anger the Muslim community and confront against Mossadegh government. They also threatened with brutal punishment other religious leaders if not supported Mossadegh. Thus, the CIA incited riots and demonstrations pretending to be Iranian citizens. That escalation of violence initiated by US and the UK left a toll of between 300 and 800 people dead.

Figure 32. Mohammad Mosaddeq.

9- Former Turkish Prime Minister Adnan Menderes admitted that the Turkish government carried out a bomb attack on its consulate in Greece in 1955 which affected the maternal home of the founder of modern Turkey and Greece blamed the fact in order to incite and justify anti-violence fretwork.

Figure 33. Attack against the Turkish consulate in Greece.

10- The British Prime Minister Anthony Eden, admitted to his defense secretary that he and US President Dwight Eisenhower approved a plan in 1957 to carry out attacks in Syria who then blamed the government of that country, as a way to achieve political change.

11- Italy admitted that the Organization North Atlantic Treaty (NATO), with the help of the Pentagon and the CIA, carried out explosions in Italy and other European countries in the early 50s, in order to attract popular support their governments in Europe in their struggle "against communism". A participant in the plot said: "You had to attack civilians, the people, women, children, and innocent people, unknown the reason was simple these people were supposed to force the Italian public to demand greater security to the state" (...) Notably Italy joined NATO before the attacks against civilians. They were also carried out attacks in France, Denmark, Germany, Greece, Holland, Portugal, United Kingdom, and other countries.

Figure 34. Operation Gladio.

12- In 1960, US Senator Smathers Georga suggested that the United States conduct a "false attack on Guantanamo Bay would be the excuse to foment a conflict that would give us the excuse to invade and overthrow Fidel Castro".

13- Official Records of the United States Department of State revealed that in 1961, the Chief of Staff and other senior military officers discussed blow up the US consulate in the Dominican Republic to justify an invasion. The plans did not materialize but all proposals were discussed as series. However, under the guise of "protecting American citizens", the US government invaded the Caribbean country on April 28, 1965, after military Dominicans to gain control over the power to demand the return of Juan Bosch as president of the Republic, after be overthrown by the military right and with support from the United States on September 25, 1963.

14- As he admitted the US government, and demonstrated in declassified documents, in 1962 the Joint Staff of the United States developed a plan to blow up American planes and commit terrorist attacks on American soil, and blaming Cubans to justify the invasion from Cuba.

15- In 1963, the State Department wrote texts that promoted attacks on nations belonging to the Organization of American States, as Trinidad and Tobago and Jamaica, of which blame Cuba.

16- The US Defense Department suggested paying an official of the Government of Fidel Castro to attack the United States, as part of "Operation Mongoose": "The only way left to consider would be to bribe one of Commanders Castro government to carry out an attack on Guantanamo".

17- On August 4, 1964, President Lyndon Johnson appeared on American television to announce to the nation that North Vietnamese forces had launched two attacks on US destroyers in the Gulf of Tonkin. On August 2, the destroyer USS Maddox claimed to have identified three North Vietnamese torpedo boats that approached him. According to Washington, the ship was in international waters, but several historians have reason to believe that the American destroyer was sailing (deliberately or not) in the territorial waters of the Democratic Republic of Vietnam. Then a fight broke out, after which warships from North Vietnam were damaged and retreated, while the US destroyer was not damaged. The second incident occurred during a tropical storm in the Gulf of Tonkin, when radar detected a US destroyer allegedly ten ships unidentified. On August 7, 1964, Congress authorized the president a large – scale military operation against Vietnam. The National Security Agency (NSA, for its acronym in English), admitted he lied about what really happened in the Gulf of Tonkin in 1964. Manipulated data to make it appear that North Vietnamese boats fired on US ships and so create a false justification for the war in Vietnam.

Figure 35. The Secretary of Defense Robert McNamara at press conference pointing pseudo location of incidents.

18- A US congressional committee He admitted that, as part of the campaign Program Contrainteligencia– the Federal Bureau of Investigation (FBI) used several provocateurs from the 50s to the 70s to make violent attacks and blaming political activists, especially African Americans. Counterintelligence Program is called in English "COINTELPRO" is an FBI program whose purpose was to investigate and demobilize the popular political organizations within the United States.

Figure 36. J. Edgar Hoover, former director of the CIA.

19– A general high level, Sabri Yirmibesoglu admitted that Turkish forces torched a mosque in Cyprus in the 1970s and blamed his Greek enemy of it. According to the general he explained during an interview: In the war of Cyprus, certain acts of sabotage were organized and blamed the enemy to increase the anger of the people against the Greeks. This we did in Cyprus; even we burned a mosque.

20– The German Government recognized that, in 1978, the German secret service detonated a bomb on the outside wall of a prison and hid "tools to escape" a prisoner member of the Red Army Faction, in order to blame him the detonation of the bomb.

Figure 37. Fraction of the Red Army.

21- A Mossad agent admitted that in 1984 the Mossad planted a radio transmitter in the complex Gaddafi in Tripoli, Libya, which broadcast false terrorist transmissions recorded by the Mossad, in order to show Gaddaffi as a supporter of terrorism. Ronald Reagan bombed Libya immediately afterwards.

22- The board of the Truth and Reconciliation Commission of South Africa in 1989 revealed that the Civil Cooperation Bureau (a secret branch of the South African Defence Force) made several false flag attacks aimed at discrediting the ANC (African National Congress). Later in the trial of several members of the ANC, the Civil Cooperation Bureau, he tried to engage the services of an expert in explosives in an operation to put a bomb in the car of the police officer in charge of investigations, to return to again blaming the African National Congress the attack.

Figure 38. African National Congress.

23– An Algerian diplomat and several officers of the Algerian army admitted that in the 1990s, the Algerian army massacred Algerian civilians and then blamed Islamic militants for the killings.

24– A research team from Indonesia investigated the violent riots in 1998, and determined that "elements of the armed forces had participated in the riots, some of which were deliberately provoked".

25– In 1999, more than 290 people died in attacks against apartment buildings in Russia. That fact was blamed both the Chechens and the KGB. The truth is that after the attack Russia invaded Chechnya.

Figure 39. False Chechen attacks in 1999.

The clamor for revenge of the population to the massacre led to the invasion of Chechnya, led by Putin as prime minister and sparked a wave of popularity for Vladimir Putin, who won an election victory the following spring as president of the Russian Federation.

Figure 40. Invasion of Chechnya.

26- According to the Washington Post, the Indonesian Police admitted that the Indonesian military killed American teachers in Papua in 2002 and blamed the killings on a separatist group in order to get that appeared before the international public opinion as an organization terrorist.

27- Former Indonesian President Abdurrahman Wahid admitted that Indonesian police and military officers probably played a role in the Bali bombings on October 12, 2002, which caused 202 deaths, in order to blame it on fundamentalists of Jemaah Islamiyah.

28- As reported by the BBC, the New York Times and Associated Press, Macedonian officials admitted that the government killed seven innocent immigrants in cold blood and pretended they were soldiers of Al Qaeda who tried to assassinate a Macedonian police, in order to join the "war on terror" launched after the attacks of September 11, 2001.

29- Police officials in Genoa, Italy, admitted that in July 2001 at the G8 summit in that city, threw two Molotov cocktails and faked the stabbing of a police officer in order to justify the violent crackdown protesters.

30- Although the FBI admitted that the Anthrax attacks of 2001 were carried out by one or more scientists from the US government, the White House tried to blame the attacks on Al Qaeda and the Government of Iraq as justification for regime change in that country.

31- Similarly, US falsely he blamed Iraq to play a role in the attacks of September 11, as shown by a memorandum by the Secretary of Defense, posing one of the main justifications for launching the Iraq war. Even after the 9/11 Commission admitted that there was no Dick Cheney declared that the evidence of Al Qaeda's relationship with the government of Saddam Hussein was "overwhelming" connection. Also he said the media were "not doing their homework". Senior US officials admit that the war against Iraq was actually executed by oil, not the 11 September or alleged weapons of mass destruction that were never found.

Figure 41. Project New American Century.

32- Former Justice Department lawyer John Yoo, suggested in 2005 that the US They should go on the offensive against Al-Qaeda, making "our intelligence agencies believe a false terrorist organization. It could have their own websites, recruitment centers, training camps and operations fundraising sites. It could launch fake terrorist operations and borrow funds to make real terrorist attacks, helping to sow confusion in the ranks of Al Qaeda, causing operating doubt the identity of others and questioning the validity of communication".

33- United Press International reported in June 2005. "US intelligence officials have reported that some of the insurgents in Iraq are using a recent model of the Beretta 92 pistols, but those guns seem to have their serial numbers erased numbers They not appear to have been physically removed; pistols seem to have left the production line without any serial numbers analysts suggest that the lack of serial numbers indicates that the weapons were intended for intelligence operations or terrorist cells with support. Government analysts speculate that these weapons are probably the Mossad or the CIA".

34- Israeli soldiers disguised admitted in 2005 that threw stones at other Israeli soldiers to blame for attacks on Palestinians as an excuse to crack down on peaceful protests of the Palestinian people.

Figure 42. False Palestinian attacks on Israel.

35- The Quebec police admitted that in 2007, the people armed with stones blew a series of peaceful protests, were in fact police officers undercover Quebec.

36- In the G20 protests in London in 2009, a British Member of Parliament saw police officers dressed as civilians who were trying to provoke the crowd to act violently.

37- The Egyptian politicians admitted that government employees priceless pieces looted from the Museum of Cairo in 2011 and damaged several mummies, to try to discredit the demonstrators protesting against the government of Hosni Mubarak.

38- A Colombian army Colonel Luis Fernando Borja, admitted that his unit killed 57 civilians, then dressed them in uniforms and claimed they were rebels of the FARC guerrillas killed in combat, known as "false positive".

Figure 43. Colonel of the Colombian army, Luis Borja.

39- The respected journalist for the Telegraph, Ambrose Evans-Pritchard, said the head of Saudi intelligence, Prince Bandar, admitted in mid-2013 that the Saudi government "controlled" the Chechen separatists.

Figure 45. Saudi Prince Bandar Bin Sultan.

40- High-level US sources acknowledged that the Turkish government, a NATO member country, carried out the attacks with chemical weapons that the Syrian government of Bashar al

Assad was blamed; also senior members of the Turkish government, were recorded admitting plans to carry out more attacks and blame the Syrian government.

41- The former chief of security of Ukraine admitted that attacks by snipers during protests euromaidan, who initiated the coup of Ukraine, were carried out to discredit the Ukrainian government of Mr Yanukovich, in order to bring about a change regime in the country, sponsored by the Government of Barack Obama.

42- The British spy agency has admitted carrying out false flag attacks "digital" on certain targets, raising or writing offensive or illegal material on certain websites or social media accounts, then blame illegal publications to their owners, in order to pursue and punish them.

This was revealed by documents released by former NSA agent **Edward Snowden** in mid-2014, showing that the British spy agency GCHQ developed numerous digital tools for espionage. Consulted Source:

http://www.washingtonsblog.com).

THE REAL FACE OF WAR IN SYRIA

"Syria will never sell their honor, their national sovereignty and personality for a piece of bread" Bashar Al–Assad

WAR IN SYRIA

Syrian or **Syrian Arab Republic** is a country in the Middle East and is located at the eastern end of the Mediterranean Sea with a coastline of 180 km. The country has an area of 185,180 km2 and a population of about 17,000,000 inhabitants (statistics 2000). Syria borders with Turkey to the north, east Iraq, west to the Mediterranean Sea and south Lebanon and Jordan and Palestine and Israel occupied the Syrian Golan Heights since the war of the six days in 1967. This is a country opposes the expansionist foreign policy of the United States and Israel. Syria was before the false "Civil War" the most developed country in the region, both economically, and politically and militarily and in turn represented a major supplier of gas and oil to medium. The reasons why the United States, its allies and Israel planned these wars are many. Israel and Turkey could not allow both Syria and Lebanon (country where Hezbollah, an ally of Syria and Iran is armed group) to acquire too much power in the area. The "leaders" of Europe want to take a portion of the Syrian cake that has a lot of oil and gas. Monarcas Gulf dictators want to expand their territories like Turkey, to establish an oil monopoly and please the US government.

Since the beginning of time –from the existence of Mesopotamia, the land had been a strategic area; also houses about one – third of natural oil reserves, was a connection point between East and West. Thus, over the centuries, the territory has been embroiled in disputes given its geographical position, this being dominated by great empires of history: Persian Empire, Roman Empire, etc. Following the breakup of the Roman Empire, there was the rise of Islam, gradually establishing itself as the official religion in the East and ending with the creation of the Ottoman Empire by the Turks, which would be established in the territory until the First World War. After the end of the Great War, the area was fragmented resulting in Arabia, Jordan, Iraq (...) and that **is when it appears what we know today as Syria.** Let's see.

THE HIDDEN FACE OF GLOBAL GEOPOLITICS

1 – The Historical Context

In 1516 the **Sultan Salim I**, who defeated the Mamelukes in the northern city of Aleppo, conquered Syria. Later, he proclaimed himself as the Caliph. It was under his successor Suleyman the Magnificent, when the complex**Mosque Takiya Sulaymaniyah** was built in the city of Damascus. The Ottomans built many **Khans** (inns) in the **souks** (bazaars) of Aleppo and Damascus. Damascus, which was the last must for pilgrims to Mecca stop, had many great Khans and souks built for this cause. However the Great Khans of Aleppo were built to European traders after the trade was opened to Europe. Aleppo, once again became the main city of the Middle East for trade with the East and West. Under the command of Ibrahim Pasha, the son of Muhammad Ali, Damascus became the centralized government of Syria. Ibrahim Pasha occupied Damascus in 1832 and founded schools, reorganized the judicial system, reform of fiscal policies and encouraged education. He also put the Christians and Jews on an equal footing with Muslims. During World War I, the Ottomans massacred between 1 and 2 million Armenians, some in the Turkish square Belsen in Deir ez Zor. TE Lawrence and the Arabs, who rebelled against the Turks, arrived in Damascus led by Emir Feisal forces, son of Hussein, Sheriff of Mecca in 1918.

In 1918 a parliamentary government was established in 1920 in Damascus and the Emir Feisal, he was declared king of Syria. Syria at this time was geographically defined by natural boundaries, from the Taurus Mountains in Turkey to Sinai in the South. The Arabs thought Syria should be a one country to govern itself, or that's what I explained to them the British. The secret Sykes-Picot agreement between the British and French however ended this dream. This agreement was created in 1916 was launched after the meeting in San Remo. Greater Syria is divided into 4 parts (Jordan, Palestine, Lebanon, and the area now known as Syria), and divided between Britain and France. The current Syria and Lebanon were the French, while Palestine and Jordan would go to the British. The British named the Emir Feisal as king of Iraq and promised the Jews the creation of the state of Israel in Palestine.

Syria was then divided by the French in the provinces or states of Aleppo, Damascus, Latakia and **Hauran**. Aleppo more was included in the state of Syria, whose capital is Damascus. In 1925, the Druze population in the Hauran revolted and marched on the capital, leading to heavy shelling of Damascus by the French. In 1939 the state of Iskanderoun (Antioquia) was given to the Turks in order to maintain its neutrality during World War II. In 1942 Hauran and Latakia were incorporated into the Syrian state. In 1945 Syria gained independence in 1946 and the last of the country French left.

Syria finally gained full independence in 1946. Three years later the country fell under the first of a series of military dictatorships that have ruled the country for most of the later period. As in the rest of the Middle East, Arab nationalism became an important political force in the 1950s and, in fact, the influence of Nasser's revolution in Egypt by Syrian was so strong that in 1958, Syria joined Egypt in the formation of the United Arab Republic.The alliance was short - lived, Syria broke this union in 1961 to form the Syrian Arab Republic. The most powerful political force in Syria since then has been the Party Ba ' ath (or Baath Arab Socialist Renaissance), which took control in the country from 1963 to the present.

In full Cold War (1947 - 1989), in Syria he came to power **Hafez al-Assad** by the year 1971; this brought numerous problems because of the Shiite condition of the president, as most of the population was made up ofSunni Muslims, this generated a deep discontent among the majority Sunni country and a true head -on collision with the objectives of the Organization of Brothers Muslims, whose ideology advocated by the Sunni supremacy in the region. The continuing sense of unease and opposition to the regime culminates with the rise to power of **Bashar al-Assad** (son of Hafez al-Assad) in 2000.

2 - The outbreak of the war

In 2011, the Arab Spring occurs to promulgate the idea of democratizing the territory, which is a series of violent clashes and numerous deaths, culminating in a civil war in Syria. At that time, the government of al-Assad is facing the Sunnis, within which is insertable called Islamists.

In turn, some of this opposition is formed by radical Islamists -movidos by the feeling of oppression and invasion idea of Western-known as Al-Nusra and ISIS (also called

Islamic State which adopts the Arab identity), which end controlling most of Syria. Since then, the Kurds launched continuous attacks to fight the radicals that are in the Syrian territory and who are against the government of al-Asad; forces are supported by countries such as Iran, China and Russia, against the opposition of countries like France, USA and England.

On March 20, thousands of people came back into Deraa to protest against the government with the slogans "God, Syria, Freedom"",overthrow the regime" or "end corruption". The peaceful protest eventually became a revolt that swept the fire at the Palace of Justice, the headquarters of the ruling Baath party in the city and the building of the telephone company Syriatel, owned by a cousin of President al-Asad. The Syrian government decided to react with a heavy hand and ordered police to use live ammunition, causing one death and several injuries among the protesters. The harsh government repression increased in the following days, exponentially increasing the number of dead and detainees, which further exacerbated the mood among opponents of the regime. In late April, the government had to deploy the army to try to quell the popular uprising.

Finally, on July 31, 2011, a group of military defectors creates the Free Syrian Army, also known as the Free Officers Movement, commanded by Colonel Riyad Mousa al-Asaad and, with the supposed aim of protecting the civilian population the repression of the regime through the use of arms. That same day, he had befallen the Slaughter of Ramadan, in which 142 people died.

In the formation of the Free Syrian Army, he followed the formation of the Syrian National Council on August 23, 2011, a body to politically represent the Syrian opposition and that allows different rebel factions can speak with one voice at the international community. In September, the Free Syrian Army began to move towards the Northern provinces in order to win control of the border with Turkey, a strategic move that would allow them to obtain supplies of arms, ammunition and medical supplies. Thus becoming a hard nut to crack for the forces of Bashar al-Assad. The Civil War was a fact.

3 – International intervention

United States and its "European allies" saw the Arab Spring as a great opportunity. They presupposed that the arrival of democracy in these countries would allow them to open new economic markets and also get new allies to strengthen their position in a conflict zone, but strategically important.

Therefore, openly they supported the rebels in most countries. This support was primarily political, but in some cases also became military: providing weapons, supplies and military advisers to the rebels, thus, a quick victory ensured them. In Libya he played out pretty badly, becoming the wake of the Arab Spring in a failed state where the different tribes struggling for power. In Egypt, the Western powers, frightened by the turn took the democratic government of the Muslim

Brotherhood, based on Islamic radicalism, had to backtrack, support, though not openly, the coup of July 2013 with which the military retook power over the country (albeit under the guise of restore democracy).

But what is really happening in Syria, does not obey the media climate that we are imposing the media, the rebels are mercenaries, the US warships are not to defend freedom and democracy in Syria, are to equip and arm these mercenaries who acted as Libya and executing terrorist attacks are civilians who are subsequently accused Syrian President Bashar al-Assad.

The Libyan model is repeated, and as there it worked perfectly, they try to export to Syria, but the Russians and Chinese are aware of reality and an attack on Syria by NATO would be a war of apocalyptic proportions, which is why financed these terrorists and professional mercenaries from Turkey, who applauds any intervention against Sira, as Turkey dreams of annexing Syria who already in the distant past was part of its territory.

In addition, Israel also welcomed any armed effort to topple the Syrian president and establish a new order that benefits the interests of those who are dominating the World.

But, what has Syria that the US, Israel and their allies want?

Syria and Lebanon are landlocked and have borders with Iraq, the country that is very close to Iran (the real and main objective of this war, greatest ally of Syria and supplier of

Hezbollah) thus defeating Syria strategically approached the Islamic Republic of Iran. If the geographical position of Syria is analyzed it can be seen that has access to the Mediterranean Sea, and this **what does it mean?** Very simple. The government of al-Assad is Russia's main ally in the Middle East, and also houses in the town of Tartus, the only Russian naval base in the Mediterranean. Therefore the establishment of a democratic and pro – Western regime in Syria would be the end for the Russian presence in the area. On the other hand, a Sunni Syria could form a bloc, along with Iraq and Saudi Arabia, to stop the expansion of the Shiites, who have their main stronghold in neighboring Iran, for the region.Besides serving to stop Iran, a pro – western Syria would no longer be a threat to the main US ally in the region: Israel. May well be terminated dispute between Syria and Israel over the Golan Heights and the anti – Israel alliance between Syria, Iran and Hezbollah. Finally, a new government in Syria could mean the end of Syrian interference in Lebanon's internal politics.

By the way the government of Barak Obama was tempted to intervene militarily in Syria, with the excuse that the government of al-Assad had weapons of mass destruction. However, Russia's support to Bashar al-Assad, the final decision on this to get rid of its arsenal of chemical weapons, and fear to turn Syria into a new Iraq that is at the grave of several thousand American soldiers, they cast for this project fret invasion.

Another way to support the Syrian rebels are undercover Special Operations (the mythical Black Ops) groups of special forces of the United States and Britain made against the Syrian regime. The London newspaper "Sunday Express" revealed that members of the SAS (Special Air Service), British special forces, stationed in Syria to fight the Islamic State (ISIS for its acronym in English, Arabic : الإسلامية الدولة, al–Dawla al–Islamiya), jihadists are often disguise for covert attacks against ISIS. Some attacks by other means, such as "syrian free press" is also made against the forces of al–Assad. Given the secretive nature of these operations, it is obvious that until several years after the conflict ended not know anything for sure about them. Source:

https://syrianfreepress.wordpress.com

4 – Intervention by radical groups: Hezbollah and the Islamic State

The risk that the War of Syria will spread to more countries in the region, such as Lebanon and Iraq, now seems content, but remains dormant. In particular, given the involvement of foreign forces in Syria and Hezbollah or the Islamic State.

4.1 – The support of Hezbollah to the Syrian government

Hezbollah (izbu'llāh) or "Party of Allah", is a Lebanese paramilitary organization, which originally emerged to fight the Israeli intervention in Lebanon in 1982. This group is mainly fed by Shiite militants in the south, and its creation is partly the work of Iran, who initially trained them, funded and provided weapons. Another of its main allies in the fight against Israel in Lebanon was precisely Syria, whose soldiers were involved in the civil war in this country since 1976.

In October 2012, Hezbollah decided to intervene militarily in the war to support the government of al-Assad, sending the country between 3,000 and 7,000 fighters, according to various sources. Hezbollah militants have been fighting since then against Free Syrian Army in the border area with Lebanon around the city of Al-Qusayr. Indeed, Hezbollah's help allowed the Syrian army retakes the town of vital strategic importance, in June 2013, after a tough battle against the rebels. The possession of this city allows the Syrian army to reopen the lines of communication between Homs and Damascus, thus accessing the Mediterranean and supplies the Russian base in the port of Tartous. Without doubt, the intervention of fervent militia Hezbollah has been, and is, a great help to the Syrian government.

4.2 – The arrival of terrorism: the Islamic State

The invasion of Islamic radical self – styled Islamic State (ISIS). This radical, an ally of the terrorist organization Al Qaeda movement emerged in Iraq in 2006. At first it is nourished by foreign fighters who come to the country to fight the US invasion and former members of the terrorist organization Ansar al Islam, formed mainly by Salafi (Sunni ultraconservative) from Iraqi Kurdistan. After a violent and fruitless struggle against US and the Iraqi authorities, the group gradually loses importance. However, the arrival in 2010 of a new charismatic leader: Abu Bakr al-Baghdadi, change everything.

In Syria, the Islamic State occupies much of the north of the country and its troops are fighting against other local forces alike attacking the regime of al-Assad and moderate Free Syrian Army rebels. Its aim is to expand the borders of their state to achieve total domination of Iraq and Syria, and then spread to more countries in the region. In the areas it controls, the Islamic State imposes its extremist version of sharia, Islamic law, extremely hard to punish anyone who violates. In addition, it persecutes religious minorities and enjoys publishing videos online bloody mass executions of captured soldiers. Clearly, the Islamic State is a return to the bloodiest and dark version of the middle Ages.

On the other hand, Congressman **Patrick Daniel Welch**, suggests that the Islamic state was created by US to fight the regime of Bashar al-Assad and that its funding and weapons come from the US, UK and Israel.

5 - Balance to present:

To date, and according to figures from Amnesty International, War Syria has caused about 250,000 deaths and displaced 11.6 million, of which about 4 million are refugees seeking asylum in other countries.

In addition, many areas in Syria suffer severe famines and epidemics, the lack of medical resources or minimal infrastructure. The lack of security has also generated a real wave of robberies, kidnappings and sexual assaults (thousands of women and young boys have been raped), which affects the whole country.

Apart from these crimes, both sides have committed serious war crimes against prisoners and civilians. The regime of al-Assad is accused of torturing and killing about 11,000 prisoners rebels, killing nearly 600 people responsible for medical and health care in rebel areas, and bomb knowingly areas occupied by civilians in order to cause terror among rebel sympathizers, causing about 9,000 deaths.

The rebels themselves have also tortured and executed hundreds of soldiers, police and supporters of the regime. World famous being the case of rebel commander Abu Sukkar, who was videotaped as he tore and devoured the heart of an enemy soldier. In addition, it accuses the rebel side of recruiting children as soldiers.

"On August 2, 2016 at 19:05 was spread in the eastern part of the city of Aleppo, which is controlled by the terrorist group Harakat Nour al-Din al-Zenki, a poisonous gas in a residential area located near Salah al Din",said the head of the Russian Center for Reconciliation of the warring parties in Syria, General Sergei Chvarkov.

"The terrorists have used weapons containing substances causing suffocation and cause damage to the nervous system", the statement said.

The Russian Defense Ministry has revealed that the terrorist group Harakat Nour al-Din al-Zenki has been responsible for the attack with chemical weapons in a residential area of the Syrian province of Aleppo on Tuesday, reports RIA Novosti.

Director of Health of the province, Muhamad Hazuri, quoted by the agency SANA said that eight more were asphyxiated as a result of the toxic effect of projectiles and were moved to nearby health facilities.

Early reports suggest that the artifacts exploded near the neighborhoods of Bab al Faraj and Bustan Kel Ab and possibly were launched by militants of the Islamic State, which in the past have used such explosives to attack Kurdish fighters and Syrian and Iraqi armies. It is assumed that production laboratories pumps, based on the use of chlorine found in the city of Mosul, in Iraq.

Martyrs in the XXI Century

Christians crucified, buried alive and stoned is not a testimony of the past, but now that many people live in Aleppo, Syria. If you do not convert to Islam are subjected to the most varied torments from ISIS.

Figure 45. Persecuted Christians.

Religion and spiritual values and sources, gives a strength to the person who professes that represents a protection against the mafias. Therefore, extremist groups and mafias first thing they do is pursue religions, in this particular case, to Christianity.

In this context, many religious movements are using social networks for help and tell the painful experiences that are living these hours. Hundreds of families torn apart, people who have been left alone, children and youth is drifting the bloody story that we collect through numerous tweets, fan pages or web sites.

Terrorism and Transnational Organized Crime, far from seeing diminished their power; continue growing and strengthening in all this failed state or country at war they find to deploy their networks. Therefore, it is disturbing to see no less than bureaucracies to their highest level continue debating whether or not to receive refugees, whether so called or called migrant or debate in eternum. Meanwhile thousands of children and women are subjected to the mafias and trafficking. Meanwhile thousands of people hoping to return someday to their land. Meanwhile, time continues and political decisions to be taken are never made.

As many will recall, **Samuel Huntington**, in his famous book "The Clash of Civilizations" forward the prospect of the post Cold War world reality, which somehow is happening. The culture has been transformed by the phenomenon of globalization and the conflict between the heterogeneous and homogeneous has accelerated in a dizzying.

Most of the belligerents in the war in Syria are gas exporting countries with interests in one or other competing pipeline to cross the Syrian territory to wage or Qatari gas to Europe or Iran, the American expert summarizes **Mitchell A. Orenstein** in an analysis published in the journal Foreign Affairs.

Despite having on the eve of the riots of March 2011 reserves of 2,500 million barrels of oil and 0.3 trillion cubic meters of gas, the battle for energy does not represent one of own resources for Syria, but which is rather due to its strategic location on the Mediterranean and its consequent potential as a corridor to Europe.

While Qatar (which controls two thirds of the site) and Iran share the world's largest reserves of natural gas, with 51 trillion cubic meters of gas buried 3,000 meters below the Persian Gulf, both aspire to draw some alternative routes.

THE HIDDEN FACE OF GLOBAL GEOPOLITICS

Agreement in Daraya

The Syrian conflict continues, although in the last hours there was an agreement that seeks to calm things down in one of the regions with more fighting in recent times: Daraya, located on the outskirts of Damascus. There, the Syrian government agreed yesterday with rebel factions to surrender their weapons in exchange for the combatants to "regularize" their situation, the Syrian Observatory for Human Rights reported.

The agreement includes the delivery of heavy and medium rebels found in the town, besieged by the government of Bashar al-Assad since 2012 weapons.

In addition, thousands of civilians remain in the city with the commitment of the Syrian government not to retaliate against them. The agreement facilitates the fighters leave the city with their families to a place that has not yet been determined.

Moreover, the official news agency, SANA, reported that this pact will allow the output of 4,000 men and women to refugee centers.

According to the Observatory for Human Rights, Daraya has been bombed since June this year by the Syrian government forces to deter rebels from Al Maza military airport. The UN has stated that there are about 4,000 people trapped in Daraya, but the Local Council of the city ensures that the number is 8,300. According to UN data, almost

600,000 people living in besieged populations of Syria, mostly in areas blocked by the government, although some others are shielded by terrorist groups.

Turkey intensifies its offensive in Syria against the Islamic State

The Turkish Armed Forces intensified yesterday after reaping the first successes on Wednesday, its military offensive in Syria, advancing down the Arab country in order to dislodge from the west bank of the Euphrates River to the jihadists of the Islamic State (EI or Dáesh) and kurdosirias YPG militia.

A dozen Turkish tanks and heavy equipment crossed the border in the morning to join the operation named "Shield of the Euphrates", after yesterday entered neighboring territory twenty tanks, the CNNTürk television reported.

The ground operation launched Wednesday is coordinated with the international coalition against Dáesh US-led and Syrian rebel factions.

According to Turkish media, between 300 and 500 Turkish soldiers involved in the operation, the most ambitious launched by Turkey on Syrian soil since the conflict began in Iraq in 2011.

But the weight of advances have led units Free Syrian Army (ELS), which suffered low although the Turks would provide them with air cover and artillery fire.

Thus, they have succeeded in wresting from the city of Jarabulus jihadists, the last major core available to the EI near the Turkish border.

According to the Turkish state agency Anadolu, in the Syrian city, which used to have about 30,000 inhabitants, about 5,000 people are alone.

INTERNATIONAL GEOPOLITICS: PIPELINE, CAUSE OF WAR IN SYRIA? 50,000 DEAD AND 11 MILLION SYRIAN DISPLACED

Enrique Montánchez in the portal www.mil21.es/ follows: has not come to build and caused the devastating war in Syria with 250,000 dead and 11 million displaced. It is the pipeline that Qatar, a US initiative, proposed tobuild in 2009 to supply gas to Europe through Saudi Arabia, Jordan, Syria and Turkey, in order to break the major source of income of Russia along with oil. Syrian President Bashar al-Assad rejected the project because it was against the interests of his ally Vladimir Putin. Obama took over the coalition to overthrow the Syrian dictator and gave the green light for Saudis and Qataris you princes would flood of money to the Islamic State. This is the story of the bloodiest pipe history. It all started in 2009 when the emirate of Qatar proposed, promoted by the United States to reduce Russia's control over energy in Europe, the construction of a large pipeline of nearly 5,000 kilometers to send the Qatari natural gas to Europe through Saudi Arabia, Jordan, Syria and Turkey.

Figure 46. Syrian President Bashar al-Assad.

Syrian President Bashar al-Assad rejected the project by understanding Gasistas prejudicial to the interests of his Russian ally, the largest supplier of natural gas to Europe. Just one year later, Al-Asad began negotiating with Iran to build an alternative pipeline that would carry gas from Iran's South Pars field to Europe via Iraq, Syria and Turkey. Qatar, supported by the US, proposed to build a 5,000 km pipeline to Europe to give a deathblow to the largest source of income of the Russian economy hit. Putin gave his approval to the project, as it had a greater control over both its Syrian ally as on the Iranian regime. At that time the specialized media reported that Damascus and Moscow were working together to block the Qatari pipeline. Experts say that was the "seed" of the Third World War in which we are immersed.

Overthrow the regime in Damascus

Obama came on the scene and saw that the only way forward with the Qatari gas pipeline and to end the main funder of the Russian economy, with oil exports, was to overthrow the government of Al-Asad. The operation allowed, incidentally, neutralizes the Iranian pipeline.

Hence one of the objectives of the negotiations between Washington and Tehran over Iran's nuclear program, an agreement that included the lifting of economic sanctions against Iran, was to convince Iranian leaders to desist oil pipeline. To maintain its control over the energy market in Europe, Putin must attend two fronts: Ukraine, with the Government of Kiev supported by the United States and NATO, and Syria with the Islamic State or Daesh and a myriad of opposition groups fighting to end the regime in Damascus.

Europe, the war at home

Meanwhile, Europe was marked as priority limit dependence on Russia and saw in the Qatari pipeline solution, confident that US resolve on the fly problems that arise.

Brussels leaders were never think to look for alternative gas supply we bring the war home jihadism hand. US decided to overthrow the Syrian dictator to allow the pipeline, but did not count on the unconditional support of the Kremlin to Al-Asad. To end the dictatorship of Bashar al-Assad, the United States could not think of better strategy than supporting the

Islamic State, at Frente al-Nusra (the franchise of Al-Qaeda in Syria) and other related organizations. A support, according to analysts and experts, has gone out of hand.

Saudi princes and Qatari finance Daesh

Saudi princes and Qataris have generously funded from the beginning to the Salafi jihadists Daesh that in parallel have been oiling their own self - financing mechanisms, such as the sale clan Erdogan of oil extracted and refined in the territories of Iraq and Syria under his control. Putin has uncovered sales to the West of thousands of barrels of oil with the Islamic State is financed. West turned a deaf ear until Russia has strong photographic evidence uncovered by smuggling hundreds of thousands of barrels whose sale below the market price has filled in the last three years Daesh coffers.

After eighteen months of theoretical bombings against Islamists by the international coalition led by the United States, the world public opinion discovered last summer that mostly are bombarding the Army of al-Asad and terrorists, well-armed weapons, roamed by controlling their respects growing Syrian and Iraqi territory.

Moscow dynamite the Islamic State

On September 30, 2015 Vladimir Putin decides to intervene and sends its most modern combat aircraft. In just eight weeks it liquidates most command posts and Daesh infrastructures and related terrorists. Obviously, protect the Army bombers of al-Asad, who begins to recover and secure areas of western Syria, the most populous and fertile territory of the country against a desert east. Behavior that triggers nervousness US sees how the scenario changes sign for Russia, Iran and China. It is also clear, according to most analysts agree that the Russian presence in Syria -apart of important military facilities that al-Asad Putin gives the Tartus naval base and air of Jmeimim-, is aimed at defending the economic interests of Moscow, preventing the construction of Qatari gas pipeline.

An illustrative description of the decisive role of gas in the Syrian Civil War is provided by the Russian analyst **Dmitry Minin**, who wrote in May 2013: **"In any of the two routes to take the pipeline, Syria ends up being a key link in this chain now tilted in favor of Iran and Russia, so Western capitals decided it was necessary to overthrow the regime in Damascus"**.

Explanation of map:

1- The purple line is drawn Qatar-Turkey pipeline.

2- Countries highlighted in red are part of the coalition that was formed when al-Asad refused to support the Qatari pipeline. Turkey had the support of NATO.

3- Syria is the only country along the purple line that is not highlighted in red.

4- After rejecting the proposal began the "civil war" in Syria. Saudi Arabia and Qatar began financing the Islamic State.

A report by the Rand advised in 2008 to instigate wars between Sunnis and CHIES to maintain dominance over the Persian Gulf oil.

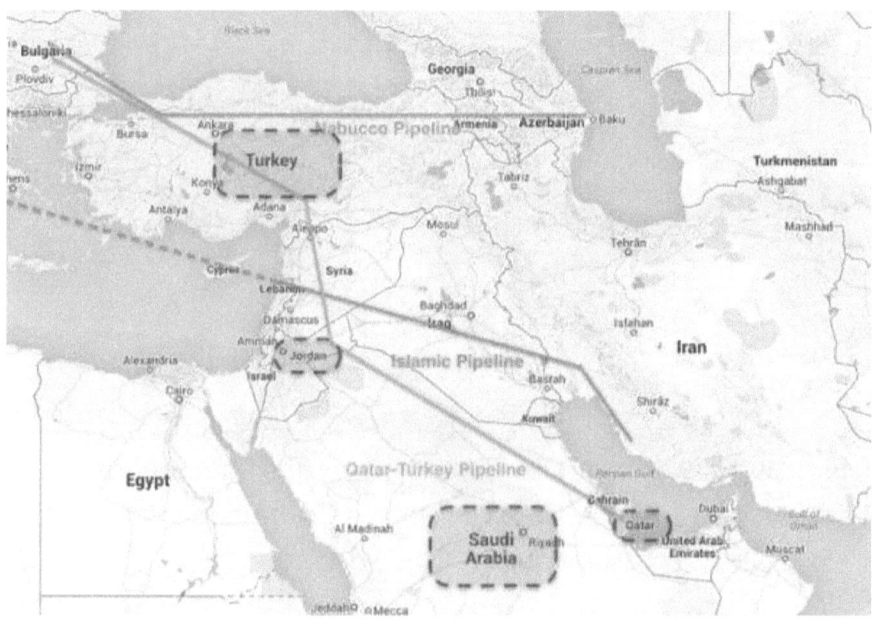

Figure 47. Gas pipeline project should pass through Syrian territory.

Much of what is happening was overtaken by a report by the Rand Corporation commissioned in 2008 by the US Army, entitled "**Unveiling the future of the protracted war** " in which it was stated that: "the geographical area of reservations proven oil matches the power base of much of the jihadist Salafist network. in the foreseeable future world oil production will be dominated by the resources of the Persian Gulf. The region will remain therefore a strategic priority that will interact with a war of long duration. "The document advised" to follow the strategy of divide and rule between Sunnis and Shiites to weaken their energies in internal conflicts and thus maintain the dominance of the Persian Gulf on oil markets.

Figure 48. Wesley Kanne Clark is a retired general of the United States Army. It was Supreme Commander of NATO during the Kosovo War.

Unconventional warfare

He proposed to the US Army that the strategy should be based largely on "covert actions, intelligence operations and unconventional warfare". Concluded the Rand document the axis on which had to turn the whole strategy should consist of: United States, United Kingdom, Turkey, Qatar, Saudi Arabia and France against Syria, Russia and Iran. Time has shown that the "advice" of the Rand worked as a self-fulfilling prophecy.

The unknown British role

A telling testimony of how the war began preparing Syria was the former French Foreign Minister Roland Dumas Affairs, who said on television gala that Britain had planned covert action in Syria and in 2009. "I was in England two years before the outbreak of violence in Syria, and met with senior British officials who confessed to me that they were preparing something in Syria. Britain gunmen preparing to invade Syria", concluded blunt the French politician.

Figure 49. Criminal devastation of Syria.

General Clark revealed after 11-S Pentagon plans to "attack and destroy Iraq, Syria, Lebanon, Libya, Somalia, and Sudan to Iran in five years". **According to the supreme commander of NATO during the Kosovo war, retired Gen.**

403

Wesley Clark, a memorandum from the Office of the United States Secretary of Defense revealed, a few weeks after 11–S, the existence of plans to "attack and destroy the governments of seven countries in five years", starting with Iraq and continuing with "Syria, Lebanon, Libya, Somalia, Sudan and Iran". In a later interview, Clark argued that this strategy was essential to control the huge oil and gas resources of the Middle East.

OTHER TESTIMONY: ALL FOR A GAS PIPELINE: A KENNEDY CLAN MEMBER REVEALS THE TRUE CAUSE OF WAR IN SYRIA

Robert F. Kennedy Jr. Nephew of John F. Kennedy – analyzes the causes of the current state of affairs in Syria in an article titled "Why the Arabs don't want US in Syria" in Político.eu. Kennedy argues that the Arab Spring in 2011 would be the deed of the civil war in Syria, but Qatar's offer to build a pipeline to Europe in 2000. The work cost 10 billion dollars and would have a length of 1,500 kilometers (through Saudi Arabia, Jordan, Syria and Turkey). It is recalled that Qatar shares with Iran the largest reservoir of natural gas in the world. Iran made the embargo prevents you sell. Meanwhile, Qatar through that pipeline could sell natural gas to Europe reaching a strategic positioning through mastery of world gas and becoming a powerful player in the Middle East. In turn, Qatar is a US ally in the region, as it allowed the installation on its territory of two US military bases.

In the article, Kennedy notes that in 2009 the Syrian President Bashar al-Assad, announced it would not allow the construction of this pipeline, which would affect its Russian ally. It should be noted that Russia would see its economy in check as it is the main supplier of natural gas to the European Union, exporting 70% of its gas to Europe. In parallel began to develop the project of Islamic gas pipeline between Iran and Lebanon would turn Iran into the largest supplier in Europe, a fact that was also regarded with suspicion from Israel. Kennedy said that secret cables reveal the intelligence services moves to grow the opposition in Syria and overthrow the authoritarian government of Bashar al-Assad. The nephew of **John Kennedy** discusses, in turn, the government of al-Assad recalling an interview the journalist Seymour Hersh, which indicates that **Bashar al-Assad** never thought of becoming president, he had his training in medical sciences and came to make a moderate secular government compared with other governments in the region. **Bob Parry**, another journalist recalls that the demonstrations that occurred in the Arab Spring in Syria were peaceful and orderly. Nothing presaged the situation would get the country. Undoubtedly, the economic Kennedy hypothesis can not be excluded, but neither asserted. Fostering the rivalry between Sunnis and Shiites; fundamentalist and terrorist groups and recent history, are links in a chain that was always fragile existence. If this is one of the many causes of this Gordian knot, time will tell.

TO BE CONTINUE

www.ingramcontent.com/pod-product-compliance
Lightning Source LLC
Chambersburg PA
CBHW030416290526
45786CB00001B/9